MIGRATIONS IN PREHISTORY

MIGRATIONS

INFERRING POPULATION MOVEMENT

YALE UNIVERSITY PRESS

IN PREHISTORY———

FROM CULTURAL REMAINS————————

IRVING ROUSE————————————

NEW HAVEN AND LONDON————————————

Copyright © 1986 by Yale University.
All rights reserved.
This book may not be reproduced, in whole
or in part, in any form (beyond that
copying permitted by Sections 107 and 108
of the U.S. Copyright Law and except by
reviewers for the public press), without
written permission from the publishers.

Designed by Sally Harris
and set in Meridien type by
Rainsford Type, Ridgefield, Connecticut.
Printed in the United States of America by
Edwards Brothers, Inc., Ann Arbor, Michigan.

Library of Congress Cataloging-in-Publication Data

Rouse, Irving, 1913–
Migrations in prehistory.
Bibliography: p. 183
Includes index.
1. Man—Migrations.   2. Anthropology, Prehistoric.   I. Title.
GN370.R68   1986   304.8   85–29514
ISBN 0–300–03612–4 (alk. paper)

The paper in this book meets the guidelines for
permanence and durability of the Committee on
Production Guidelines for Book Longevity
of the Council on Library Resources.

10 9 8 7 6 5 4 3 2 1

To José M. Cruxent and the late Gary Vescelius
with gratitude for their part
in developing the methods used here

CONTENTS

ILLUSTRATIONS

PREFACE

The purpose of this book is to explain the methodology and illustrate the results of research on prehistoric migrations. It is addressed to colleagues and students in anthropology and related subjects, especially to those whose interest has been aroused by writers who postulate migrations without the benefit of adequate training and experience. I aim to show that, while this group of writers includes prominent scientists (e.g., Fell 1976, 1980), they have abandoned the scientific method in shifting from natural to human subjects and have failed to adjust to the differences between natural and human behavior.

When I began the book, I intended to limit it to the inference of prehistoric migrations from cultural remains, which is my specialty. I soon found that the best results have been achieved by a combination of archeological, linguistic, and physical anthropological research. Culturally oriented archeologists bring to this collaboration the best information about relative chronology and hence about the direction of movement, while linguists and physical anthropologists provide the best evidence of continuity between migrating populations. Consequently, I have included all three lines of research in the book, although the main emphasis is upon archeology, as is indicated by my subtitle.

Like other anthropologists, I had come to regard culture, language, and race as independent variables, to be studied separately. I now realize that, because they vary independently, they can be used to check each other. As a result, the book contains an unanticipated message to my fellow anthropologists: the current trend towards specialization in our discipline tends to blind us to opportunities for collaboration such as those discussed herein. The excesses of Nazi anthropologists and other racists in proclaiming a one-to-one relationship among language, race, and culture have contributed to the trend toward specialization. These excesses have convinced many of us that the relationships among the three variables are not worth studying. We ought, however, to be working out the true nature of the relationships in order to forestall future excesses; and research in prehistoric migrations, which have brought together the members of different cultural, linguistic, and racial populations, is one of the better ways to do so.

The book is also intended to demonstrate to my anthropological colleagues that the inference of population movements from archeological evidence is still a viable pursuit. It was a popular activity when I entered the discipline, but the ambiguity of its results has caused it to lose favor. This point has been well documented by Adams, Van Gerven, and Levy in an article entitled *Retreat from Migrationism* (1978). They survey the results of research on prehistoric population movements by archeological, linguistic, and physical anthropologists and conclude that linguists have achieved the most success and archeologists the least. They do not, however, cover the cases discussed in this book, in which culturally oriented archeologists have collaborated with linguists and physical anthropologists and, as a result, have shared in their successes.

The study of migrations is viewed here as part of overall research on peoples and cultures, their origin, and their development. A. L. Kroeber (1962, pp. 15–16) commented as follows on this general subject: "It must be admitted that systematic developmental classification of the lower or backward cultures (corresponding roughly say to the invertebrates in the animal kingdom) has not been carried as far or pursued as energetically . . . as might be. . . . I regard such formulation as one of the things that the world of learning has the right to expect from anthropology. It is one of our responsibilities." The archeological retreat from this responsibility has opened up a gap, which outsiders are attempting to fill but without having acquired the necessary expertise. The book is intended to make that expertise available to them.

My interest in population movements was aroused when, as a graduate student in 1935, I listened to an exchange of views about it between Froelich G. Rainey, who was then writing his doctoral dissertation on the subject, and Cornelius Osgood, his faculty adviser. I pursued the interest in my own dissertation and have had the good fortune to be able to continue with it ever since, thanks to my participation in the

Caribbean research program of the Yale Peabody Museum and my teaching of a course in World Archeology in the Yale Department of Anthropology. This book is a distillation of the two experiences.

Over the years I have sought, or taken advantage of, opportunities to improve my knowledge of the subjects discussed in each of the non-Caribbean chapters of the book. My treatment of migration theory (chap. 1) has benefited from participation in three symposia on the subject. The first, sponsored by the Society for American Archaeology and held at Harvard University during July 1955, resulted in a paper on the study of culture contact situations within that subdiscipline (Willey et al. 1956). At the second, which took place in Chicago during the 1958 annual meeting of the American Anthropological Association and covered migration research in all the subdisciplines, it fell to me to summarize the results (Rouse 1958). I have also benefited from participation in a similar symposium at the annual meeting of the Northeastern Anthropological Association in Skidmore College during March 1981, which was organized by Professor Jack A. Lucas of Central Connecticut State University.

An invitation to lecture at the University of Hawaii in 1967 enabled me to observe the progress made by local archeologists in their research on the peopling of Polynesia (chap. 2). I am indebted to Patrick Kirch and Thomas Dye, students at that university who subsequently came to Yale to obtain doctorates in anthropology, and to Barry Rolett, another Yale student with a Polynesian background, for helping me to keep up with the subject.

It was Cornelius Osgood, my principal professor at Yale, who introduced me to Eskimo archeology (chap. 3). I was fortunate to be able to learn more about it from my wife, who worked in that field while a student at the University of Alaska, from the late Louis Giddings, a classmate of hers who subsequently became professor at Brown University, and from my former students John M. Campbell and Edward S. Hall, Jr., now professors at the University of New Mexico and the State University of New York at Brockport respectively.

Thanks to a grant from the Japan Society for the Promotion of Science, I was able to spend three months in Japan in 1979, investigating the origins of its prehistoric peoples (chap. 4). I wish to express my appreciation to Professor Shozo Masuda, of the University of Tokyo, for kindly acting as my sponsor, and to Kimio Suzuki, of Keio University, for making its facilities available to me and for organizing my stay in such a way that I was able to proceed with maximum efficiency despite my lack of knowledge of the Japanese language. Among the archeologists I consulted in Japan, Gina Barnes, Charles T. Keally, J. Edward Kidder, Koichi Mori, Takashi Okazaki, Makota Sahara, Shosuke Serizawa, and especially Kensaku Hayashi and Kimio Suzuki, were most helpful. I obtained further advice and encouragement from Richard Pearson when he later came to Yale as a visiting professor.

Originally I had planned to include a chapter on Bantu migrations. To broaden my knowledge of the subject, I taught in 1977 at the University of Cape Town in South Africa. I am indebted to Professor Nikolaas J. van der Merwe for inviting me there as an Oppenheim Visiting Associate and to Francis and Anne Thackeray and David Killick, three students of his who subsequently came to Yale, for their helpful suggestions. Unfortunately, I found it necessary to omit the Bantu research because its results in the field of prehistory, which which I am here concerned, do not measure up to those achieved in the field of history.

Since Taino archeology (chap. 5) is my specialty, it is impossible for me to acknowledge all the people who have helped me with it. I would, however, like to single out for special mention Ricardo E. Alegría, Juan J. Arrom, Louis Allaire, and Aad Boomert, if only because they have helped me to overcome my lack of proficiency in the Spanish, French, and Dutch languages, in which much of Caribbean research is undertaken.

The strategy of seeking the data with which to test hypotheses (chap. 6) became a special interest of mine as the result of an invitation to discuss it at the Wenner-Gren Foundation's International Symposium on Anthropology in 1952 (Rouse 1953b). I wish to acknowledge my debt to the participants in that conference and to the others with whom I have discussed the subject in my classes, lectures, and writings. Without their comments I could not have produced this book.

I am grateful to my wife for suggesting that I do the book and for her constant advice and encouragement. Portions of the manuscript have been read by Francis J. Black, Aad Boomert, Thomas Dye, Jay Custer, Richard Pearson, Barry Rolett, Anna C. Roosevelt, Mary and Peter Rouse, David R. Watters, John W. M. Whiting, and Katherine Wright. Their criticisms and those of Elizabeth Kyburg, who typed the manuscript, have been most helpful. David Kiphuth did the illustrations.

New Haven 1985   IRVING ROUSE

1 INTRODUCTION

When archeologists are asked about the origins of finds, they are expected to answer in terms of the people who produced the finds. Did that people migrate from another area, displacing or absorbing the local people and supplanting the latter's culture with its own? Or did it develop its culture locally? Or did it borrow most, if not all, of its culture from neighboring peoples?

Archeologists who study historic peoples are able to decide among these three possibilities by consulting documents and oral traditions. They have to turn to the peoples' artifacts and other cultural remains only when it is advisable to check the historic record. Students of proto- and prehistoric peoples must use the opposite procedure. They are obliged to infer the possibilities from the peoples' cultural remains and, if any writings are available, can use them only as supplemental evidence.

This book focuses on prehistory, and hence upon the use of cultural remains to solve problems of origin. Prehistoric archeologists begin by making assumptions of migration, local development, and borrowing. Then they test the assumptions against the remains, seeking to determine which of the assumptions is valid. They call each assumption a "hypothesis" and often preface that noun with the adjective "working" in order to indicate the need for a test.

In the present chapter, I shall consider the formation of hypotheses about origins. Then I shall examine a number of cases in which archeologists have successfully generated and tested them. Finally, I shall attempt to determine the reasons for success and, by so doing, to explicate the testing procedure.

A. *Strong Inference*

The idea of probability is central to the scientific method (Jeffreys 1937, pp. 6–7). One cannot "prove" that a hypothesis is correct; one can only show that it is more likely to be correct than any possible alternative. One must proceed from alternative to alternative, eliminating the weaker hypotheses and ending with the one that is most probable.

Thomas C. Chamberlain (1890) has named this procedure the "method of multiple working hypotheses." He notes that persons who limit themselves to single hypotheses become emotionally attached to them and find it difficult to knock them down. Each person tends to research for facts which support his or her hypothesis and to overlook the contrary evidence. When, however, one works with multiple hypotheses, one is less likely to identify with any of them and is more likely to become aware of contrary evidence because the facts which support one hypothesis will cast doubt upon the others.

Local development and borrowing, the two alternatives to migration mentioned above, illustrate the need to work with multiple hypotheses. By weighing the possibility of migration against its two alternatives, one may avoid the fallacy of considering only the evidence in favor of migration.

Chamberlin was a geologist who used multiple hypotheses in order to draw conclusions about the history of the earth, testing them against evidence obtained by means of fieldwork. But the method is equally applicable to laboratory experiments. In a review of the use of working hypotheses in this context, biophysicist John R. Platt (1964) pointed out that molecular biologists and high-energy physicists have achieved the greatest success because:

1. Like Chamberlin, they proceed by elimination, testing and discarding a number of alternative hypotheses until they reach one that passes its test.
2. From the validated hypothesis they develop a second set of alternatives and subject them to the same process of elimination.
3. They repeat step 2 as many times as is necessary to reach their

objective. In effect, they follow a linear, branching strategy, stopping at every point in their procedure to eliminate the unlikely hypotheses and using each surviving hypothesis as the basis from which to formulate and test a further set of alternatives.

Platt refers to this approach as "strong inference." According to him, "the conflict and exclusion of alternatives that is necessary to sharp inductive inference has been all too often a conflict between men, each with his single Ruling Theory. But whenever each man begins to have multiple working hypotheses, it becomes purely a conflict between ideas. It becomes easier then for each of us to aim every day at conclusive disproofs—at *strong* inference—without either reluctance or combativeness" (Platt 1964, p. 350).

In advocating strong inference, Platt makes a significant advance over Chamberlin. Instead of looking at each set of alternative hypotheses in isolation, he considers them within the context of an overall strategy which proceeds logically from one set of hypotheses to another. When one studies migrations, for example, one needs to distinguish local populations before attempting to determine whether any of them moved from one area to another.

Strong inference should be as efficient in archeology as in natural history and the experimental sciences. It will be used here as a standard against which to judge the effectiveness of migration research.

B. *Terminology*

If this book is to meet scientific standards, I shall have to be precise in my terminology. I need to clarify beforehand what is meant by "migration" and other key words in our archeological hypotheses. Let me begin with the units of study and then consider the terms used to process them. (For a more detailed discussion of the subject, see Rouse 1972.)

1. *Cultural units.* As stated at the outset, proto- and prehistoric archeologists work primarily with cultural remains, that is, with artifacts and other kinds of materials deposited by human beings. Each deposit is termed an *assemblage.* The inhabitants of an area who have laid down similar assemblages may be said to comprise a culturally homogeneous population or *people.*

From a people's assemblages are inferred its standards, customs, and beliefs, for example, its artifact types, burial practices, and knowledge about the environment. These are called its *cultural norms,* and collectively they make up its *culture* (Rouse 1972, fig. 11).

A people carries its culture with it when it migrates. We may therefore trace its movement by plotting the distribution of the norms that characterize its culture.

2. *Social units.* We must also take into consideration the *societies* into which each local population or people organized itself and through which it carried out its activities—groups such as villages, hunting parties, and religious or political elites. These are inferred from the nature and distribution of the people's assemblages. Each society may be thought of as a division of the people, although some societies such as confederacies, extend to neighboring peoples.

The principles according to which a people organized its societies may be called its *social norms.* Collectively, these norms comprise the people's *social structure* (Kroeber and Parsons 1958, p. 583).

Social structures leave fewer material traces in the ground than do cultures. Consequently, prehistorians find it advisable to start by studying cultural norms, after which they turn to the social correlates of those norms. Both cultural and social norms can and should be employed in tracing migrations, but I shall here limit myself to cultural norms in order to simplify the discussion.

3. *Spatial and temporal units.* Archeologists construct chronological charts—a phrase often shortened to *chronologies*—for use in dating their assemblages. Such a chart is a modified form of map, in which the vertical dimension denotes the passage of time and the horizontal dimension is marked off in a series of areas, combining latitude and longitude (fig. 1,*a*). Chronologies have an obvious advantage over maps in testing migration hypotheses; one can use them to trace the progress of peoples or their constituent societies along potential routes of movement.

The units marked across the tops of chronological charts are known as *local areas.* Archeologists divide the columns thus formed into sequences of *local periods,* keeping each period small enough to be culturally as homogeneous as possible (fig. 1,*a*). They name each local period after a typical site and define it by listing the cultural norms that are distinctive of its assemblages. These norms serve as *time-markers,* with which to date newly discovered assemblages.

4. *Integrative devices.* The overall trends evident in a chronological chart can be conceptualized by adding a set of *general periods* along its

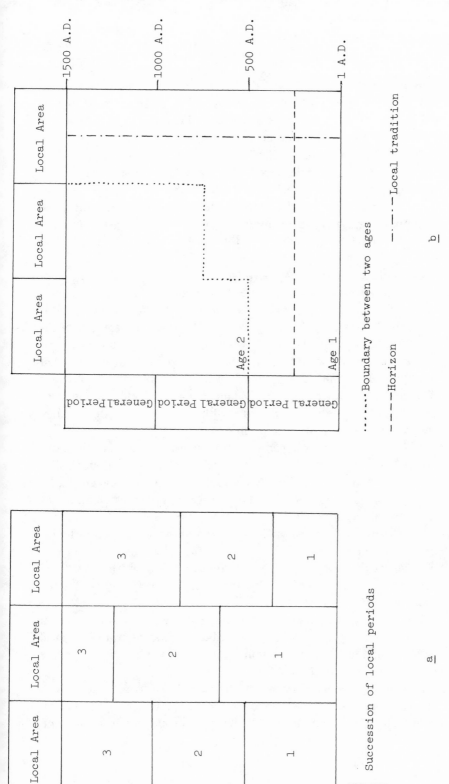

Fig. 1. Chronological Charts: (*a*) basic units, (*b*) integrative devices.

side (fig. 1,*b*). This procedure is effective only when dealing with trends that took place simultaneously wherever they occurred. Trends which differed in time from locality to locality should instead be plotted within the body of the chart, in order to show when they took place within each area. The units thus formed are known as *ages* (fig. 1,*b*).

General periods may be considered an absolute measure of time because they extend across each chart horizontally, like latitude on a map. Ages are said to be relative, because they vary in height within the columns of a chart, like the contour lines on a map. Each general period or age is defined by its innovations, that is, by the norms which are new to it (see 5 below).

Chronological charts may be quantified by placing calendric dates along their sides (fig. 1,*b*). Such dates are obtained by various techniques, foremost among which is *radiocarbon analysis*. This technique depends upon the fact that all living organisms contain a fixed amount of radioactive carbon, which decays when they die. The dates of a local period may be calculated by measuring the amount of radioactivity left in its organic remains and applying to that amount the rate of decay worked out by studying historically dated remains. All radiocarbon dates are estimates, hence must be regarded with suspicion. Nevertheless, they give some idea of the passage of time.

5. *Distribution of cultural norms.* Chronological charts, like maps, can be used as a frame of reference on which to plot the distribution of a variety of phenomena, including cultural norms. When one enters the norms on a chart, one usually finds that some of them extend more or less horizontally through the local areas within a general period (fig. 1,*b*). Such norms are known as *horizons* and are considered to be diagnostic of the periods in which they occur. Other norms extend vertically through a number of periods within a single area. They are called *local traditions*, and serve to define the areas to which they are limited (fig. 1,*b*).

The term *tradition* is also used more generally to refer to any norm or combination of norms whose distribution extends from one local period to another, in any direction. Each tradition is assumed to be the result of the process of diffusion.

Literally, the word *diffusion* means transmission by contact, and it will be so used in this book to refer to the spread of norms from one person to another and, on a broader scale, from the people of one local period

6

to those of another local period. It is analogous to *gene flow* in biology; just as a gene may "flow" from one biologically defined population group to another by means of interbreeding among members of the two groups, so a norm may "diffuse" from one culturally defined population group (a people) to another as the result of interaction among members of the two groups.

Biologists make a distinction between gene flow and migration. In the former case, individual genes pass from one local population to another, and in the latter, a single population carries it entire pool of genes into another area. Similarly, I shall here distinguish between the spread of individual norms through diffusion and the spread of a people's total repertoire of norms, that is, its culture, by means of either migration or acculturation (see 11 below).

6. *Development of individual norms.* Both biologists and archeologists also study the changes that take place in genes and norms respectively as they pass from one individual to another. Biologists say that genes *mutate* and archeologists, that norms *develop* one from another. By development is meant the pattern of change from norm to norm, as opposed to the pattern of distribution produced by diffusion from one person or people to another.

Individual norms that appear to have evolved one from another are known collectively as *series of norms* (Colton and Hargrave 1937, fig. 1). If the norms in a series become more complex with the passage of time, the series is said to be progressive. If they become simpler, the series is regressive.

Many archeologists overlook the need to augment their study of the distribution of individual norms with research on the changes from norm to norm. For example, they map the distributions of pottery types and plot their frequencies on chronological charts without also investigating the manner in which one type evolves into another. This is a mistake. It is not enough to view norms only as horizons and traditions, that is, in terms of their occurrences; one should also study them as members of series, from the standpoint of their progression or regression (see 10 below).

7. *Definition of cultural units.* Since the areal and temporal divisions of a chronological chart are made culturally as homogeneous as possible, each combination of the two of them, in the form of a local period, ought to contain a different people and culture (fig. 2,*a*). We may apply

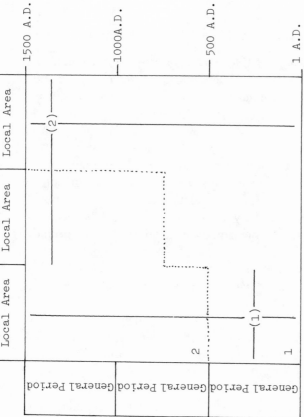

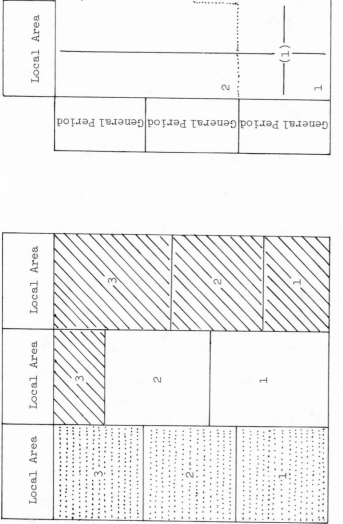

Fig. 2. Use of Charts to Show the Distribution of Peoples and Cultures.

the name of the period to its people and culture, and use the period's time-markers to define and identify both of them. When employing the time-markers in this way, archeologists call them *cultural complexes*.

Such complexes are alternatively termed styles or phases. *Style* is more appropriate when referring to a complex as a discrete unit, since that term designates the norms distinctive of a local people, as in the phrase "life-style." *Phase* is more appropriate when referring to the changes from one complex to another, because it implies that each complex is a component of a pattern of change.

8. *Local migration*. We may use a people's complex to trace its migrations, but not within a local period since by definition that unit contains only one complex. *Seasonal movement* and other kinds of intra-areal migration must be traced by other means. In the case of seasonal movement, for example, archeologists compare the tool kits and food remains they obtain from neighboring sites in order to determine whether the occupants moved from site to site, seeking the resources available around each one as they became available at different times during the year. I have chosen not to include local movements such as these in the present study since they require specialized techniques that are better discussed in other contexts.

9. *Interareal migration*. If a household- or village-site yields an alien complex, we may assume that its former inhabitants intruded from the homeland of that complex (see, e.g., chap. 5,D). I shall refer to such intrusion, whether hostile or peaceful, as *immigration*.

If the immigrant groups are few in number, small in size, and socially passive, they will sooner or later adopt the local complex and will thereby become absorbed into the local population by the process of *assimilation*. Their sites will then be difficult, if not impossible, to find. There will be so few of them, and they will be so insignificant, that looking for them will be like seeking a needle in a haystack. For this reason, prehistoric archeologists have made little headway in studying immigration and it does not figure prominently in my book.

If, on the other hand, the invading social groups are numerous enough and large enough, they may drive out the local population or else absorb it. I shall refer to this more drastic kind of migration as *population movement*. The migrants may be said to have repeopled the area, unless it had previously been virgin territory, in which case *peopled* is the appropriate term.

10. *Cultural hierarchies.* We should not expect to be able to trace population movements in terms of single cultural complexes. As a people migrates from area to area, it will encounter different natural and cultural conditions and will modify its complex accordingly. Moreover, replacement of an entire population takes time, and culture changes of its own accord with the passage of time. In addition, the migrants may be atypical of their parent population, in which case they will not carry their entire cultural complex with them. (This phenomenon was first recognized by population biologists, who call it the founders' principle; MacArthur and Wilson 1967.)

For all these reasons, population movements have to be inferred from patterns of change in peoples' complexes. Many archeologists refer to the patterns as traditions, but this term is inappropriate because it implies lack of change. We need to draw the same distinction here that is drawn in studying individual norms, between the occurrences of complexes and the changes from one complex to another (cf. 5 and 6 above). To meet this need, J. M. Cruxent and I have substituted *series* for *tradition* in our Caribbean research reported in chapter 5, and I employ this term throughout the book. Each series consists of a set of complexes that have developed one from another. It is commonly named by adding the suffix *-oid* to the name for a typical complex or relevant locality. Alternatively, the name of a typical artifact may be used.

Since a series is developmental, it can be divided into stages, each of which I shall call a *subseries.* Following the late Gary Vescelius (1980), I name each subseries by adding the suffix *-an* to the term for one of its constituent complexes, or else I conform to local usage by naming it after a distinctive artifact type.

There are two ways of plotting the distribution of subseries and series in the bodies of chronological charts. One is to start with the basic configuration of local periods (fig. 1,*a*). As we have seen (7 above), each period may be regarded as a local culture, defined by its cultural complex. One may use different kinds of shading to indicate the series or subseries to which each local culture and its complex belong (fig. 2,*a*). The second alternative is to omit the local cultures, treating their boundaries merely as frames of reference like the lines of latitude and longitude on a map, and to plot only the distributions of series and subseries. I have found it most practicable to use crossed lines for this purpose, a vertical line to show maximum persistence in time and a horizontal line to indicate greatest geographical distribution (fig. 2,*b*). The first procedure is preferable when working locally and the second is more practicable when tracing migrations on a broad scale, as I do in this book.

11. *Alternatives to migration.* When one plots the distribution of series and subseries on a chronological chart in terms of their constituent complexes, one finds that most extend irregularly from period to period and from area to area (e.g., fig. 5). Insofar as a series or subseries is distributed through time, we can consider it a *local development.* If it is also distributed through space, we can say that it expanded from one area to another. We are then faced with the problem of explaining the expansion.

The term *interaction* is central to this problem. It means contact among individuals and social groups while carrying out cultural activities. Interaction is the mechanism whereby cultural norms diffuse internally among the members of a local population, first increasing in popularity and eventually declining and disappearing. It is also the means of external diffusion from the members of one local population or people to another. Interacting peoples exchange norms back and forth. Archeologists refer to the area in which such an exchange takes place as an *interaction sphere* (Caldwell 1964).

Levi-Strauss (1971, p. 4) has arbitrarily divided interaction into two categories, weak and strong. Weak interaction consists of trade, intermarriage, religious pilgrimages, and other kinds of sociable activity. Strong interaction includes warfare, political control, economic pressure, and other kinds of forcible activity.

Weak interaction within a sphere will normally result in local development. The peoples involved will exchange norms and, as they do so, will integrate them into their own cultures, modifying them to fit local conditions. Each people will thus retain its own cultural identity. I shall call this process *transculturation.* (I am here extending the original usage of the term; Malinowski 1947 and Ortiz 1947, pp. 97–103, coined it to refer to the exchange of norms that takes place when immigrants enter a new area.)

Strong interaction, on the contrary, may lead to loss of cultural identity. One people within an interaction sphere may become so dominant that the other peoples within that sphere will acquire its distinguishing traits and will thereby assume its identity. Alternatively, the subordinate peoples may retain their separate identities but pass from their own subseries or series to that of the dominant people. I shall call this process *acculturation*. (I am here using the term in its special sense, referring to the complete or partial capture of a subordinate culture by a dominant one; Kroeber 1948, pp. 425–28.)

Whenever one seeks to explain the expansion of a series or subseries from one area to another, one must be careful to consider acculturation and the interaction that causes it as a possible alternative to population movement. In acculturation, the peoples involved move two ways, to and from each other's territory. The few individuals or social groups who do settle down among the other people are assimilated into the local population. Consequently, the changes in cultural norms that result from the interaction are not accompanied by a corresponding change in the overall nature of the people.

In population movement a people invades another's territory, traveling only in one direction, and establishes residence there. Its presence becomes so overwhelming that it is able to replace or to assimilate the local population. As a result, there is a change of people as well as culture.

We may decide between the alternatives of acculturation and population movement by comparing the former people's complex with that of the new people. If the change from one to the other is gradual, and the traits of the new people are integrated into the structure of the old complex, we may conclude that acculturation has taken place. If the change is abrupt and the structure of the previous complex is replaced by a foreign structure, we may come down on the side of population movement.

12. *Explanation of migrations.* After a population movement has been demonstrated, we want to know what caused it. This brings up the problems of *adaptation* to the natural, cultural, and social environments. For example, a people may have left home because of pressure from its neighbors. If it went in a particular direction in order to remain in the kind of environment to which it was accustomed, we may say that it did so because it was *preadapted* to conditions in the new area. If instead it expanded into different kinds of environment, it will be conforming to the process known as *adaptive radiation* (Simpson 1949, pp. 114, 117).

In studying problems of adaptation, archeologists shift their focus from the material remains through which they trace population movements to the behavior of the migrants. Two kinds of behavior have attracted the most attention, because both are well documented archeologically: *settlement pattern*, by which is meant a people's choice of places in which to live and to perform its activities; and *subsistence strategy*, or its selection from among the available foods. A migrant people tends to seek out the places in which it can maintain its distinctive settlement pattern and can continue its previous subsistence strategy, as we shall see in chapters 2–5.

c. *Generating Hypotheses*

The three alternative hypotheses posed as questions at the beginning of this chapter may be rephrased in the foregoing terminology as follows:

1. *Population movement*, in which the people of one area expands into another area replacing the latter's population. This process should not be confused with immigration, in which individuals or social groups from one population penetrate the territory of another population without overwhelming it. We shall use *migration* as a cover term for both processes.
2. *Local development*, in which two or more peoples separately evolve through a succession of cultures without losing their own identities. The peoples may mutually influence each other through the process of transculturation.
3. *Acculturation*, in which one people adopts the culture of another people, thereby losing its separate identity. Like transculturation, this process is a special form of diffusion, resulting from the spread of norms among the members of interacting populations.

How are we to generate hypotheses of these three kinds for consideration in accordance with the principle of multiple working hypotheses? It is common practice to concentrate on hypothesis 1 and to infer it from the archeological record. The investigator searches for similarities in culture between two areas and, when he finds them, assumes that they are the result of movement from one area to the other. He then "tests" his hypothesis by compiling a list of additional similarities.

This procedure does not meet Platt's standards for strong inference (see above, sec. A). The investigator formulates a "Ruling Theory" and seeks to convince us that it is correct. He does not actually test his theory; he only offers additional evidence to support it—more evidence of the same kind. One can "prove" any plausible migration hypothesis in this manner, no matter what its validity relative to alternative hypotheses, for the reasoning is circular.

The circle may be broken by bringing the alternative hypotheses into consideration. We need to distinguish the similarities in culture that are the result of local development or acculturation from those that are due to population movement.

This may be accomplished by following the example of the linguists, who have been most successful in inferring migrations from their data (Adams, Van Gerven, and Levy 1978, pp. 505–13). Linguists generate migration hypotheses and their alternatives by classifying languages in such a manner as to reveal historical relationships. When they encounter a relationship that seems to have resulted from population movement, they plot the distribution of the languages involved in order to test whether a movement did indeed take place (Dyen 1956).

It is a central thesis of this book that archeologists, too, should classify their data before inferring migration and its alternatives from them. They should start with the local area-period units established through chronological research and should define those units in terms of their diagnostic cultural norms in order to produce complexes of norms, each indicative of a local population or people and its culture. They should organize the cultures hierarchically into subseries and series of cultures, corresponding to the subfamilies and families of languages. Then they may infer hypotheses of population movement, local development, and acculturation from the historical relationships indicated by the hierarchies (see above, sec. B:6,9,10).

After generating hypotheses by means of classification, archeologists will be able to test them by plotting the distribution of the subseries and series on their chronological charts and studying the changes that have taken place within these taxonomic units. They will thus be able to test their hypotheses independently against different kinds of data. The testing procedures will be discussed later (chap. 6,A).

For help in generating hypotheses, archeologists may turn to other disciplines. If, for example, the peoples under study were protohistoric, investigators may utilize the conclusions reached by historians, as indicated at the beginning of the chapter. They may likewise project historians' conclusions back into prehistory, although this is a less reliable procedure, especially as one goes farther back in time.

Archeologists have had better success working with linguistic conclusions. Languages are so complex, so distinctive in their underlying structure, and so slow to change their structures that they provide the best evidence for deciding between population movement and its alternatives. Unfortunately, linguistic research is limited by the nature of its data to protohistoric and late prehistoric time.

In theory, archeologists should also be able to obtain reliable hypotheses from the physical anthropologists to whom they entrust the study of the human teeth and bones they find in their sites, for these objects supply direct, empirical evidence about the local populations. Some success has been achieved with teeth but, regrettably, bones do not preserve well and their range of variation is often too small to rule out the possibility of local development.

Physical anthropologists who study living populations have the advantage that they are able to work with genetically transmitted traits that do not survive archeologically, for example, blood groups, hair form, and skin color. The find it difficult, however, to disentangle the complicated skein of events that has produced the present combinations of these traits; the farther back in time they go the more difficult this task becomes. Sociocultural anthropologists, who also study contemporary or historic populations, encounter even greater difficulty because their data are more subjective and less highly structured.

The conclusions reached by biogeographers and paleontologists about the migrations of plants and animals are also worth consulting, if only because wildlife and humans face similar problems of adaptive radiation (see above, B:12). The ways in which wildlife solved the problems may provide clues to human solutions.

In final analysis, though, archeologists must rely upon their own knowledge of population movement and its alternatives. They should learn as much as possible about these subjects from the other kinds of specialists discussed above and from their own colleagues. Just as detectives use their experience with previous crimes to solve the ones they are investigating, so archeologists must use their general knowledge about migration and its alternatives to generate their hypotheses.

Archeologists refer to the leads they obtain from other kinds of specialists and from their own colleagues as *models*. Since the movement of human populations is an anthropological problem they rely primarily upon the theoretical and comparative literature of that discipline, for example, the demonstration by Whiting, Sodergren, and Stigler (1982) that migrants have tended to remain within the ranges of winter temperature to which they are accustomed. Archeologists have also developed models by experimentation, and, in recent years, through computer simulation. Heyerdahl's (1950) voyage in the Kon Tiki from Ecuador to Polynesia is a good example of experimentation; its purpose was to demonstrate the feasibility of such a voyage (chap. 2,B). Levinson, Ward, and Webb's (1973) computer study of the possible effects of environmental factors on migration into Polynesia exemplifies simulation (chap. 2,E).

Models are statements about conditions or events which may have happened and which explain the nature of archeological finds. In order to determine whether the conditions or events stated in a model did, in fact, happen in any specific instance, we must separate the model into its component parts and frame a set of alternative hypotheses for each part, taking care to include all possibilities within that set. We can then proceed to eliminate the possibilities one by one in accordance with the linear, branching strategy that Platt calls strong inference. (The use of this kind of strategy by archeologists is discussed in chapter 6, section B.)

D. *Overcoming Cultural Bias*

Nineteenth- and early twentieth-century archeologists explained their finds by generating single hypotheses. They regarded each hypothesis as a postulate, to be taken for granted, and became aware of the need to consider alternative hypotheses only when they produced conflicting conclusions and were forced to defend their own hypotheses against those of their colleagues. They were also unaware of the range of potentialities that we have reviewed in sections B and C of this chapter. They had to base their hypotheses on the knowledge and experience available to them at the time, which was rudimentary at best.

Western archeologists were led by their training and experience to hypothesize rapid, long-distance migrations. They had been taught about, and were witnesses to, the ongoing colonization by Westerners of Africa, India, Australia, Oceania, the Americas, Central and Northern Asia, and parts of Eastern and Southeastern Asia. They were predisposed by this knowledge to use hypotheses of rapid, long-distance migration to explain the similarities in proto- and prehistoric remains they encountered in different parts of the world.

South and East Asian archeologists had different biases. Since they had been brought up within relatively stable populations, they were more inclined to postulate local development in the case of the Indians and Chinese, and acculturation in the case of the Southeast Asians and Japanese, who lived on the fringes of Indian and Chinese civilization and were influenced by them.

When Western archeologists began to extend their research into South and East Asia, they proceeded to postulate migration and acculturation from the Western world in order to explain the rise of Indian and Chinese civilizations. This brought them into conflict with the local archeologists (e.g., Sankalia 1962, pp. 98–99; and Creel 1937, pp. 38–39). The conflict did not last long, however. Opinion shifted to the side of the local archeologists as new evidence made it increasingly clear that Indian and Chinese civilizations are local developments, subject to transculturation form the West but to little, if any, migration or acculturation (e.g., Fairservis 1975, pp. 227–39; and Chang 1977, pp. 267–81).

Specialists in Southeast Asian and Japanese prehistory, both foreign and indigenous, are also beginning to place more emphasis upon hypotheses of local development and transculturation. They now recognize that the customs and beliefs which diffused from India and China were absorbed into the local civilizations, where they became attached to long-standing local traditions and were modified to fit them. Southeast Asian and Japanese civilizations are, therefore, syntheses of traits drawn from various sources (e.g., Aikens and Higuchi 1982).

The archeologists who specialize in the parts of Europe beyond the frontiers of the classical civilizations have come to similar conclusions. They too have been turning away from hypotheses of migration and acculturation and have begun to infer hypotheses of local development and transculturation (e.g., Clark 1966 and Renfrew 1973). In fact, there has been a worldwide "retreat from migrationism" (Adams, Van Gerven, and Levy 1977). Archeologists everywhere have become disillusioned with the use of migration hypotheses to explain similarities in cultural remains.

The disillusionment has come about for a number of reasons. One is the discovery of evidence favoring alternative hypotheses, as just noted. Recent research in anthropology and the other social sciences has also had an effect; it has sensitized archeologists to the need to discriminate among the kinds of migration discussed in sections B and C of this chapter, seasonal movement, immigration, and population movement, as well as the interaction resulting from visits by non-residents.

Current events have further reduced the Western bias in favor of migrationism. The decline of colonialism since World War II and the consequent retreat of Westerners from large parts of the world—Africa and India in particular—has caused archeologists to realize that the effects of the various kinds of migration are not so great nor so long lasting as they had supposed. They have also become more conscious of ethnic differences and of the persistence of ethnic identities and, as a result, are better able to appreciate the importance of local development.

Finally, archeologists have become disenchanted with migration hypotheses because they have been unable to resolve their disagreements about them. They have too often reached opposite conclusions—for example, about the direction of the movements—and, in the absence of adequate testing procedures, have failed to reconcile their differences, as the following chapters will illustrate.

Paradoxically, while this retreat from migrationism has been taking place, archeologists in several parts of the world have achieved breakthroughs in studying the problem. By using strong inference, greater sophistication in generating hypotheses, and more exacting test procedures, these archeologists have succeeded where their predecessors failed. In the following chapter, I shall consider four such cases. In all four, the archeologists involved had occasion to reject their predecessors' migration hypotheses, but they recognized that these are set up to be knocked down and did not retreat in discouragement. Instead, they formed and tested new hypotheses in accordance with the principles advocated here.

The four cases have not been uniformly successful. Each has its weak points, which I shall note as I go along. Indeed, one of the lessons to be learned from the cases is that migration hypotheses can be satisfactorily generated and tested only when sufficient evidence is available, which it often is not. Nevertheless, the cases do show, in my opinion, that "migrationism" is a viable pursuit, provided that it is done properly and under favorable circumstances.

___ 2 THE POLYNESIANS ___

Polynesia is an especially favorable place in which to study migrations because it was the last major part of the earth's surface to be settled by mankind. It has yielded no archaeological remains earlier than 1300 B.C., and the first settlers did not reach its peripheries until after 500 A.D.

When studying the original movement into an area, we need not concern ourselves with the processes of transculturation and acculturation, for there was no prior population with which the migrants could have interacted. We can assume that the earliest remains to be found in any region are entirely the result of migration. In most parts of the world, this happened so long ago that its effects have been obscured by subsequent events, and as a result archeologists find it difficult if not impossible to work back from historic time to the original peopling of a region.

Not so in Polynesia. The time of occupation was so short—an average of two thousand years—and the isolation of the islands so great that the local archeologists have experienced little difficulty in proceeding back from the historic inhabitants to the first settlers. And from the latter they have been able to trace the ancestors of the Polynesians back along the route they traveled to reach their present homeland.

A. *Setting*

Some knowledge of geographic and ethnographic conditions during historic time is needed in order to understand the problem of Polynesian origins. Polynesia itself occupies a triangular area in the center of the Pacific Basin (fig. 3). The Hawaiian Islands form the apex of this triangle and its base extends from New Zealand in the west to Easter Island in the east.

There are two principal routes of access to the Polynesian triangle from the west. Both begin in the Indonesian Archipelago, which lies between the continents of Asia and Australia. One route passes through Micronesia, the tiny islands to the north of the Equator, and the other route goes through Melanesia, large islands accompanied by small outliers, to the south of the Equator. The two routes converge on Samoa and Tonga in the middle of the west side of the Polynesian triangle.

The triangle can also be approached from the east via two parallel routes. One leads from the North Pacific Coast of Canada and the United States to Hawaii, at the apex of the triangle, and the other goes from the Pacific coast of South America to Easter Island, at the base of the triangle. While these routes require long voyages, both are favored by the trade winds, which blow eastward from North and South America respectively into the central Pacific.

Since the Polynesians have occupied their present homeland for such a short time, one would expect them to be closely related in race, culture, and language to the peoples along the route through which they entered the central Pacific. Racially, however, they are unique. Garn (1965, fig. 21) distinguishes three "geographical races" on the Pacific Islands—Polynesian, Micronesian, and Melanesian—and considers them to be as distinct as the European, African, Indian, Asiatic, and American races in other parts of the world.

The Polynesian race contrasts strongly with the Melanesian race, which occupies the southern migration route from the west. The Polynesians are relatively tall, light skinned, and broad headed, and they have a high incidence of straight and wavy hair. They share most of these traits, as well as the shovel-shaped incisor and epicanthic eye-fold, with both Asiatic and American races. By contrast, the Melanesians are often called "Oceanic Negroes" because of their dark skin, narrow heads, wooly or frizzy hair, and thick everted lips.

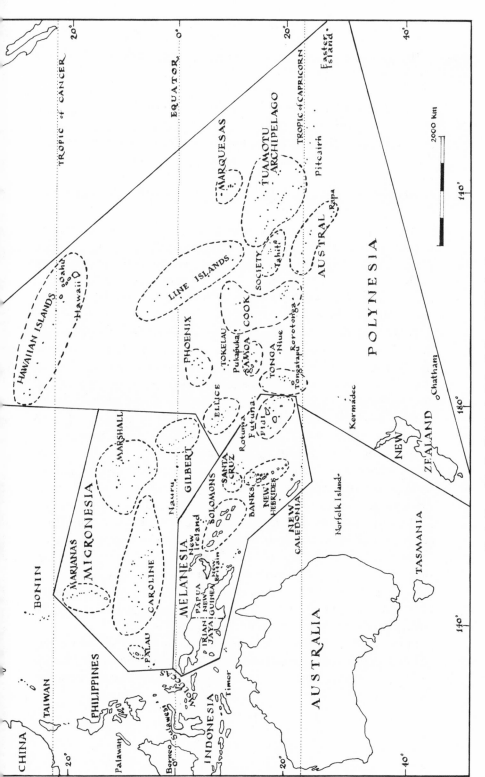

Fig. 3. Map of the Pacific Islands. (After Bellwood 1978, fig. 1)

The Micronesian race, along the northern migration route from the west, is intermediate between the other two. Overall, the Micronesians are light skinned like the Polynesians, but subgroups in the west, center, and east are darker, apparently as the result of gene flow along island chains that provide access from Melanesia to the south (chap. 1,B:5). The Micronesians are also transitional between the Polynesians and the Melanesians in stature and head shape. A computer study of the anthropometric traits of the three populations has indicated that the Micronesians are closer in these traits to the Melanesians than to the Polynesians (Howells 1970).

The fact that the Polynesians are racially so distinct, even though they have existed as a separate population only for the last 3,200 years, illustrates the difficulty of using contemporary biological traits to trace migrations (chap. 1,C). Polynesian racial traits are too different from those of all the surrounding races to serve as reliable indicators of population movement.

At the time of their discovery by Europeans, the Polynesians also differed from the Melanesians in culture and social structure. They made their canoes, houses, and other woodwork primarily with rectangular stone adzes, whereas the Melanesians used petaloid celts (i.e., axes). The Polynesians lacked pottery, preferring to bake their food in the ground rather than boil it in clay vessels as the Melanesians did. Both people grew root crops, but the Polynesians emphasized taro and the Melanesians yams. The Polynesians were ruled by descendants of the chiefs who had led them on their voyages of settlement, while the Melanesians had village headmen. The Polynesian chiefdoms became more hierarchical the farther that people proceeded out into the Pacific.

The Micronesians were intermediate in culture and social structure, as in race. Those in the west resembled most closely the Indonesians; those in the center, the Melanesians; and those in the east, the Polynesians. Polynesians, Melanesians, and Micronesians were more alike than any of them was like the tribal peoples of the Northwest Coast, on the northern migration route from the east, or the civilized peoples of the Andes, on the southern migration route from the east.

In language, too, Polynesia's affinities are clearly to the west rather than the east. All the Polynesian and Micronesian languages and most of those in Melanesia belong to a single family, known as Austronesian or Malayo-Polynesian. As the latter name implies, this family extends from the Malay Peninsula in Southeast Asia to Polynesia in the central Pacific, with an offshoot on Madagascar Island along the east coast of Africa. On New Guinea and the adjacent islands of northwestern Melanesia, Austronesian languages overlap those of another group, Papuan, in such a way as to suggest that Papuan speakers were there first and were pushed back into pockets by Austronesian speakers.

B. *Hypotheses*

Early anthropologists assumed that the Polynesians must have come from the west because their language pointed in that direction. The only question that seemed to be worth investigating was whether the Polynesians had taken the northern route, through Micronesia, or the southern route, through Melanesia. The northern route was considered more likely because the modern Polynesians appeared to be racially and culturally more like the Micronesians than the Melanesians.

Thor Heyerdahl shattered the anthropologists' complacency by voyaging from Ecuador to the Tuamotu Archipelago on a South American-style raft, which he named Kon Tiki. As already noted (chap. 1,c), he did not aim to show that the Polynesians had migrated along that route buy only to demonstrate that it would have been possible for them to do so. He thus set up a model of movement from east to west in opposition to the linguistically based model of movement from west to east that was being assumed by the anthropologists.

Heyerdahl was a professional sailor and, as such, had been impressed by the feasibility of the routes from the east. He was predisposed by his training and experience to use a navigational rather than a linguistic model. He did not deny the existence of a linguistic connection to the west but argued that it would have been just as easy for the Austronesian speakers to have followed the great circle route up from Indonesia past Japan and Alaska to the North Pacific Coast and thence back into Polynesia from the east. The Austronesians who settled in Madagascar appear to have followed a similarly circuitous route; starting out from Borneo, they migrated past India and East Africa to reach their present homeland (Murdock 1959, pp. 214–15).

Heyerdahl was led by his navigational model to hypothesize two successive migrations from South America to Polynesia, the first from

Bolivia and Peru to Easter Island in order to explain certain resemblances in stone statues between the two areas, and the second from the North Pacific Coast to Hawaii to account for the diffusion of Malayo-Polynesian languages along the great circle route. He proceeded to compile a large number of cultural and racial similarities along the two routes to support his hypotheses (Heyerdahl 1953). In addition, he undertook archeological field work in both the Galapagos Islands, off Ecuador, and Easter Island, in Polynesia, seeking to confirm his hypothesis of migration along the southern route (Heyerdahl and Skjölsvold 1956; Heyerdahl and Ferdon 1961–65).

Heyerdahl deserves great credit for generating his two hypotheses. If he had not proposed them, Oceanic specialists might have continued to assume that the Polynesians came from the west, without ever investigating whether in fact they had done so. He called attention to a problem that needed to be investigated.

But his test of the hypotheses was faulty. Instead of taking all possible hypotheses into consideration and demonstrating that his were superior to the others, in accordance with the principle of multiple working hypotheses (chap. 1,A), he limited himself to the data pertinent to his own hypotheses. He did not make use of the evidence favoring migration from the west, and as a result he was unable to determine which combination of hypotheses best fits both sets of data.

It remained for the linguistic and archeological specialists to complete Heyerdahl's tests by bringing the missing data into consideration. The linguists proceeded to refine their classification of the Austronesian family and to work out the nature of the proto-languages from which the modern languages have developed. They were then able to reconstruct the sequence of routes along which the proto-languages spread and to study the manner in which the subsequent languages differentiated as their speakers became geographically separated from the speakers of the proto-languages.

With the aid of a substantial grant from the National Science Foundation in the United States, the archeologists organized a program to undertake chronological research along the routes of migration indicated by the linguists. They worked out the sequences of cultural complexes at strategic points in order to determine the time when each of the points they studied had first been settled and the direction from which the settlers had come. They used the technique of radiocarbon analysis to date each sequence (chap. 1,B:4).

In effect, the linguists and the archeologists were making separate tests of Heyerdahl's hypotheses. The linguists demonstrated that there had been only one migration and that, contrary to Heyerdahl's belief, it had proceeded from west to east via Melanesia. The archeologists confirmed this conclusion, showing among other things that the dates of first habitation become progressively more recent from west to east.

The archeologists have not, however, abandoned the navigational model on which Heyerdahl based his hypotheses of migration in the opposite direction. They have found remains of the sweet potato, which is a South American cultigen, in protohistoric sites on Easter Island, Hawaii, and New Zealand (Rosendahl and Yen, 1971). It is not clear whether the plant was introduced by prehistoric voyagers or by the first European explorers, but they both would have followed the route originally popularized by Heyerdahl in the voyage of the Kon Tiki. This is a good example of the operation of the principle of multiple working hypotheses; Heyerdahl's hypothesis of population movement from Peru to Polynesia has been replaced by one of immigration or trade between the two places and of consequent diffusion of the sweet potato in accordance with his navigational model (Finney 1985, pp. 19–20).

As we proceed to examine the results of the linguistic and archeological tests of Heyerdahl's hypotheses, we should bear in mind that languages and archeological cultures can, and often do, vary independently. Both imply the existence of population groups—the speakers of each language vs. the possessors of each culture—but the members of the two groups are not identical. The speakers of one language may possess several different cultures, as do the English speakers who live in different parts of the world today, and, conversely, the speakers of different languages may share the same culture, as is the case in Switzerland today. The speakers of one language may adopt the culture possessed by the speakers of another language, or the members of one cultural group may learn and use the language of another group.

When testing migration hypotheses, therefore, it is desirable to work separately with linguistic and archeological evidence. Linguists should define their own population groups, date them, and trace their development in terms of linguistic evidence alone. Archeologists should create a different set of population groups, based upon the remnants of material culture they find in the ground, and should date them and trace their development in terms of this material-culture evidence. Linguists and archeologists would then be making separate tests of their respective migration hypotheses and would be in a position to compare their results. Agreement between the results would provide further support for the respective hypotheses. Discrepancies, on the other hand, need not be significant, for linguistic and cultural development may be expected to vary in details (Green 1981).

c. *Linguistic and Physical Anthropological Tests*

Linguists could not find traces of Austronesian languages along the great circle route advocated by Heyerdahl. There is no linguistic evidence, either, of migration from west to east through Micronesia, as assumed by the early anthropologists. Instead, the evidence indicates that Western Micronesia was settled from Indonesia; central Micronesia, from Melanesia; and eastern Micronesia, from both Melanesia and Polynesia (Bellwood 1979, pp. 124–30).

Having thus followed the process of elimination that is essential to strong inference, linguists were left with the west-to-east route through Melanesia into Polynesia. They have been able to draw the following conclusions (Bellwood 1978, pp. 28–30; 1979, pp. 124–30; Green 1981):

1. All the modern Polynesian languages belong to a division of the Austronesian family known as Oceanic. Its original language, Proto-Oceanic, is believed to have developed in western Melanesia by 3000 B.C. (fig. 4).
2. Around 2000 B.C., the Proto-Oceanic speakers expanded from western to central Melanesia and there produced a new language known as Proto-Eastern Oceanic, from which the modern Eastern Oceanic languages of that area are descended.
3. Some Proto-Eastern speakers moved on through eastern Melanesia into the western side of the Polynesian triangle, where further fission resulted in the formation of a language called Proto-Central Pacific. This language appears to have arisen about 1500 B.C. in Fiji, which is the easternmost island group in Melanesia, and on Tonga and Samoa, just across the Polynesian boundary (fig. 3).
4. The speakers of the Proto-Central Pacific language subsequently

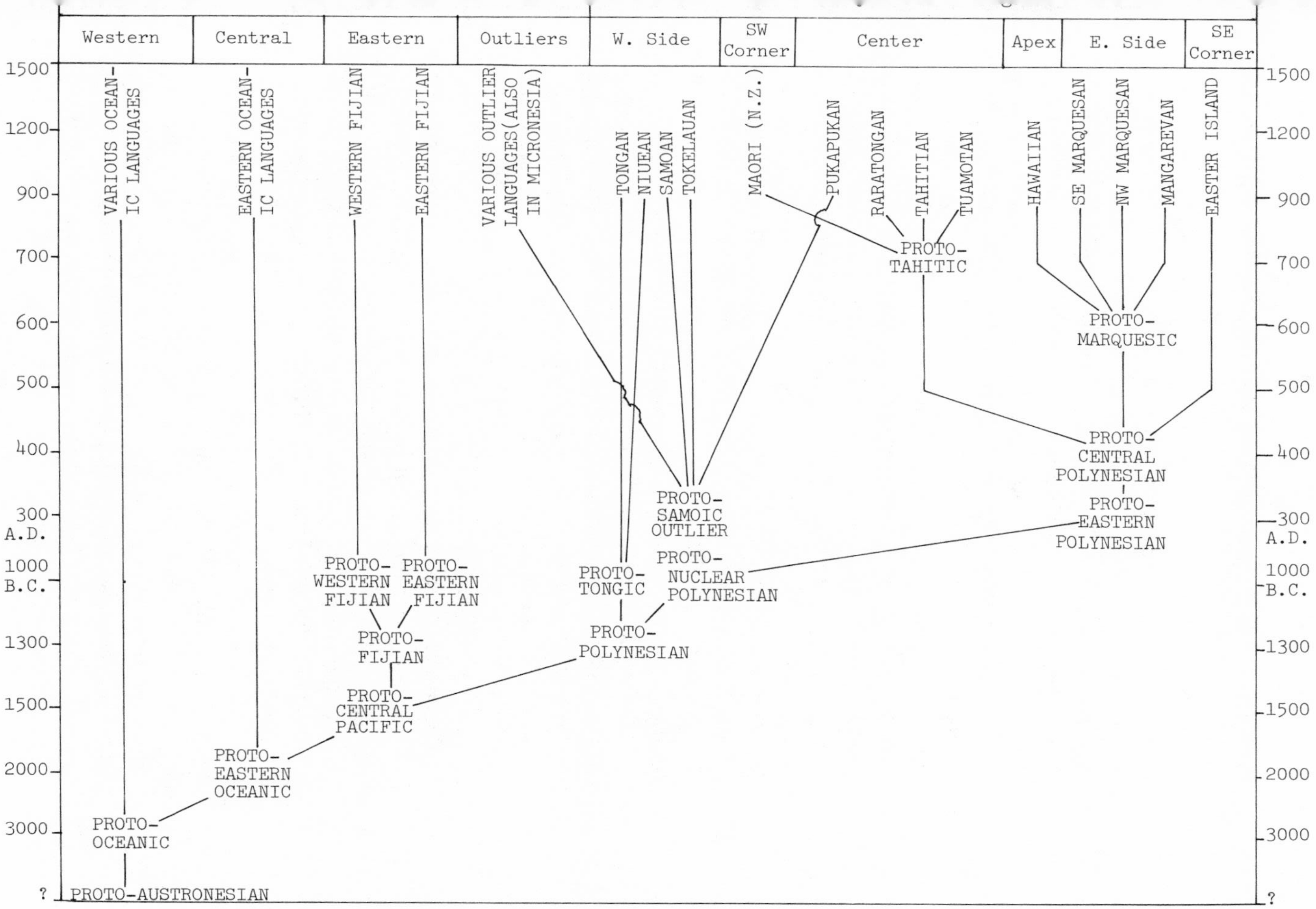

Fig. 4. Phylogeny of the Austronesian Languages. N.Z. = New Zealand.

split in two. Those in the Fijian Islands gradually produced the languages and dialects now present there (fig. 4). Those in Tonga and Samoa gave rise to Proto-Polynesian. Archeologists equate this language with the earliest known cultural complexes, which are radiocarbon dated about 1300 B.C.

5. In Tonga and Niue, the Proto-Polynesian language evolved through Proto-Tongic into the two languages present on those islands today. There was a parallel development in the Samoan group from Proto-Polynesian into Proto-Nuclear Polynesian, which became fully differentiated about 1000 B.C.

6. If the archeological chronology is correct, the Proto-Nuclear Polynesian speech community remained stationary on the Samoan Islands, in the middle of the western side of the Polynesian triangle, throughout the first millennium B.C. Then the following events took place:

   a) There was an in situ development from the Proto-Nuclear Polynesian language to Proto-Samoic-Outlier and from the latter to modern Samoan.

   b) As the name Proto-Samoic-Outlier implies, some speakers of that language radiated westward and northwestward to the outlying islands of Melanesia and Micronesia respectively. They also expanded onto two west-Polynesian outliers, Tokelau to the north of Samoa and Pukapuka to its northeast. These movements are thought to have taken place during the latter half of the first millennium A.D.

   c) Meanwhile, the Proto-Nuclear Polynesian speakers of Samoa had resumed colonization of the large islands. They expanded eastward across the Polynesian triangle to the Marquesas group in the middle of its eastern side. In this isolated locality, their language changed from Proto-Nuclear Polynesian to Proto-Eastern Polynesian and subsequently to Proto-Central Polynesian. the first of the new languages had begun to develop by 300 A.D., if the archeological chronology is correct.

7. By 500 A.D., the Proto-Central Polynesian speech community had expanded from Marquesas to Easter Island, in the southeastern corner of the Polynesian triangle, and by about 700 A.D. it had reached Tahiti and other islands of the Society group, in the center of the triangle.

8. Back in the Marquesas group, the Proto-Central Polynesian language developed into Proto-Marquesic. Speakers of the new language moved into Hawaii, at the apex of the Polynesian triangle, ca. 600 A.D.

9. In the Society group, the Proto-Central Polynesian language evolved into Proto-Tahitic, and the speakers of the new language spread to New Zealand, in the southwestern corner of the Polynesian triangle. The latter event is believed to have taken place shortly before 1000 A.D.

10. There is no linguistic evidence of major population movements after the one into New Zealand. The modern languages of Polynesia all seem to have developed locally from those in place by the end of the first millennium A.D.

The foregoing summary of the results of the linguistic test contains references to radiocarbon dates obtained by archeologists, and these dates are incorporated in the accompanying phylogeny (fig. 4). They are not essential to the test, however; they only add a measure of time to conclusions already reached by studying the development of the languages. Nevertheless, by compromising the independence of the linguistic test, they weaken its validity.

Full independence could have been achieved by using the technique of glottochronology. In it, linguists work with a "basic vocabulary," consisting of words, such as those for parts of the body, which are not likely to have been affected by the cultural milieu and which may therefore be expected to have changed at a constant rate. They compare the basic vocabularies in each pair of divergent languages, count the number of differences, and determine the time required for these to develop by applying to them the rate of change in the basic vocabularies of historic languages. Thus they obtain a measure of the amount of time that has elapsed since the two languages began to diverge. It is not a very accurate measure (chap. 3,c) but is better than guesswork, and it provides an independent check on the validity of the radiocarbon dates.

Physical anthropologists have lagged behind linguists in studying population movements in the Pacific. Recently, however, Sergeantson, Ryan, and Thompson (1982) have investigated the frequencies of leukocyte antigens among the aborigines of Australia, New Guinea, Melanesia, and Polynesia. Their classification of the local populations in terms of these linked genetic traits has disclosed substantially the same lines of divergence as those revealed by linguistic research, hence it has independently confirmed the linguistic hypotheses.

D. *Archeological Test*

Oceanic archeologists (e.g., Clark and Terrel 1978) have long recognized the need to study culturally defined population groups, paralleling the linguistically and biologically defined groups. At first, the archeologists treated these groups solely as discrete units, to be dated so as to determine the order of original settlement of the islands (see above, B:7,9). Recently, they have also become interested in the changes that took place in the groups' diagnostic complexes as they moved from island to island (above, B:10). Just as linguists study the differentiation of languages among the migrants who settled new islands and became separated from their homelands, so archeologists are beginning to investigate the differentiation of cultural complexes under similar circumstances. As a result, archeologists are now in a position to make an independent test of the linguistic conclusions that were summarized in the previous section.

To facilitate this, Golson (1971, p. 75) and Kirch (1978) have introduced into Oceanic archeology the concept of series discussed in chapter 1, section B:10. The other workers in the area have not followed suit, however. They still make no distinction between a local people's cultural complex and the pattern of change that results when that people moves from island to island, repeatedly modifying its complex as it does so and eventually giving rise to a new series of complexes. For example, they continue to apply the term *Lapita* not only to the local complex distinguished at the site of that name on the island of New Caledonia but also to the related complexes in other parts of Melanesia and in Western Polynesia. Following the lead of Golson and Kirch, I shall instead refer to the set of related complexes as a Lapitoid series. And I shall divide that series into two subseries, Lapitan and Plain-ware.

My complexes, subseries, and series are intended to be comparable to languages, their subfamilies, and their families. Just as a language consists of the norms through which the members of a speech group communicated with each other, so a complex consists of the norms through which an artifactually defined population made and used its

30

items of material culture. And just as linguists study the development of speech norms from language to language within each subfamily and family, so archeologists may study the development of artifactual norms from complex to complex within each subseries and series.

In figure 5, a chronological chart for Melanesia and Polynesia, I have plotted the distribution of the subseries and series pertinent to the problem of Polynesian migrations. I have arranged the vertical columns of this chart in the order of the migration routes worked out by the linguists, so as to facilitate comparison of the linguistic and archeological tests.

The earliest, Papuoid series began long before the time shown in the chart. It goes back to the final part of the Pleistocene epoch, when great ice sheets covered much of Europe and North America, drawing water from the ocean basins and lowering the sea level so that New Guinea was attached to Australia (Bellwood 1979, fig. 2.9). Humans settled the resultant continent of Greater Australia ca. 38,000 B.C. The assemblages (chap. 1,B:1) by which we identify the settlers consist of pebbles sharpened on one edge to convert them into choppers and of flakes struck from pebbles for use as knives and scrapers.

About 25,000 B.C., the descendants of the original settlers in New Guinea and northern Australia learned to make oval axes by extending the chipping from the edges of pebbles over both surfaces. They also began to sharpen the cutting edges of the axes by grinding them, an innovation in which the Eastern world led the West (chap. 4,D).

Thus the Papuoid series was born. The final stages in its development are shown on the left side of figure 5 by a vertical line extending from 2000 B.C. at the bottom of the chart to 1500 A.D. at its top. The dashed line extending horizontally from the name of the series across the Melanesian columns indicates there is some reason to believe that the Papuoid peoples had expanded into that region before the arrival of the ancestors of the Polynesians. So far, the only good artifactual evidence for this expansion consists of a preceramic assemblage from Balof Cave on the island of New Ireland, close to New Guinea (White and Downie 1978). However, scattered finds of non-pottery and atypical pottery assemblages throughout the rest of Melanesia suggest that Papuoids may also have reached the other islands (Green 1979, pp. 47–48).

If this hypothesis proves to be correct, all of Melanesia had been peopled by 2000 B.C., the earliest date indicated in figure 5. Accordingly, the hatched line that marks the time of first settlement begins at the

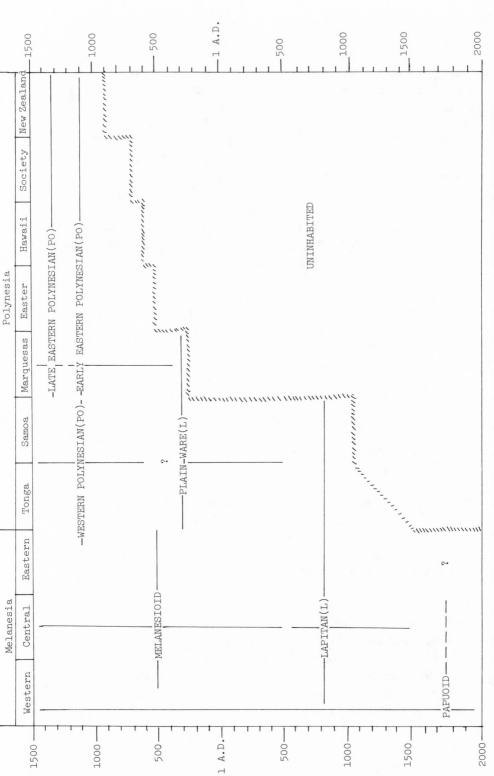

Fig. 5. Chronology of the Peoples and Cultures in Melanesia and Polynesia. (L) = Lapitoid series. (Po) = Polynesioid series.

boundary between Melanesia and Polynesia. It will be seen that the line rises steadily as one proceeds along the route of migration worked out by the linguists. This confirms the results of the linguistic test summarized in section c above.

Further confirmation is provided by the nature of the earliest classifiable assemblages, shown immediately above and to the left of the hatched line in figure 5. According to this evidence, people of the Lapitan subseries, which has been mentioned above, were the first settlers of Polynesia. Lapitan assemblages are ceramic, unlike most of the presumed Papuoid assemblages. They include perhaps the most elaborate combinations of shape and decoration to be found in the Western Pacific: subglobular pots, shouldered jars, bell-shaped bowls, and flat-bottomed dishes, decorated with horizontal bands of dentate-stamped, notched, and incised designs (fig. 6,a,b). Plano-convex adzes and sling shots are also used to identify the Lapitan people (fig. 6,d,c).

Lapitan complexes have been found all the way from New Britain, off New Guinea in western Melanesia, to Tonga and Samoa, the first islands in western Polynesia (fig. 5). The sites of that subseries are limited to the coasts of the larger islands and to small satellite islands, which suggests that the Lapitan people were immigrants who left the interiors of the main islands to their previous Papuoid inhabitants. This hypothesis is further supported by the fact that pottery and its associated artifacts are basically the same throughout the whole vast area of Lapitan distribution.

Nevertheless, there are differences. Roger C. Green, of the University of Auckland, his students, and his colleagues have made detailed, computer-assisted analyses of the pottery. "The results revealed an overall west-to-east trend indicative of distance delay in the Lapitan design system, from the rather ornate curvilinear and fairly elaborate rectilinear design patterns of the western Lapitans to the more simplified and generally rectilinear forms of the eastern Lapitans. They also indicate that exchange of motifs among the more westerly sites continued to occur, while in the eastern area Fiji, Tonga, and Samoa tended to remain in contact with one another but not with the regions to the east" (Green 1979, pp. 42–43).

In the west, the Lapitan assemblages retained their elaborate shapes and decoration until around 500 B.C., when the subseries came to an end there and its assemblages were succeeded in the archeological record

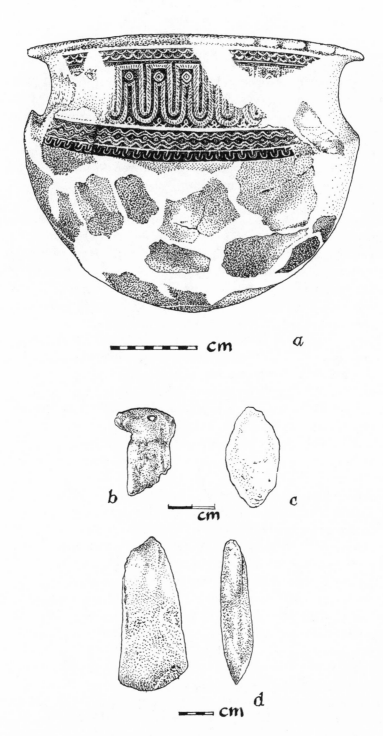

Fig. 6. Typical Lapitan Artifacts: (*a*) pottery jar, New Hebrides; (*b*) bird's head of modeled pottery, Santa Cruz Islands; (*c*) sling shell, Santa Cruz Islands; (*d*) plano-convex adze, Santa Cruz Islands. (After Green 1979, figs. 2.7, 2.6, 2.5,*h*, 2.4; *a*, courtesy of J.D. Hedrick)

by Melanesioid ones with different kinds of pottery. It is presumed that this change resulted from assimilation of the Lapitans with the previous Papuoid inhabitants of Melanesia. Apparently, the Lapitans contributed their Austronesian languages to the mix and the Papuoids, their racial traits, while Melanesioid culture was a blend of the traits of the two groups. This parallels the outcome of the migration of Austronesian speakers from Borneo to Madagascar a few centuries later (Oliver and Fagan 1975, pp. 199–202).

In the eastern Lapitan assemblages, on the contrary, the vessel forms gradually became simpler and the decoration began to disappear (Green 1979, pp. 43–44). By 500 B.C., only globular jars and simple bowls with little or no decoration were being produced. At this point, we may say that the Lapitan subseries had evolved into another Lapitoid subseries, which the specialists call Plain-ware.

The Plain-ware subseries lasted in the east from 500 B.C. to ca. 300 A.D. (fig. 5). To date, its assemblages have been found only in Tonga, Samoa, and Marquesas. It appears to be transitional between the Lapitoid series as a whole and modern Polynesian culture, which I shall call Polynesioid. The boundary between the two is marked by complete abandonment of pottery, which took place more or less simultaneously in Tonga, Samoa, and Marquesas (fig. 5).

The Polynesioid series is distinguished from its Lapitoid predecessor not only by the absence of pottery but also by the presence of new types of non-ceramic artifacts, including adzes with quadrangular cross sections (fig. 7,c). Bellwood (1978, p. 164) has divided the new series into three subseries: (1) Western Polynesian, which succeeded the Plain-ware subseries in Tonga and Samoa and spread to the outlying islands settled from there; (2) Early Eastern Polynesian, which followed the Plain-ware subseries in Marquesas and spread from there to the rest of the islands, including Hawaii at the apex of the Polynesian triangle, Tahiti in its center, and Easter Island and New Zealand in its southeastern and southwestern corners respectively; and (3) Late Eastern Polynesian, which developed out of subseries 2. The three subseries are plotted in figure 5.

The Western Polynesians retained the relatively simple fishing techniques of the ancestral subseries, while the successive Eastern Polynesian groups developed a variety of fishhooks, which archeologists have been able to use as time- and people-markers (fig. 7,a; Kirch 1980, p. 45).

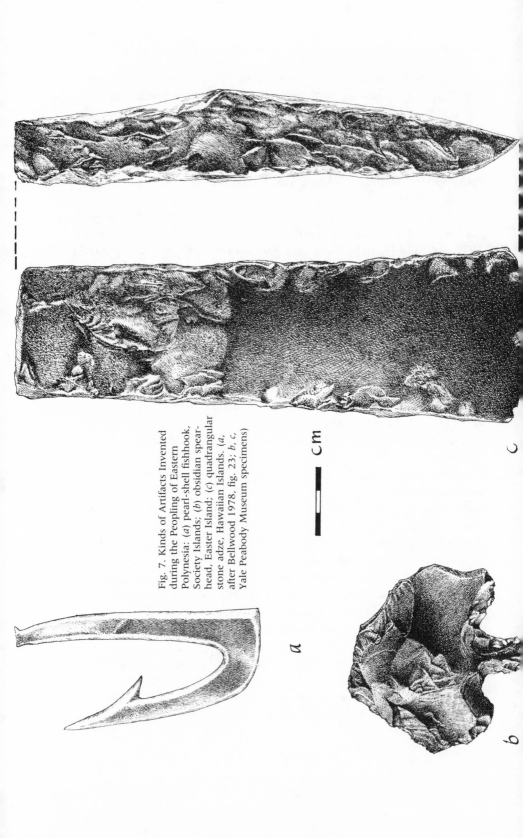

Fig. 7. Kinds of Artifacts Invented during the Peopling of Eastern Polynesia: (*a*) pearl-shell fishhook, Society Islands; (*b*) obsidian spearhead, Easter Island; (*c*) quadrangular stone adze, Hawaiian Islands. (*a*, after Bellwood 1978, fig. 23; *b, c,* Yale Peabody Museum specimens)

Cm

The migrants also adapted their agricultural techniques to the differences in climate and topography they encountered as they moved (Kirch 1982). The Western Polynesians made ceremonial buildings of perishable materials, while the Eastern Polynesians constructed increasingly complex platforms and enclosures of masonry. Upon the platforms, the Easter Islanders erected the statutes that attracted the attention of Heyerdahl, elaborating on a tradition of sculpture begun by their ancestors in central Polynesia (fig. 8,*b*,*c*,). They were perhaps driven to the use of stone for this purpose and for making houses and spearheads (figs. 8,*a*; 7,*b*) by exhaustion of the forests on the island. This is another example of how culture changes during the course of population movement.

E. *Summary and Conclusions*

The early Eastern Polynesians are the people Heyerdahl derived from Peru, while the Late Eastern Polynesians are his supposed migrants from the North Pacific Coast of the New World. The linguistic, physical anthropological, and archeological tests of his hypotheses have all shown to the contrary that these two groups are the latest in a series of local developments that took place as the ancestors of the Polynesians migrated into the Pacific from the direction of Asia.

There can no longer be any doubt, therefore, that the ancestors of the Polynesians moved through Melanesia from west to east, entering it via the smaller islands off New Guinea and leaving it through Fiji. From there, they passed into Tonga and Samoa on the east side of the Polynesian triangle (fig. 3). Present evidence indicates that they then crossed the triangle to the Marquesas Islands on its east side, whence they radiated to Easter Island in its southeast corner, to Hawaii at its apex, to Tahiti in its center, and finally to New Zealand in its southwest corner (figs. 4, 5). Their entry into Polynesia is dated around 1300 B.C., their settlement of Marquesas about 300 A.D., and their arrival in New Zealand ca. 900 A.D.

There is general agreement among the three tests about what happened in the Polynesian triangle. We can credit that agreement to the fact that Polynesia was virgin territory, without previous languages, cultures, and races that would have blended differentially with those of the migrants. Such a one-to-one relationship between language, culture, and race does not occur in less isolated parts of the world.

Professional linguists, archeologists, and physical anthropologists have

37

Fig. 8. Forms of Masonry and Sculpture Developed in Eastern Polynesia: (a) reconstructed stone house, East Island; (b) stone statue, Austral Islands; (c) stone statues, Easter Island. (a, c, courtesy of Roger Pardo-Mauer b, after negative no. 107935, Dept. Library Services, American Museum of Natural History)

been able to improve upon Heyerdahl's conclusions for the following reasons:

1. They used the results of each other's research as models, from which to derive their own working hypotheses. By so doing, they were able not only to check each other's progress but also to avoid wasting time and effort in needless trial and error (chap. 1,C).
2. They formulated alternative hypotheses, instead of limiting themselves to a Ruling Theory as Heyerdahl had done. This enabled them to discover and take into consideration the evidence not favorable to his theory (chap. 1,A).
3. They traced the migrations in terms of complexes of linguistic, cultural, or genetic traits, each indicative of a local population, instead of working with single traits as Heyerdahl had done. Complexes provide empirical evidence of population movement (chap. 1,B:7). Study of single traits, on the other hand, shows only that each trait has spread from one area to another. Such study does not indicate whether the spread was due to migration or to intercommunication, interaction, or interbreeding (chap. 1,B:5; see also Rouse 1980).
4. The experts examined the patterns of divergence from complex to complex, instead of working only with similarities as Heyerdahl had done. He had assumed that a people's language, culture, and race remain the same while they migrate, when in fact they are found to change (chap. 1,B:10).

Heyerdahl took it for granted that the ancestors of the Polynesians had developed their present form of culture either in the Americas or in the western Pacific and had brought it unchanged into the central Pacific. It never occurred to him that the migrants might have arrived with a previous, Lapitoid series of cultures and developed their distinctive Polynesioid series *after* they arrived in their present homeland. Kenneth Emory (1959), dean of Polynesian archeologists, was the first to suggest this possibility, and subsequent research has proved him right.

The research shows, as we have seen, that the Lapitoid peoples were making elaborate pottery when they first entered the Polynesian triangle. They gradually simplified this pottery and eventually abandoned it entirely. Simultaneously, they invented more elaborate fishing equipment and developed ceremonial platforms, with statues on some of them. These are but a few selected examples of the artifactual changes that

39

took place as the Lapitoid peoples transformed themselves into Polynesioids. The specialists are still working out the details and are also using the artifactual changes as a base line along which to trace the accompanying behavioral developments, for example, in settlement pattern, subsistence strategy, and social organization (Green 1979, pp. 34–40). The extent of these artifactual and behavioral changes is all the more remarkable because first the Lapitoids and then the Polynesioids were moving into a vacuum and were unable to obtain fresh ideas through interaction with previous inhabitants.

The Polynesians have preserved oral traditions about the manner in which they settled the islands. These traditions can be used to test parts of the linguistic and archeological conclusions. For example, the Maori, who live in New Zealand, tell us that their ancestors first settled there in the tenth century A.D. (Buck 1954, pp. 277–78). This date agrees nicely with the linguistic and archeological estimates.

According to the Maori, there were two subsequent migrations into New Zealand, one in the twelfth century and the other in the fourteenth century, the former by members of a single family and the latter by a fleet of canoes (Buck 1954, pp. 277–78). Neither of these events could have caused a repeopling of New Zealand; they are examples of immigration rather than population movement (chap. 1,B:9). Nevertheless, they may have touched off the change in subseries from Early to Late Eastern Polynesian, which happened more or less simultaneously.

But can we be sure that both events actually took place? Subsequent individuals may have claimed to be descended from the leaders of fictitious migrations in order to justify chiefly status. This possibility could be eliminated archeologically by searching for sites containing the cultural complex diagnostic of twelfth- and fourteenth-century Tahiti, whence the migrants are said to have come. In the absence of such evidence, the two traditions of immigration must be considered untested hypotheses.

Assuming that the traditions are valid, Duff (1950, pp. 18–20) has attempted to determine which cultural traits were introduced by each group of migrants. This illustrates the role of individual traits in the study of immigration and population movement. The traits should be regarded not as markers of the migrants but as a consequence of their movement.

Another lesson to be learned from the tests of Heyerdahl's hypotheses is that peoples do not move at a steady pace. As figure 5 indicates, the ancestors of the Polynesians paused for more than one thousand years in Tonga and Samoa before penetrating the heart of the Polynesian triangle. Bellwood (1978, p. 57) refers to these places as a bottleneck; *frontier* would be a more appropriate term.

The theory of preadaptation is applicable here (chap. 1,B:12). The halt at the Tongan-Samoan frontier must have been due, at least in part, to the need to develop new equipment and techniques with which to travel the far longer distances between islands in the heart of the Polynesian triangle. Discovery of a sailing canoe at an early site on Huanine Island, near Tahiti, has provided us with knowledge of the equipment (Emory 1979, pp. 202–04). This canoe had an estimated length of sixty-five feet, was double hulled, and, to judge from historic examples, contained a cabin (Sinoto 1983).

As for techniques, Polynesianists have conducted a series of experimental voyages in native-type canoes, seeking to determine how the peopling of the islands took place. They have been particularly concerned with the migrants' solution to the problem of sailing into the prevailing trade winds, which blow from the northeast above the equator and from the southeast below the equator, because Heyerdahl had based his hypotheses of population movement from the New World on the assumption that the migrants sailed before these easterlies. Finney (1985) has shown that the migrants could have waited for intervals in which westerlies temporarily replaced the trade winds and made it possible to sail from Melanesia to Polynesia.

Here we have an example of the need to take into consideration historical as well as functional factors. Heyerdahl reasoned only in terms of the most efficient use of sailing canoes. He did not stop to think that these canoes had been more highly developed in the western Pacific than in the New World and that, as a result, migrations were more likely to have proceeded against the prevailing winds.

The authorities have also debated whether the ancestors of the Polynesians made intentional voyages of colonization or accidentally drifted to new islands. A computer-assisted study of the possibilities indicates that intentional voyages are more likely to have been the case. Westerners, who are used to the emptiness of the Atlantic Ocean, find it difficult to conceive that anyone would intentionally seek islands in an unknown sea. However, the migrants into Polynesia came from seas that were full of islands, hence they must have had greater confidence in their ability to find new land (Levinson, Ward, and Webb 1973, pp. 62–64).

When the migrants first advanced into the central part of the Polynesian triangle, they encountered the same moist, tropical conditions from which they had come. When they continued on into the corners of the triangle, however, they had to adapt to different conditions— subtropical in the case of Easter Island and Hawaii, which they settled next, and temperate in the case of New Zealand, at the end of their journey. This is a good example of the process of adaptive radiation (chap. 1, B:12; see also Kirch 1980).

In the central part of the triangle, for instance, they relied both upon taro, grown in paddies like those used elsewhere for rice, and on yams, grown in dry fields cleared by the slash and burn technique. They were forced by the relatively dry, cool conditions in the corners of the triangles to place more emphasis on yams, and on the sweet potato when this became available from South America (Kirch 1982).

It is important to note finally that the reliability of conclusions about the Polynesians and their ancestors decreases as one moves back along the route of their migrations (from the right to the left side of figure 5). If one were to continue still further back through Indonesia to Southeast Asia, or through the Philippines and Taiwan to the mainland of China, whence the ancestral Lapitoid peoples are believed to have come, one would be indulging in speculation. There is not yet sufficient evidence from these areas to be able to test migration hypotheses.

The greater reliability of the Polynesian columns in figure 5 is partially due to the fact that more research has been done there. But, in addition, experience elsewhere indicates that the final stages of a migration are easier to study than its beginning. As one moves back toward the beginning, the changes become so great that it is difficult to determine whether one is still dealing with the same lines of development. Nevertheless, further research may ultimately be expected to solve the riddle of the origin of the Austronesian family of languages, which the Polynesians speak, and to establish its racial and archeological correlates.

3 THE ESKIMOS

The Eskimos have attracted the attention of students of migration because they are the only people known to have lived jointly in the Old and New Worlds at the time of European discovery. Prehistoric Eskimo remains have been found all along the Subarctic and Arctic coasts from the Chukchi Peninsula in northeastern Siberia to Greenland and Labrador (fig. 9). The Eskimos must have peopled this vast territory very recently, for their original speech has only had time to become differentiated into two languages. Nevertheless, they do not know how they reached their present territory. Anthropologists have therefore been faced with the task of determining whether the Eskimos developed in Siberia or in some part of northern North America.

Solution of this problem has been complicated by the fact that the Eskimos were not, like the Polynesians, the first occupants of the land where they now live. Both sides of the Bering Strait, in Siberia and Alaska, were originally peopled by the first inhabitants of the New World, who were able to cross the strait on a land bridge formed by the same last-glacial fall in the sea level that caused the island of New Guinea to become part of the continent of Australia (see chap. 2,D). And even in Greenland and Labrador, at the eastern end of Eskimoan territory, archeologists have found remains of earlier peoples. Consequently, we cannot, as in Polynesia, trace the Eskimos in terms of the

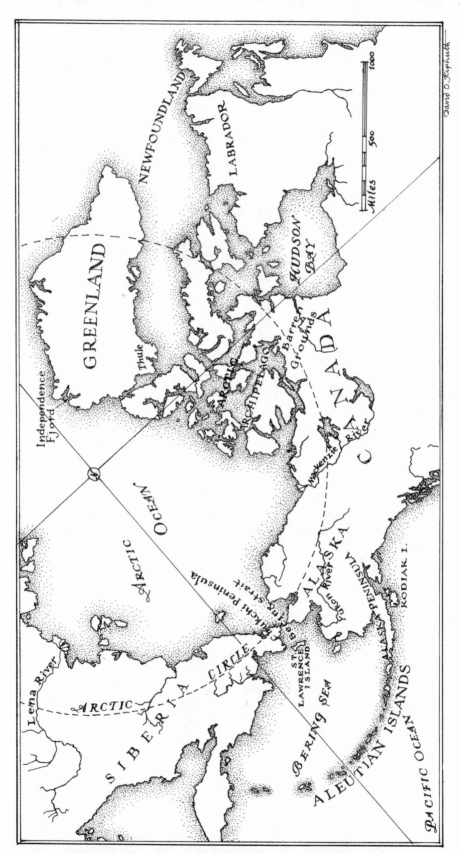

Fig. 9. Map of Arctic America. (After Dumond 1977, fig. 9)

David O. Kaplaluk

first settlement of each local area. We must rely instead upon the patterns of continuity and change in material culture from locality to locality, taking advantage of the fact that there has been relatively little time for change, whether in language, race, or material culture.

A. *Setting*

No discussion of Eskimo origins would be complete without reference to their close relatives, the Aleuts. These people live on the outer part of the Alaska Peninsula and on the Aleutian Islands, which jut far out into the Pacific Ocean from that peninsula.

At the time of first European contact, the Eskimos—or Inuits, as they now prefer to call themselves—occupied the base of the Alaska Peninsula and the land on either side of it, including most of the southern shore of Alaska proper and all of its western and northern shores (Oswald 1967, map 2). They also inhabited St. Lawrence Island at the end of the Chukchi Peninsula on the Asiatic side of the Bering Strait. From northern Alaska they extended along the Arctic coast of Canada to Labrador. Their remains are to be found throughout the Arctic Archipelago, a large triangular mass of islands whose base rests upon the Canadian coast and whose apex leads into northwestern Greenland. From it, they were able to expand all around Greenland, although they survive there only in isolated communities (Dumond 1977, fig. 6). At the northern tip of Greenland they came within 500 miles of the North Pole.

The Aleuts and most of the Eskimos are shore dwellers, living off the sea. A few Eskimos have moved inland along several rivers in western and northern Alaska and on the Barren Grounds in north central Canada, just east of Hudson Bay. Elsewhere, American Indians occupy the interior.

Soviet physical anthropologists have grouped the Aleuts and Eskimos with the Chukchis and neighboring tribes of northeastern Siberia into an Arctic-Mongoloid subrace, which is more closely related genetically to the Asiatic (Mongoloid) geographic race than to the American (Indian) race. The Arctic Mongoloids are relatively short, strongly built, and flat faced. They are also distinguished by brown skins, coarse black hair, and, except in the central and eastern Arctic, by a tendency towards broad-headedness.

The languages of the Eskimos and Aleuts are classified within a single

45

Eskaleutian family, along with the speech of the Chukchis. The broader affiliation of this family is unknown.

Aboriginally, the two groups shared a distinctive complex of cultural equipment, which differentiated them from both their Asiatic and their American neighbors. During the winter they lived in semisubterranean houses built of sod, stone, bone, and/or driftwood, and during the summer they moved about, living in skin tents. They had two types of skin boats: the small, decked kayak and the large, open umiak, which they used for hunting seal and whale respectively. From sea mammals like these they obtained not only their food but also skins for their houses, boats, and clothing; ivory and bone for implements and ornaments; and oil for the stone lamps with which they heated their homes.

Elaborate harpoons were employed to catch sea mammals. The harpoons had detachable heads, the lines from which were held in the hand when hunting from the ice and attached to skin floats when using boats. The floats enabled the hunters to retrieve animals after they had become exhausted. The harpoon heads were made of bone or ivory and had stone blades with which to cut through the animals' skins (fig. 12, a). Each base was beveled so that, when the harpoon head had entered the animal's flesh, it was pulled crosswise and acted as a toggle.

Two groups of Eskimos departed significantly from the diagnostic complex just described. The so-called Caribou Eskimos, on the Barren Grounds west of Hudson Bay, and the Central Eskimos, on the coasts and islands farther north (fig. 9), spent the winter in igloos made of snow-blocks, sometimes supplemented with skins. They used these temporary shelters in place of semisubterranean houses because they had to travel long distances overland or on ice floes in search of caribou and musk-ox, in the interior, and seal, on the coast.

Both the Eskimos and the Aleuts lived in small family groups without formal chiefs or headmen. They had shamans (medicine men), who cured the sick, foretold the future, and acted out events in the spirit world, using for this purpose masks and figures carved of wood, bone, and ivory which turn up in the archeological sites under favorable conditions of preservation.

B. Hypotheses

A number of late nineteenth-century archeologists were so impressed by the similarities in race and culture between the Eskimos and the

Magdalenian people, who inhabited much of western Europe at the close of the last glaciation, that they hypothesized a relationship between the two. W. Boyd Dawkins (1874) of Great Britain theorized that, when the climate became warmer at the end of the last glaciation and the musk-ox and reindeer consequently retreated to the north and east, the Magadalenian people followed them, eventually crossing the Bering Strait and becoming the Eskimos. W. J. Sollas (1924) continued to derive the Eskimos from the Magdalenians until well into the present century.

This early use of the model of population movement is patently wrong, for it assumed that a people on the move for ten thousand years, along a route that took it most of the way around the world, would have ended with the same culture with which it started. The model's protagonists made the same mistakes as Heyerdahl; they inferred a migration from similarities at each end of a presumed route without also considering the alternative ways in which these similarities might have come into existence and without being able to test their hypothesis by examining the patterns of change in race, language, and culture along the route. Subsequent study of these patterns has shown that they developed vertically, on chronological charts, rather than horizontally, as would have been the case if a migration had taken place (e.g., Chard 1974, pp. 56–108).

As in Polynesia, more recent attempts to determine the origin of the Eskimos have focused on the places where they now live. It is agreed that they developed their unique blend of physical, linguistic, and cultural traits either on the Chukchi Peninsula of northeastern Siberia or somewhere along the coasts of northern North America. The question is, where in that range?

Social anthropologists were the first to address this question. They were attracted to it by the fact that the Eskimo expansion appears to have taken place so recently as to be almost ethnographic. In *The History of Greenland*, Cranz (1767) came close to the mark when he stated that the Eskimos originated in northeast Asia and did not arrive in Greenland until the fourteenth century A.D. Rink (1887) derived them instead from Alaska; he thought they were local Indians who had moved to the coast and had there developed a maritime adaptation that enabled them to expand eastward. But Boas (1888) concluded from a study of Eskimo legends that they had originated in central Canada rather than Alaska.

More recent ethnologists have combined the foregoing hypotheses in various ways. Most importantly, Birket-Smith (1929, p. 608) was led by his research on the Caribou Eskimos to propose the following sequence:

1. Like Boas, he assumed that the original Proto-Eskimos were hunters who lived inland in the central area. He considered the Caribou Eskimos to be their modern survivors.
2. Some Proto-Eskimos moved to the shore and developed seal-hunting, thereby converting themselves into a new cultural group, Paleo-Eskimo. This group expanded along the shore, eastward into Greenland and westward into Alaska and Siberia.
3. The Paleo-Eskimos who went west learned to hunt the whale and thus evolved into Neo-Eskimos. The new group spread eastward along the coast, replacing the rest of the Paleo-Eskimos. It was ancestral to most of the modern Eskimos.
4. In the central area, however, descendants of the Proto-Eskimos subsequently moved to the shore and took the place of the Neo-Eskimos, forming a fourth group, the Eschato-Eskimos.

Birket-Smith developed these hypotheses as a member of the Fifth Thule Expedition of 1921–24, which was so called because the previous expeditions had worked in the district of that name in northwestern Greenland, near the point of entry from Central Canada (fig. 9). The fifth expedition aimed to trace the movement of the Eskimos from Canada through Thule into the rest of Greenland.

In furtherance of this aim, the expedition's archeologist, Therkel Mathiassen (1927), conducted excavations in the territory of the central Eskimos, on the route leading from the Canadian coast to Thule. The artifactual remains he found there were so similar to those of northern Alaska and Thule that he grouped all three into a "Thule culture" and concluded that they marked the eastward movement of the Neo-Eskimos that had been hypothesized by Birket-Smith. He was unable, however, to find traces of Birket-Smith's other three groups, the Proto-Eskimos, Paleo-Eskimos, and Eschato-Eskimos, and he expressed doubt that they had existed (Mathiassen 1930).

Birket-Smith (1930) responded by predicting that further archeological research in the central Arctic would turn up remains of the three missing groups. This has not happened, however. The pre-Thule remains that have been found do not fit Birket-Smith's predictions. And the post-Thule discoveries are in the Thule tradition. Consequently, archeologists now agree that the modern Eskimos developed in the west and that the Thule culture marks their movement eastward into Canada and Greenland.

Nevertheless, Birket-Smith, like Heyerdahl, deserves credit for calling attention to a problem that needed to be investigated. In effect, he set up alternative hypotheses to be knocked down, in accordance with the procedure of strong inference (chap. 1,A). Let us now examine the ways in which his hypotheses have been disproved.

c. *Linguistic and Physical Anthropological Tests*

As in Polynesia, linguists have studied the divergence of the local languages in an effort to determine the order and direction of their development. The results are summarized in figure 10, which is adapted from Dumond (1977, fig. 117). I have used the form of the Austronesian phylogeny (fig. 4).

The dates on the sides of the figure are glottochronological (chap. 2,B). They, too, come from Dumond (ibid.). He presents each date in the form of a range of the results achieved by different investigators; I have substituted means for the ranges, in accordance with radiocarbon practice. He notes a further bias. Whereas divergence was able to take place at its natural rate in Polynesia, because the local languages were widely dispersed on isolated islands, the speakers of divergent languages in the Arctic remained in communication with each other. This slowed the natural rate of change, and as a result the glottochronological dates are younger than they would otherwise be.

If figure 10 is correct, the original Eskaleutian language arose somewhere along the coast on either side of the Bering Strait. Glottochronology indicates that it had come into existence some time before 2500 B.C. Its speakers subsequently expanded through the Alaska Peninsula onto the Aleutian Islands, where they developed a new Aleutian language. Back in their Southwest Alaskan and Siberian homeland, there was a parallel development from Eskaleutian into Eskimoan. These events took place prior to 200 A.D.

The Aleutian language is still spoken on the islands of that name, but Eskimoan split in two some time before 1700 A.D. In Siberia and/or Southwest Alaska it developed into Western Eskimoan, and this language in turn spread to South Alaska. Meanwhile, other Eskimoan

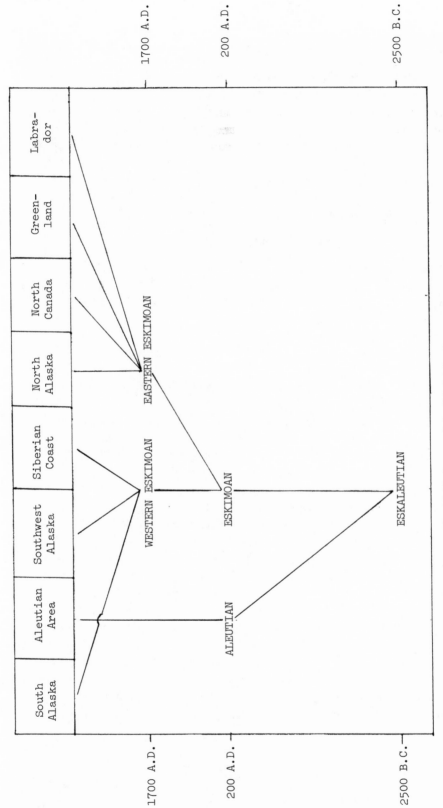

Fig. 10. Phylogeny of the Eskaleutian Languages.

speakers had expanded into north Alaska and, thus isolated, had produced an Eastern Eskimoan language, which they subsequently carried into North Canada, Greenland, and Labrador.

The expansion of Eastern Eskimoan speakers coincides nicely with Birket-Smith's hypothesis of a Neo-Eskimo migration from Alaska eastward and with Mathiassen's conclusion that there had not previously been true Eskimos in the east, as both Boas and Birket-Smith had supposed.

Dumond (1977, pp. 151ff.) has summarized the results of the research on physique. He reports, "little more can be gleaned than (1) that the skeletons of Arctic Mongoloids, of whom Eskimos and Aleuts are a part, are said to be distinguishable from those of American Indians, (2) that Eskimos and Aleuts are said to be distinguishable from each other in certain cranial features, such as the height of the vault, and (3) that all skeletal material [yet known] from the present territories of Eskimos and Aleuts are those of, respectively, Eskimos and Aleuts."

These results confirm the conclusion that the Eskimos and Aleuts must have originated somewhere within their present territories, presumably in the west since that is where the early split between the two took place. A study of dental morphology by Turner (1983) indicates more specifically that the origin was in Asia but tells us nothing about the time and route of migration. We do not yet have enough securely dated skeletal finds to determine the latter.

D. Archeological Test

The archeological test is illustrated in figure 11. This chronological chart has the same set of areas across its top as does the linguistic chart (fig. 10). The figures along its sides are, however, based upon radiocarbon analysis rather than glottochronology, and the units within its body consist of population groups defined in terms of their artifactual remains rather than their languages.

Synthesizers of Arctic prehistory have approached the problem of cultural differentiation in two ways. Bandi (1969, pp. 198–99) and Giddings (1967) have worked solely with individual complexes. They have preferred to discuss the relationships among the complexes informally and individually, instead of expressing them formally by means of a developmental classification, although Bandi has indicated overall lines of development in his chronological chart. In contrast, Dumond (1977,

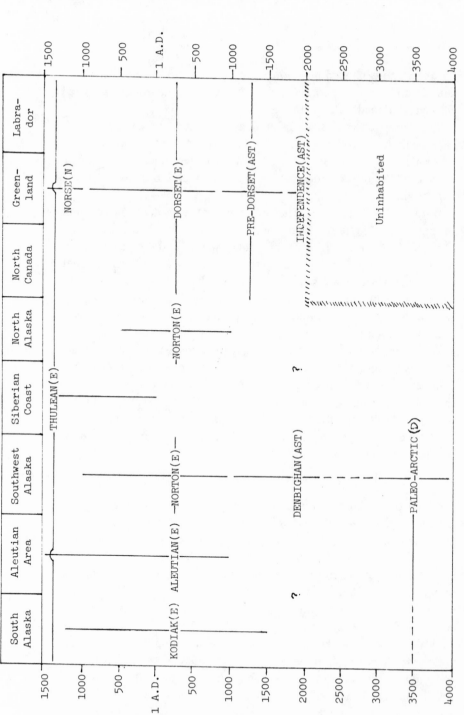

Fig. 11. Chronology of the Peoples and Cultures in Arctic America. (D) = Diuktoid series, (AST) = Arctic Small Tool series, (E) = Eskimoid series, (N) = North European series.

p. 155), MacNeish (1959, chart), Maxwell (1980), and Willey (1966, fig. 7–3) have grouped the complexes into formal "traditions," comparable to Mathiassen's Thule culture. They do not, however, agree upon the nomenclature for these traditions and upon the assignment of complexes to them, nor have they paid much attention to the developments within and among them. Consequently, I have devised my own classification, based upon the principles discussed in chapter 1.

Mathiassen's Thule culture is the Arctic equivalent of the so-called Lapita culture in Polynesia. I shall handle it in the same way, treating it as a subseries and adding the suffix -an to the term Thule in order to indicate that status. Following Dumond (1977, pp. 118–24, fig. 118), I shall also assign to it all of the subsequent Eskimo remains, since they appear to have evolved from it, and all of the previous complexes in the western Arctic that he considers to be ancestral to it (fig. 11).

Dumond (1977, fig. 118) distinguished four other late prehistoric traditions—Kodiak, Aleutian, Norton, and Dorset—which I shall likewise term subseries (fig. 11). Following Willey (1966, pp. 419–45), I assign these four, together with Thulean, to a single Eskimoid series. (He calls it "the Eskimo tradition.") In so doing, I have shortened Dumond's Kodiak and Aluetian "traditions" by excluding their original complexes, since these do not have the distinctively Eskimo and Aleut traits that were discussed in the previous section. The complexes I have omitted do not show in figure 11, because I am unable to assign them to subseries (the plain names in the figure) and series (the names in parentheses).

Three other series are included in figure 11. The Norse intruded into Eskimoid territory during protohistoric time; and Diuktoid and Arctic Small Tool peoples were there before the Eskimoids.

The earliest, Diuktoid series is named after finds in Diuktai Cave, northeastern Siberia, which their Soviet excavator dates between 20,000 and 8,000 B.C. (Rouse 1976). This series is represented within the Eskimoid area by a single, Paleo-Arctic subseries (Dumond 1977, pp. 36–46).

At the time, a great ice sheet extended all the way across northern North America, from the Alaska panhandle to Greenland and Labrador. Northeastern Siberia and the main part of Alaska were open, however, because they lacked sufficient precipitation to support glaciation; and the worldwide lowering of the sea level had caused the Bering Strait and adjacent seas to become a broad land bridge. As a result, Alaska formed part of the Asiatic continent, cut off from the rest of the Americas by the ice barrier to its east and south.

The Paleo-Arctic subseries reflects these conditions. For an indefinite time before 7000 B.C. it was the easternmost representative of the Diuktoid series, prevented by the ice barrier from expanding farther into the New World. When the barrier broke up after 7000 B.C., Paleo-Arctic spread into British Columbia, where it gave rise to a new subseries, Northwest Microblade, which does not concern us here.

The Paleo-Arctic subseries, like the rest of those in the Diuktoid series, is characterized by narrow, more or less parallel-sided slivers of flint or obsidian (volcanic glass), so small that they are called microblades. The artisan formed a wedge-shaped core by chipping a piece of obsidian on both sides and then exerted pressure on the blunt end of the wedge, successively removing a number of microblades. Next he appears to have prepared antler or ivory points. He grooved them on either side and inserted one or more microblades in each groove, for which reason they are known as side blades. Multiply hafted side blades like these are typically Asiatic and contrast strongly with the much larger, singly hafted end blades that were being used at the time by Folsomoid peoples south of the ice barrier (Dumond 1980, Rouse 1976).

The Paleo-Arctic artisans made hand tools in the same way they produced their wedge-shaped cores, by chipping away the surfaces on one or both sides of a stone flake. They used these unifacially or bifacially worked tools as choppers, knives, or scrapers, depending upon size and shape.

The people lived in bands, moving from camp to camp in order to hunt caribou, musk-ox, and other land mammals. It is believed that they followed the animals from Siberia across the Bering land bridge into Alaska, where they were stopped by the ice barrier. Unfortunately for us, they did not have the custom of intentional burial and so we lack information about their racial type. It is not impossible that they had already become differentiated into the Arctic Mongoloid subrace of the modern Eskimo and Aleut (sec. B, above).

When the ice barrier broke up after 7000 B., the Paleo-Arctic peoples came into contact with the Folsomoid and subsequent Archaic Indians south of the ice, and many of them adopted those Indians' practice of making bifacially chipped end points, often as alternatives to their own side-bladed points. This was the situation around 4000 B.C., when our chronological chart (fig. 11) begins.

Some time during the next two millennia, the Asiatic tradition of making side-bladed points and the American tradition of making end-bladed points coalesced, and a new Arctic Small Tool series was born. As the name of that series implies, its artisans continued the Asiatic practice of miniature stone chipping; even their end-bladed points are relatively small compared with American Indian practice. At the same time, they began to develop a greater variety of tools designed for specialized purposes, a trend which foreshadows later Eskimoid practice.

The original subseries of the Arctic Small Tool series will be called Denbighan, after the Denbigh Flint complex discovered by Giddings (1967, pp. 248ff.) on the Alaska coast just south of the Bering Strait. It was limited to the American side of the strait, extending from the Alaska Peninsula in the south through northern Alaska (Dumond 1982, fig. 2), and is radiocarbon dated between 2200 and 1000 B.C. It probably began earlier than that, however (fig. 11).

Denbighan is characterized by exquisitely made end and side blades, often bipointed, which appear to have been inserted in antler foreshafts. These were in turn attached to wooden shafts. The artisans also made small, chisel-like gravers, known technically as burins, with which to cut and groove the foreshafts. They were the first Arctic peoples to use the technique of stone grinding; they produced adze blades with polished bits and also ground the cutting edges of burins.

The Denbighan peoples lived primarily in the zone of tundra inland from the shore, where they hunted caribou and musk-ox. They visited the coast in summertime to obtain seal and went to the rivers to fish during salmon runs. They also began to settle down in semisubterranean houses during the winter. Thus they started to develop the subsistence and settlement patterns of the modern Eskimos and Aleuts.

These innovations enabled them to expand eastward into northern Canada and Greenland, which had previously been uninhabited. They followed the shore past the mouth of the MacKenzie River and then moved into the Arctic Archipelago, from which they spread all around Greenland, including its northernmost tip (Dumond, 1977, p. 86).

As they moved, they developed two new subseries. The first, known as Independence, lasted from ca. 2000 to 1700 B.C. (fig. 11). Its artisans added stems to their end blades, abandoned stone grinding, and pro-

55

duced the first harpoon heads of bone that have survived in the archeological record. The second subseries, Pre-Dorset, is dated between 1700 and 800 B.C. Stone grinding reappears and is now used to make slate knives and an occasional stone lamp. The Pre-Dorset people expanded southward from the Arctic Archipelago onto the mainland of Canada, taking advantage of a cooling trend which caused the Arctic climate to which they were accustomed to move southward.

The Arctic Small Tool series gave way to the Eskimoid series ca. 1500 B.C. in South Alaska, 1000 B.C. farther north in Alaska, and 800 B.C. in the central and eastern Arctic (fig. 11). The change appears to have been the result of acculturation or transculturation rather than migration, that is, the traits diagnostic of the Eskimoid series spread from one Arctic Small Tool people to another with little or no population movement. Four subseries developed in this manner: Kodiak in South Alaska, Aleutian in the adjacent peninsula and islands, Norton along the west coast of Alaska, and Dorset in the central and eastern Arctic (fig. 11).

The Norton peoples will serve to illustrate how this happened. Like their Denbighan predecessors, they were limited to the Alaskan side of the Bering Strait. They date back to 1000 B.C. both north and south of the strait, a distribution which may be ascribed to strong interaction and consequent acculturation among the local communities up and down the coast (fig. 11). Their culture gave way to Thulean ca. 500 A.D. in North Alaska and 1000 A.D. in Southwest Alaska, which suggests that Thulean migrants replaced them.

They joined the other emerging Eskimoid peoples in abandoning the manufacture of wedge-shaped cores and microblades, replacing them with bifacially chipped side blades, made in the same way as their end blades. The late survivors of the subseries in Southwest Alaska subsequently changed to the ground slate blades and knives that had developed among the rest of the Eskimoid peoples.

Like all Eskimoids, they had modern Eskimo settlement and subsistence patterns. They lived along shores and the major streams in order to hunt sea mammals and catch salmon, but at the same time continued to place greater reliance on land mammals than most of the modern Eskimos. They made harpoon heads of antler and ivory, but, with a few exceptions, these were relatively crude. They lived in pit houses and most used stone lamps to heat them.

The Norton peoples were the first of the Eskimoids to make pottery.

They tempered their clay with fibers to prevent it from cracking during the firing process and roughened the surfaces of the vessels by beating them, originally with sticks and later with carved paddles. They were also the first to practice art, but only sporadically and crudely except in the case of Iputiak, a late Norton people in northwest Alaska who joined the contemporary Thuleans of Siberia in engraving the bone and ivory objects in their burials. Both the pottery and the art are believed to have diffused form East Asia, where they have a long history of development. (Pottery goes back to the end of the Ice Ages in Japan; see chap. 4, D.)

Thulean was the last of the Eskimoid subseries to make its appearance. Like the previous ones, it seems to have resulted from acculturation. U.S. archeologists have found its earliest remains on St. Lawrence and Punuk Islands, off the southeast coast of the Chukchi Peninsula (fig. 9), and have securely dated them there back to at least the time of Christ. Soviet archeologists have obtained similar remains on the adjacent Siberian coast. Since Norton was still solidly entrenched on the American side of the strait at this time, we must conclude that Thulean began in Asia. It crossed the strait to North Alaska about 500 A.D. and, after a five hundred-year interval, resumed its advance in two directions, into Southwest and South Alaska and through the coast and islands of northern Canada to Greenland and Labrador (fig. 11).

The earlier Thulean peoples continued to chip side and end blades but the later peoples, after 1000 A.D., ground them from slate (fig. 12,a). They developed an impressive array of specialized tools and implements, which recall those of modern dentists in their variety and ingenuity. Among them were the first toggled harpoon heads, employed in catching both seal and whale; the kayak and umiak; floats and ice picks, which were likewise for pursuing sea mammals, as described in section A above; bird darts and boards with which to throw them; fish spears; bows and arrows for hunting land mammals; women's ulus and other kinds of knives of polished slate; sleds, snow goggles, bone needle cases, combs, and many more. Most of these are made of perishable materials, which have survived because so much of the ground is permanently frozen.

Whale was now a basic food, along with seal, and in the areas where the two were plentiful the Thuleans were able to settle down and build up large middens (piles of refuse). They constructed elaborate pit dwellings, with sunken entrance passages that trapped the cold air from outside, raised sleeping platforms, and occasionally a separate cooking

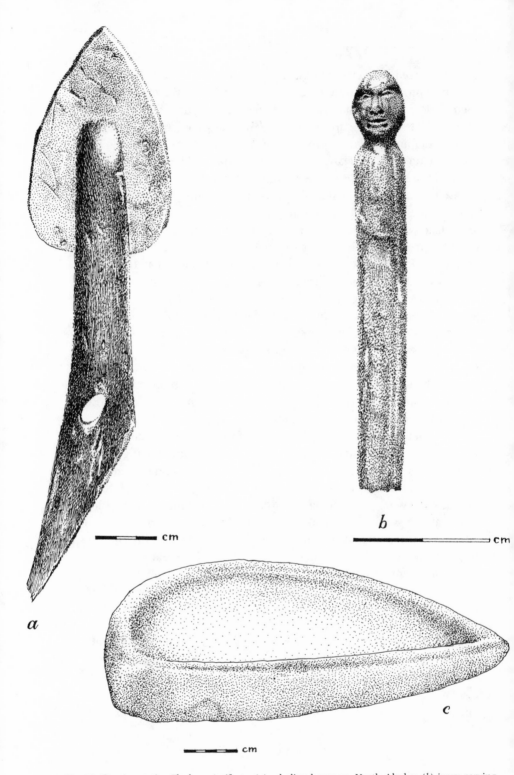

Fig. 12. Representative Thulean Artifacts: (a) whaling harpoon, North Alaska; (b) ivory carving, Southwest Alaska; (c) stone lamp, North Alaska. (After Dumond 1977, figs. 114, 115, 110)

chamber (fig. 13). Stone lamps and clay pottery continued in use (fig. 12,*d,c*); the latter gradually became gravel tempered and plain surfaced.

The earliest Thulean cultures, on the Asiatic side of the Bering Strait, are characterized by elaborate engraving and carving of organic materials, including harpoon heads and toys or ceremonial objects. The style is mostly geometric and curvilinear but also portrays human and animal figures (fig. 12, *b*). While it became simpler with the passage of time, it never died out and has experienced a renaissance among modern Eskimos. It was done with the help of iron tools obtained by trade from farther south in Asia.

The foregoing description applies primarily to the remains found in Siberia, where the series originated, and in north Alaska, to which it spread during the latter half of the first millennium A.D. That spread appears to have been the result of population movement; the Thulean pattern of change continued uninterrupted in north Alaska, without a significant admixture of traits from the preceding Norton population. The archeological evidence does not clearly indicate whether the further expansion into Southwest and South Alaska about 1000 A.D. was due to population movement or acculturation, but the fact that the Siberian, Southwest Alaskan, and South Alaskan Eskimos all speak the same language suggests a second migration from Siberia.

The Thulean migration eastward into Greenland and Labrador remains to be considered. Recent research has confirmed Mathiassen's conclusion that the migration proceeded from north Alaska through northernmost Canada to northwest Greenland (sec. B, above). It is radiocarbon dated in the tenth and eleventh centuries A.D. Given the rapidity of the movement, one might expect it to be traceable in terms of artifact similarities, but instead the archeologists have relied "heavily on stylistic variation of harpoon heads, which fortunately alter in regular progression" (Maxwell 1980, p. 171). As in Polynesia, the migrants gradually abandoned the use of pottery (Dumond 1977, p. 144) and modified their house types to fit local conditions, building their permanent dwellings of masonry rather than driftwood and adding snow-block igloos for temporary purposes (fig. 13).

The Thuleans took the same route as their Arctic Small Tool predecessors. They followed the coastline to the Arctic Archipelago and then turned into the islands, leaving the rest of the mainland to the previous

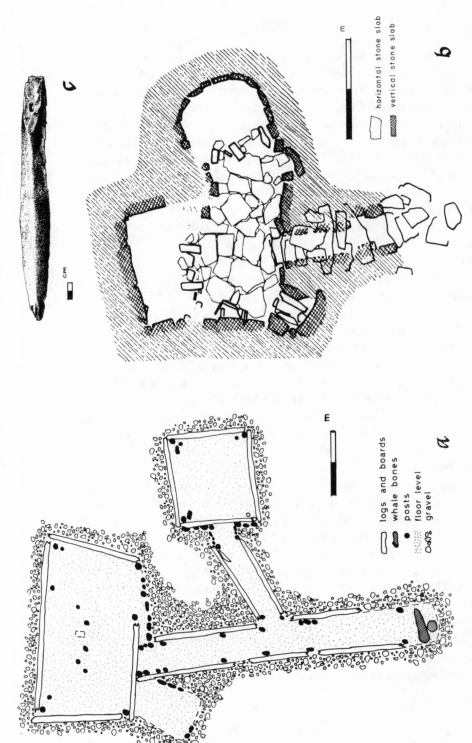

Fig. 13. Changes in House Type during the Thulean Migration: (a) ground plan of a Western Thule pit dwelling, Alaska; (b) ground plan of an Eastern Thule pit dwelling, Greenland; (c) bone knife presumably used to make snow-block houses in North Canada. (a, b, after Bandi 1969, figs. 47, 67; c, Yale Peabody Museum specimen)

Dorset peoples. They continued into northwestern Greenland but did not immediately occupy the rest of that island.

While the Thuleans were expanding eastward, the Norse were moving in the opposite direction, first into Iceland and then into southwestern Greenland. There, they found remains of Dorset peoples, who had previously abandoned the area. They were able to make contact with the people themselves only when they voyaged to the mainland (Dumond 1977, pp. 10–11).

It is no accident that the Norse movement westward coincided with the Thulean migration eastward. The climate was becoming warmer at the time, and this made life in the Arctic easier for the Norse, who were dairy farmers, as well as for the Thuleans, who depended on sea mammals (Hatt 1953, pp. 66–99).

In Alaska, the Thuleans had hunted whales in leads or narrow channels in the pack ice along the shore. The warming trend is believed to have reduced the area of the ice and caused the hunters to venture into the open sea, whence they expanded through the Arctic Archipelago into northeast Greenland in order to take advantage of the land-bordered channels and fjords available there. According to an alternative theory, the Thuleans relied more on seals than on whales, overexploited them in Alaska, and moved eastward as the ice opened up in order to obtain a fresh supply. Still other authors have suggested that population pressure in the west may also have played a role in their migration (Maxwell 1980, p. 172).

In Canada, the Thuleans coexisted with the Dorset peoples from the tenth to the fourteenth centuries, the former in the Arctic Archipelago and the latter on the mainland. Sites of both peoples have been found side-by-side along the boundary between the two. Subsequently, the Thuleans assimilated their neighbors, not only in the frontier zone but also farther south along the coasts of Hudson Bay and Labrador.

The climate was turning colder at the time, and this may have given the Thuleans an advantage over the Dorset people, since the Thuleans were accustomed to live under more Arctic conditions. They were also more flexible. When the two groups first came into contact, the Thuleans adopted a variety of items of Dorset material culture, including snow houses for travel during the winter and soapstone lamps and vessels, which they substituted for the pottery they had made in the west. The

Dorset people, on the other hand, only copied several features of Thulean house construction.

A similar sequence of events took place in Greenland. When the Thuleans arrived in northwestern Greenland, they came in contact with the Norse, who had previously colonized the southwest coast. The two groups traded with each other, the Thuleans obtaining iron artifacts to replace those which they had procured from Asia when they lived in the west. Again, the Thuleans were more receptive to new ideas; for example, they began to make buckets and barrels, using whalebone for the purpose in place of the wood which the Norse imported from Europe. The Norse rigidly retained their own culture, like the Dorset people on the mainland. Consequently, when the climate deteriorated with the onset of the Little Ice Age in the fifteenth century and disturbances in Europe cut the line of supplies from Europe, the Norse declined and the Thuleans, with their superior adaptability, were able to replace them (Hatt 1953, pp. 90–99).

As the climate continued to deteriorate during the sixteenth century, the Thuleans were forced to make further adjustments. Growth of the pack ice kept whales from entering the channels through the Arctic Archipelago and along the coast. The local Thuleans turned instead to the hunting of seals through the ice, which they did from snow houses, giving up the practice of constructing pit dwellings. They continued to live in tents during the summer in order to fish and hunt caribou, and thus they developed the migratory pattern of the modern Central Eskimos. During the nineteenth century a group of them moved out onto the Barren Ground in order to concentrate on fish and land mammals, and they became the modern Caribou Eskimos. Only in the subarctic parts of Alaska and Greenland were they able to continue their previous emphasis on seal- and whale-hunting from kayaks and umiaks. In Alaska, too, some expanded inland as their population increased, in order to exploit the rich supply of fish (Dumond 1977, pp. 147–49).

Thus the modern Thuleans developed a variety of settlement and subsistence patterns in order to take full advantage of the variety of resources available to them in different parts of the Arctic. Insofar as possible, however, they continued to make and to use the distinctive complex of portable artifacts through which their movements have been traced. All are still recognizable, therefore, as members of the Thulean subseries.

62

E. *Summary and Conclusions*

The linguistic, physical anthropological, and archeological tests have all confirmed the validity of Mathiassen's Thulean hypothesis and his rejection of Birket-Smith's four-part Eskimo sequence. If, however, Birket-Smith had conceptualized the parts of his sequence as general periods rather than as peoples, it too would have been valid (cf. chap. 1,B:4,7). His Proto-Eskimo would then have become the time of the Arctic Small Tool peoples; his Paleo-Eskimo, the time of the Kodiak, Aleutian, Norton, early Thulean, and Dorset peoples; his Neo-Eskimo, the time of the Thulean expansion; and his Eschato-Eskimo, the time of Thulean adaptation to the Little Ice Age.

Periods like these are worth formulating in the Arctic, as opposed to Polynesia, because the time of habitation was so much longer and the range of cultural development so much greater. Periods divide long time perspective into more manageable segments and make it easier to obtain an overview of the peoples who lived during each segment.

Birket-Smith put the cart before the horse. Instead of proposing a set of hypotheses about peoples and their origins, he would have been better advised to focus on the more fundamental problem of chronology. If he had couched his ideas about Arctic prehistory in a chronological framework, archeologists could have used it as a model from which to derive hypotheses about the local sequence in each area. This would have helped them in setting up the sequences, after which they could have converted the local periods into peoples, as advocated above (chap. 1,B:3,7), and could have organized those peoples into subseries and series, as I have done here. I shall treat Birket-Smith's units as general periods in the following summary.

Archeological research has shown that the Eskimos are rooted in the Diuktoid peoples, who inhabited northeastern Siberia, the Bering land bridge, and Alaska at the end of the Ice Ages. Diuktoid gave rise to the Arctic Small Tool series in Siberia and Alaska, which had become reseparated by the Bering Strait at the beginning of the Proto-Eskimo period about 3000 B.C.

During the latter part of that period, between 2000 and 1000 B.C., the Arctic Small Tool peoples moved eastward into the Arctic Archipelago and Greenland. They were the first to settle those areas. Their movement is marked not by a uniform culture but by a succession of three subseries, all three of which have incipient forms of the Eskimo settlement and subsistence patterns. These make Birket-Smith's term *Proto-Eskimo* an appropriate label for the period.

In the subsequent Paleo-Eskimo period, beginning about 1000 B.C. the Arctic Small Tool peoples became Eskimoid. They shifted from tiny, chipped-stone tools to large ground-slate tools, perfected the Eskimo type of pit dwelling, and developed seal-hunting from boats, in accordance with Birket-Smith's Paleo-Indian concept. These changes must have been the result of acculturation rather than population movement, for they took place at different times and in different ways in the various parts of the Arctic, producing separate Kodiak, Aleutian, Norton, Dorset, and Thulean subseries. The last arose on the Siberian side of the Bering Strait during the latter part of the Paleo-Eskimo period, between 1 and 500 A.D.

Thus the stage was set for the Thule expansion during the Neo-Eskimo period (fig. 11). It began as a migration from Siberia to North Alaska ca. 500 A.D., causing the Eskimoan language to split into Western Eskimoan, in Siberia, and Eastern Eskimoan, in North Alaska. the Thuleans who spoke Western Eskimoan expanded into Southwest and South Alaska after 1000 A.D. Those who spoke Eastern Eskimoan moved into the central and eastern Arctic about the same time. They followed the route previously traveled by the Arctic Small Tool peoples and, like them, reached north Greenland, the land closest to the North Pole. Their movement was facilitated by a warming trend about 100 A.D., which opened up the central and eastern Arctic to the typically Neo-Eskimo activity of whaling in the open sea.

During the Eschato-Eskimo period, finally, the Thuleans adapted to the Little Ice Age that began during the fifteenth century A.D. They were able to continue sealing and whaling for kayaks and umiaks in the subarctic parts of the western and eastern Arctic, but in the central Arctic had to turn to sealing from the ice, if they lived along the shore, and to caribou hunting, in the interior. There was also an expansion up the river valleys in Alaska to take advantage of the salmon runs and the animals in the adjacent forests.

The migration of the Thuleans into the central and eastern Arctic was intermittent. Like the Arctic Small Tool peoples before them, they originally colonized only the Arctic Archipelago and northwest Greenland.

After a pause of nearly five hundred years, they continued southward into the territory of the Dorset Eskimoids, on the Canadian mainland, and the Norse colonists, in southern Greenland. They had the advantage over both these groups that they were more willing to adjust their culture to the changing conditions of the time. This trait has also enabled them to make a better adaptation to European civilization than their Indian neighbors.

It is clear from the foregoing summary that the Bering Strait played a key role in the origin of the Eskimos. Most authorities (e.g., MacNeish 1964, p. 386) have assumed that it was a corridor through which human populations migrated back and forth between the Old and the New Worlds. The late J. L. Giddings (1952, p. 102) has argued on the contrary that "from the distant past a locally modifying population and culture, based upon the combined food resources of the land and sea, . . . has served as a narrow conduit through which diffusion has freely vibrated in both directions."

Recent research has proved Giddings to be right. In current terminology, the Bering Strait was an interaction sphere, in which locally based populations exchanged ideas and developed new forms of culture. First the Arctic Small Tool and then the Thulean peoples carried the forms they developed there into Canada and Greenland. These two peoples did not pass through the Bering Strait; they started from it.

This is a good example of the fallacy of interpreting the past in terms of present conditions. For us, the Bering Strait is a boundary, to be traversed in order to reach the places in Siberia and America where developments are taking place. For the Eskimos and their predecessors, the strait was a center from which traits spread to peripheries in the interior of Asia and North America. We are oriented towards the land, prefer to travel by it, and hence regard the sea as a barrier to communication. the Eskimos, on the contrary, were a coastal people, more at home on water than on land, hence they were more likely to communicate by sea. The Eskimos on St. Lawrence Island, for example, used to meet regularly with their Siberian counterparts until the Soviet authorities prohibited contact (Geist and Rainey 1936, p. 17).

In chapter 2, we found that the archeologists tracing the Polynesian migration began at its end and moved back toward the center from which it started. They have encountered increasing difficulty the closer they have come to the center. The same is true in the Arctic area. The original and most successful research on the Eskimo migration has taken place in its eastern periphery and the results became less clear and less reliable the closer we move to the center on either side of the Bering Strait. To judge from these two examples, and from the others to be discussed below, research on migrations is more easily conducted in peripheries than in the centers of cultural development.

Since the Eskimos have lived in a harsh environment and have been faced with the problem of adapting to it, one is tempted to trace their movement in terms of their adaptations. Birket-Smith succumbed to this temptation, another reason why his hypotheses have proved to be wrong. One cannot assume, as he did, that a migrating people will retain its distinctive adaptation when it enters an area where conditions are adverse. Some peoples, like the Norse, have done so, but others, like the Thuleans, have successfully adjusted to the new conditions. Consequently, we cannot treat migration and adaptation as dependent variables, and we are not justified in using one to study the other.

A further reason for keeping migration and adaptation separate is that each requires a different data base. Population movements are best traced in terms of technological and stylistic norms, such as the chipped stone industries and harpoon-head styles used by Arctic archeologists. Ecological adaptation, on the other hand, is best studied in terms of functionally defined artifact types and the ways they have been used to insure the survival of particular social groups within a given population.

In anthropology today, the first of these two approaches is known as structuralism and the second, as functionalism (e.g., Leach 1973, Johnson 1982). Many anthropologists consider the two to be alternatives and argue about which is the better approach to use in all circumstances. The experience of the Arctic specialists shows that the two are instead complementary and that it is advisable to select one or the other depending upon one's objectives.

Certainly, migrations are better traced through structural than functional traits. Structural traits are relics of the past and, as such, provide the continuities anthropologists seek when studying migration, evolution, and other problems of origin. Functional traits, on the contrary, are phenomena of the present and hence more suitable for working with problems of adjustment to current conditions. I shall return to this subject in chapters 5,E and 6,B.

4 THE JAPANESE

Japan is a favorable place in which to study migrations because its islands form a linear chain, through which people could have moved in either direction (fig. 14). The large islands of Kyushu, Shikoku, and the western end of the largest island of Honshu cluster together in the center of the chain, enclosing a body of water known as the Inland Sea. Honshu continues in an easterly direction beyond the Inland Sea and then curves northward to within a few miles of Hokkaido, a fourth large island at the top end of the chain. The much smaller Nansei (Southern) Islands extend southward from Kyushu at the bottom end of the chain.

The chain parallels the east coast of Asia but can be reached from there only via the Korean Peninsula in its center, Siberia at its northern end, and Taiwan at its southern end. Between Korea and Siberia, it is separated from the mainland by the Sea of Japan, and between Korea and Taiwan, by the East China Sea.

Korea is the main point of entry. From its southeastern corner, one need only cross the relatively narrow Korea Strait to reach the Tsushima Islands, which are Japanese. One can then continue over Tsushima Strait to Kyushu Island and on into the Inland Sea. Korea and Tsushima Straits play the same central role in the study of Japanese origins that the Bering Strait plays in research on the origin of the Eskimos.

From southern Siberia one can reach the northernmost Japanese is-

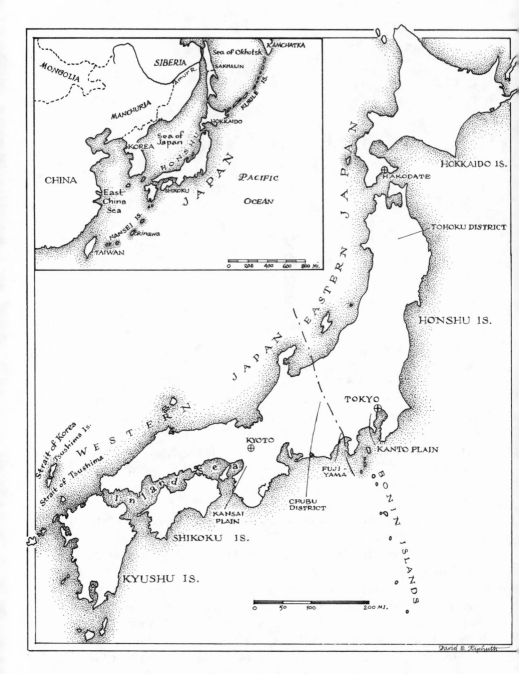

Fig. 14. Map of the Japanese Archipelago.

land of Hokkaido via the Amur River valley and the island of Sakhalin, which is at its mouth. This route, however, is roundabout, relative to the center of civilization in China, and is handicapped by a cold climate. The third route, from the south China coast through Taiwan, does not have these disadvantages, but the Nansei Islands, which link Taiwan with Kyushu, are too far apart and too open to the sea for easy passage. Nevertheless, the Black Current favors movement from south to north (Pearson 1969, pp. 19–20).

Since Japan is on the Pacific Rim, it can also be reached via the segments of that rim at either end of its chain of islands. The Bonin Islands and Micronesia connect it with the rest of Oceania to the southeast; and the Kuril Islands and Kamchatka Peninsula, with the Bering Sea to the northeast. Thus, Japan was accessible to both of the peoples already discussed, the Polynesians and the Eskimos, but over distances too great for direct contact. The Japanese appear to have been culturally influenced by the peoples of the Pacific and the Arctic, but we must look to the continent of Asia for their origins.

Japan was almost certainly peopled before either the Pacific Islands or the New World. The Korea and Tsushima Straits, like the Bering Strait, were dry during the periods of Pleistocene glaciation, and they are far enough south to have been traversed by the first humans who expanded out of tropical Asia into its temperate parts (Aikens and Higuchi 1982, fig. 2.1). It is not clear to what extent the northern and southern ends of the Japanese archipelago were also connected to the mainland (for another version, see Groot 1951, map III). In any event, Japan's longer time of occupation increases the difficulty of distinguishing later arrivals from the original inhabitants.

A. *Setting*

Most summaries of Japanese archeology are limited to the large islands of Kyushu, Shikoku, Honshu, and Hokkaido (e.g., Aikens and Higuchi 1982). We shall also include the Nansei Islands in order to be able to take into consideration all possible migration routes, in accordance with the principle of multiple working hypotheses.

The Japanese divide their country into two parts, Western and Eastern, drawing the line between the two through Fujiyama and the other mountains in the central part of the main island of Honshu (Fig. 14). Western Japan begins on the Kansai (west of the mountains) plain and continues through the Inland Sea and Kyushu to the Nansei Islands. Eastern Japan begins with the Kanto (east of the mountains) plain, on which Tokyo is situated, and continues through the rest of Honshu to Hokkaido Island at the northern end of the archipelago.

The two regions differ in climate and vegetation. Western Japan is subtropical, especially in the south, and has evergreen forests. Eastern Japan is temperate and has deciduous forests, which give way to conifers at higher altitudes and in the north (Koyama 1978). The Black Current flows from south to north along the Pacific side of the islands, ameliorating the climate and providing a wealth of seafood. Heavy snowfalls occur on the Asiatic side of Eastern Japan.

Since the Japanese people are civilized, they cannot be defined in terms of their folk artifacts, that is, in terms of the pottery, stonework, and other equipment used by the ordinary people, as was possible in the case of the Polynesians and the Eskimos. We must focus instead upon the artifacts of their vocational specialists—the buildings erected to house them, the tools of their professions, and the luxury goods they consumed.

Their artifacts may be viewed in two different ways. On the one hand, they provide us with a record of the standards, customs, and beliefs that define the Japanese people and comprise its civilization; on the other hand, they document the existence of the social entity that we call the Japanese state. The Japanese people and its civilization have to be considered coterminous, for the former is defined by the latter, but the Japanese state is not. Just as the Classical Greek people and its civilization were divided among a number of small states, so parts of the Japanese population have from time to time rejected the authority of the Japanese state or have lived beyond its limits. In the following discussion, therefore, I shall carefully distinguish the history of the Japanese people and its civilization, which is my primary concern, from the history of the Japanese state, which is not.

The earliest historical records about the inhabitants of Japan come from Chinese who settled in northwest Korea during the first two centuries B.C. (Pearson 1978a). These intruders participated in trade with the islanders, whom they called the Wa (dwarf) people. Their historians tell us that the Was were skilled farmers and fishers, adept at weaving and warfare. They were organized into one hundred "countries," which varied in size from one to seventy thousand households. They had hereditary rulers, nobles, and officials to collect taxes (Reischauer and Fairbanks 1958, pp. 462–64).

The Chinese and Koreans exchanged envoys with the dominant kingdom of Yamatai, which was ruled between 183 and 248 A.D. by a queen named Himiko. To reach Yamatai, the historians say, it was necessary to cross the straits of Korea and Tsushima to northern Kyushu Island and then to undertake another long sea voyage (fig. 14). The direction and distance of this voyage is unclear but if, as many modern historians believe, it passed through the Inland Sea, Yamatai would have been situated on the Kansai plain at the far end of that sea (Kidder 1977, p. 44, map).

It can hardly be a coincidence that the present imperial dynasty arose in a district called Yamato on the Kansai plain. Several other parts of the historical record also relate Queen Himiko to that dynasty. Her name means "sun daughter" and the members of the dynasty trace their descent from the sun goddess, Ameratsu. She had priestly functions like theirs, and upon her death she was buried in a huge mound, as they used to be. It is reported that hers measured more than one hundred paces in diameter and that she was accompanied to her grave by more than one hundred attendants (Miller 1967, p. 25).

The Chinese records indicate that the Was were a Japanoid people but had not yet become specifically Japanese. They were only approaching the status of civilization. Their range of full-time professional specialists does not seem to have extended much beyond the activities of politics and warfare.

With the downfall of the Chinese outposts in northwest Korea during the fourth century A.D., Japan receded from protohistory into prehistory. Our knowledge of subsequent events in the islands is derived from local traditions written down after the adoption of Chinese historiography at the beginning of the eighth century A.D. Between 300 and 600 A.D., according to these traditions, the imperial dynasty arose in Yamato and extended its rule as far as southwestern Korea. Professional experts entered Japan from that country and contributed to the development of specialized vocations.

In this way, the Wa people gradually acquired such elements of Chinese civilization as its writing, administrative structure, palace architecture, urban planning, historiography, and the Buddhist religion. The local Was adapted these foreign traits to their own indigenous lifestyle by

71

means of the process of transculturation (chap. 1,B:11), thereby transforming themselves into the Japanese people and becoming fully civilized (Hall 1970, pp. 24–47).

Japanese civilization thus arose at the beginning of the historic era, some time after the formation of the Japanese state. The historic era is divided into three ages, Ancient, Medieval, and Modern, each of which may also be viewed substantively as a stage in the development of the civilization (fig. 15). Let us proceed in terms of these ages.

The Ancient Age lasted roughly from 600 to 1200 A.D. During the 600s, the Japanese people and its civilization were limited to the territory from northern Kyushu, in Western Japan, through the Kanto Plain in the east. During the 700s, the inhabitants of southern Kyushu and parts of Honshu immediately north of the Kanto plain became acculturated to the civilization as a consequence of strong interaction (chap. 1,B:11) between the Japanese state and its neighbors to the south and north, but it was not until the end of the Ancient Age, ca. 1200 A.D., that the state and its civilization reached the northern end of Honshu Island.

The Japanese called the barbarians beyond the northern limit of their state Emishis or Ezos (Hall 1970, p. 19). Since these people practiced farming, had metal tools, and occasionally buried their dead in mounds, they must be considered Japanoid. They were in effect survivors of the way of life that had existed in central Japan before the introduction of elements of Chinese civilization (Aikens and Higuchi 1982, p. 291).

The previous way of life also survived on the Nansei Islands, to the south of the Japanese state. Here, however, interaction was weaker, consisting primarily of trade (e.g., Ryūkyū Island Archaeological Research Team 1981, pp. 141–42).

Nothing is known historically about the situation during the Ancient Age on Hokkaido Island, at the northern end of the archipelago. That island was just as isolated at the time as Hawaii and Alaska were during the foundation of the United States. Too remote for direct contact with civilized peoples, it remained completely prehistoric.

During the Medieval Age, which lasted in round numbers from 1200 to 1600 A.D., the Japanese people finally began to interact with the inhabitants of Hokkaido as well as the Nansei Islands. They developed both commercial and political relationships with the two outlying peoples, but did not influence them strongly enough to affect their separate identities.

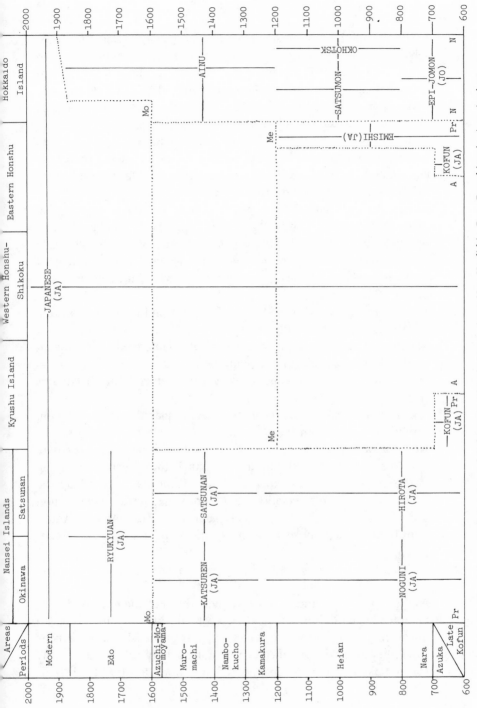

Fig. 15. Chronology of the Peoples and Cultures in Historic Japan. Ages: N = Neolithic, Pr = Protohistoric, A = Ancient, Me = Medieval, Mo = Modern. Series: (Jo) = Jomonoid, (Ja) = Japanoid.

They found the Nansei islanders to be more or less related to themselves. The islanders possessed a rudimentary Japanoid culture (Pearson 1969, pp. 134–35). Their language, Ryukyuan, and the Japanese language belong to the same family, Altaic (Miller 1971, pp. 43–46); and both they and the Japanese are classified within the Asiatic geographic race, otherwise known as Mongoloid (Garn 1965, p. 133).

Hokkaido Island, on the contrary, was populated by an unrelated people, the Ainus, who lived by hunting and fishing rather than agriculture and had customs, such as a bear cult, that are reminiscent of the natives of Siberia and Alaska. Their language is considered non-Altaic; and their light skin, rugged faces, and abundant body hair led many of the earlier authorities to classify them as Caucasoid in the now outmoded tripartite division of the world's population into typologically defined races. The Ainus have since been reclassified as a separate local race within the Asiatic geographical race, to which the Japanese also belong (Garn 1965, p. 148).

Both the Nansei Islands and Hokkaido became fully Japanized during the Modern Age, after 1600 A.D., but in very different ways. The Nansei islanders were acculturated, passing through an intermediate Ryukyuan stage before acquiring Japanese civilization (fig. 15). Like the inhabitants of the main islands, they retain many elements of their local folk cultures (Pearson 1969, pp. 21–22).

The Ainus of Hokkaido, in contrast, were displaced, and the few who survive are being assimilated. Japanese colonists began to enter southwest Hokkaido in the seventeenth century but remained stationary there until late in the nineteenth century, when their government, responding to the threat of Russian expansion through Siberia, rounded up the Ainus, put them on reservations, and encouraged further immigration from the south (fig. 15). These events paralleled the expansion of Americans into Alaska at the expense of its natives, the Eskimos and Indians (chap. 3).

B. *Hypotheses*

As the Japanese expanded into Hokkaido, they became interested in its natural and cultural resources. They recorded Ainu customs and began uncovering traces of the previous occupants of the island. As early as 1764, they noted the presence of prehistoric pottery at Kamiyama, now part of Hakodate, the principal port of entry from Honshu Island (Haniwara et al. 1968). During the following century, they made similar discoveries on most of the other main islands. They called the pottery they found *Jomon* (cord-patterned), because much of it bears the impression of strings or other organic materials.

When Westerners were admitted to Japan during the latter part of the nineteenth century, they rediscovered Jomon pottery. Edward Morse (1897), an American zoologist, noticed a shell heap at Omori on Tokyo Bay, collected Jomon pottery from it, and was able to show by excavation that the pottery had been laid down by hunters and fishers, like the Ainus.

These events led to the formulation of a Jomon people and culture and to a belief that the Jomons were ancestral to the Ainus. Projecting the historic situation in Hokkaido back into prehistory, and relying on the fate of the Eskimos and Indians in Alaska as a second model, both local and foreign archeologists concluded that the Jomon people were the aborigines of Japan, had been displaced by Japanoid migrants from the mainland, and in the process had developed into the Ainus (e.g., Watson 1963).

Historians accepted this conclusion and proceeded to identify the Emishis who lived in northern Honshu Island during the Ancient Age as Ainus. They viewed the conquest of the Emishis as part of the migratory process whereby Japanese replaced Ainus throughout the archipelago (e.g., Sansom 1968, pp. 196–203). In so doing, they overlooked the alternative possibility that the Emishis might have been Japanoids not yet affected by the rise to civilization in central Japan, as now appears to have been the case (fig. 15).

Meanwhile, archeologists had begun to investigate the Japanoid remains. They were able to distinguish two successive peoples and cultures, Yayoi and Kofun. The former, named after a site in the Tokyo metropolitan area, was characterized by plain pottery, rice cultivation, and the gradual development of metallurgy. The latter was marked by large mounds (*kofun*), after which the people and its culture are named. The mounds contain the burials of persons of high status accompanied by clay figures (*haniwa*) portraying warriors, servants, and other attendants, together with the material equipment needed in an afterlife. Thus they illustrate the development of vocational specialists (Beardsley 1955, figs. 2–7).

The Yayoi people and the earlier Kofuns can be identified as the Was who interacted with the Chinese intruders and contemporary local peoples in Korea, for their sites have yielded bronze mirrors, coins, and other trade objects in the style of the dynasties that ruled China at the time. Their remains correspond remarkably well to the Chinese historians' description of Wa culture, if it be assumed that *haniwa* were buried with Queen Himiko as surrogate attendants (Kidder 1966, pp. 91–94).

The later Kofun sites obviously date from the time when the imperial dynasty was emerging among the Wa people on the Kansei plain. Japanese scholars have been able to identify particular sites as the burial places of emperors mentioned in the traditional sources. Chinese trade objects now disappear from the mounds; their place is taken by comparable artifacts made locally (Amakasu 1973, pp. 169–78). These goods bear witness to the increasing professionalism that was to lead to the emergence of the Japanese people and its civilization at the beginning of the historic era.

Secure in the belief that they had solved the problem of their origin through the Jomon-Yayoi-Kofun classification, the local archeologists moved on in the period immediately before and after the second World War to chronological research. They discovered a new Preceramic culture and worked out a chart for it. They also set up separate charts for the Jomon, Yayoi, and Kofun cultures. The Jomon chart, for example, has local areas marked off across its top and a set of general periods along its sides. The body of the chart is composed of local periods, as is my figure 1, each defined in terms of its diagnostic pottery types (e.g., Kamaki 1965). A system of ages was also established to serve as a means of tying together the four charts. Both the general periods and ages are modeled after those for the historic era (fig. 15).

The charts have provided Japanese archeologists with a frame of reference through which to study changes in ceramic style and in other aspects of artifactual and behavioral culture. On northwest Kyushu Island, they were surprised to find a pattern of gradual development extending through the Late and Final Jomon periods into Early and Middle Yayoi. This contradicts the theory that a Yayoi people and culture, ancestral to the modern Japanese, had invaded Japan from Korea and had driven its previous, Final Jomon population northward into Hokkaido Island, where they became the modern Ainus. It has caused many archeologists to assume instead an in situ development of Yayoi culture under influence from the mainland (e.g., Akazawa 1982).

As a result, we are now faced with two alternative hypotheses, one of which assumes a repeopling of Japan by Yayoi immigrants from Korea and the other, transculturation of all except the most remote Jomon people to mainland customs. I shall test these two hypotheses against the linguistic, physical anthropological, and archeological evidence.

c. *Linguistic and Physical Anthropological Tests*

The Japanese have done little comparative (i.e., classificatory) research on their own language. It remained for an American linguist, Roy Miller (1967) to hypothesize that Japanese, Ryukyuan, and Korean all belong to the Altaic family, which comes from the heart of Asia. He has since worked out a phylogeny of the family (Miller 1971, fig. 1) and, through lexical research, has reconstructed the route of its expansion into Japan (Miller 1980, pp. 52–56, 92–103).

In presenting Miller's phylogeny here (fig. 16), I have modified it to conform to the format used elsewhere in the volume and to my understanding of his 1980 publication. The areas marked off on the top of my chart are based upon the latter. The dates along the sides are his glottochronological estimates (1967, pp. 82–83), with one exception that will be noted later. The dates are to be considered minimum values (for an explanation, see chap. 3,c). The dates in round numbers are my own interpretation of the historical evidence.

The following conclusions may be drawn from the genetic relationships and geographic distributions indicated in figure 16:

1. The original, Proto-Altaic language arose on the West Siberian steppes, between the Caspian Sea and the Altai Mountains, many thousands of years before the time of Christ.
2. The Proto-Altaic speakers migrated eastward into the Altai Mountains, where they separated into two groups, one speaking the Proto-Western Altaic language and the other, Proto-Eastern Altaic.
3. Proto-Western Altaic gave rise to Turkish and other West Asian languages. (They are omitted from the figure since they are not pertinent to our discussion.)
4. Some Proto-Eastern Altaic speakers moved in a southeasterly direction onto the Mongolian steppes, where their language developed through Proto-Mongol into today's Mongol.
5. Others turned to the northeast and settled in the Siberian forests.

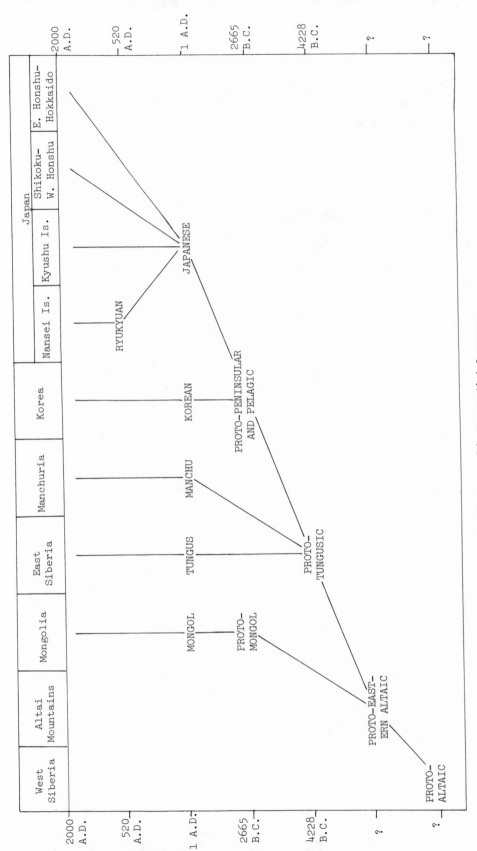

Fig. 16. Phylogeny of the Eastern Altaic Languages.

Their language progressed through Proto-Tungusic to Tungus, which is spoken by the present natives of the forests.

6. Some of the Proto-Tungusic speakers proceeded eastward into Manchuria, settled down there, and created the Manchu language.

7. Others continued on into the Korean peninsula. Intercommunicating within this isolated territory, they produced a separate, Proto-Peninsular and Pelagic language. It came into existence some time before 4000 B.C.

8. The speakers of Proto-Peninsular and Pelagic eventually split into two groups, one remaining on the peninsula and the other moving eastward into the Japanese archipelago. The peninsular group developed the Korean language and the island group, Japanese. This divergence took place prior to 2665 B.C.

9. In conformity to the geographic configuration of the islands, the Japanese speakers formed three dialects, which are indicated in the figure by unnamed lines. One centered around the Inland Sea in Western Japan, a second occupied Eastern Japan, and the third developed in the relative isolation of Kyushu Island (Miller 1980, p. 6).

10. Several poorly known dialects in the Nansei Islands are grouped together under the name Ryukyuan. Since this language is farthest removed from the linguistic center around the Inland Sea, one might expect it to be a separate offshoot of the ancestral language, Proto-Peninsular and Pelagic. Instead, it appears to have become differentiated from Japanese in the extreme isolation of the Nansei Islands (Miller 1967, pp. 83–87). This process began to take place some time before 526 A.D. (Bleed 1972, p. 10).

The glottochronological date of 2665 B.C. for the separation of Korean and Japanese is surprisingly early (Miller 1967, pp. 83–84). It implies that the speech community which produced the modern Japanese and Ryukyuan languages had reached Japan several thousand years before the appearance of the first Japanoids, who had traditionally been thought responsible for introducing Yayoi culture and, with it, the Japanese language. Miller did not pursue this implication immediately, but the subsequent discovery of archeological evidence for a transition from Jomon to Yayoi culture within Japan aroused his interest in it (Miller

1980, pp. 120–25). He searched the Jomon literature for evidence of an invasion from Korea that might be correlated with the arrival of the ancestral Japanese speakers and found it in a ceramic horizon that is variously termed Comb-pattern, Geometric, Rectilinear Incised, and Sobatan (Kim 1978, pp. 10–52; my fig. 17). If he is correct, the Proto-Insular and Pelagic speakers who were to develop the Japanese and Ryukyuan languages moved from Korea into Kyushu Island during the Early Jomon period, between 5000 and 3500 B.C. Miller further concludes that the Japanese speakers did not expand into the rest of Japan "until much later, perhaps as late as the two-century period from 100 B.C. to 100 A.D.," which would be the Middle Yayoi period in my terminology (Miller 1980, p. 128; my fig. 17). In this way Miller is able to reconcile an early arrival of the Japanese language from Korea with the much later rise and spread of Yayoi culture throughout Japan. He hypothesizes that Japanese speakers long resident in Kyushu developed Yayoi culture there by borrowing agriculture, metallurgy, and the other distinctive Yayoi traits from the mainland, and that they subsequently carried that culture and the Japanese language into the rest of Japan by population movement.

J. J. Chew (1978) has proposed an alternative way of resolving the discrepancy between the early date for the development of the Japanese language and the late date for the Yayoi people and culture. Instead of locating the divergence of the Japanese and Korean languages within their present homelands, he moves it back to an unspecified place in the heart of Asia. He hypothesizes that the Korean speech community was the first to reach its present homeland, that it was joined there after a long period of isolation by the Japanese speech community, and that the latter eventually moved on to the islands, arriving there at the start of the Early Yayoi period.

Chew (1978, p. 196) bases his hypothesis on the fact that "Japanese and Korean share much more of their syntax and semantics than two languages which have been separated for over 4500 years should." He concludes that this could only have happened if the Japanese and Koreans had come into intimate contact after a long period of separation.

He might have added that the inhabitants of southern Korea in Yayoi time had a Plain-pottery culture which was quite similar to that of Yayoi. Together, the two constitute a second ceramic horizon, succeeding the

Geometric-pottery horizon cited by Miller (Kim 1978, pp. 53–117). Either horizon could mark the spread of the ancestral Japanese language through Korea into Japan.

In the following section, I shall consider the archeological evidence for and against population movement into Japan during the time of each horizon. Here, I shall limit myself to the linguistic evidence in accordance with the principle of separately testing linguistic and archeological hypotheses (chap. 2,c). From this standpoint, Chew's hypothesis has to be rejected because it does not fit the patterns of genetic relationship and geographic distribution evident among the languages diagrammed in figure 16. These patterns indicate that the Korean and Japanese speech communities became differentiated after their joint ancestor had arrived on the Korean Peninsula. Moreover, Chew assumes a kind of movement that does not seem appropriate to the situation: immigration of small groups of people speaking different languages along routes that took them in and out of contact with each other, as opposed to a population movement in which thousands of immigrants proceeded in waves that engulfed and repeopled whole areas.

On the other hand, the patterns of relationship and distribution do allow a second alternative to Miller's hypothesis. The Korean and Japanese languages may have arisen side by side on the Korean Peninsula, the former in the Han River Basin of central Korea and the latter in the Naktong River basin at the end of the peninsula (Richard Pearson, personal communication). If this had happened, the Japanese speakers could have moved from the peninsula to the archipelago as late as Final Jomon time, and we would not need to reject the traditional belief that they brought Yayoi culture with them. This hypothesis, however, is inconsistent with Chew's evidence that the Korean and Japanese speech communities lost contact and then came together again; the two groups would have continued to intercommunicate so long as both were on the peninsula.

Miller's hypothesis does account for Chew's evidence. Had the Japanese originally become separated from the Koreans by an overseas migration, we would expect that, coming from the mainland, they would have been oriented towards the land rather than the sea. If so, they might well have lost contact with Korea until they succeeded in becoming seafarers, after which they would have reestablished contact and have developed the interaction sphere that linked Japan with Korea at the beginning of the historic era (sec. A, above). On balance, therefore, Miller's hypothesis is preferable to the other two.

What were the languages of Japan before the arrival of Proto-Insular and Pelagic and its transformation into Japanese and Ryukyuan? Ainu place names are widespread in eastern Japan (Chew 1978, pp. 198–99). This fact enables us to project the historically known conquest of Ainu speakers by Japanese speakers back from Hokkaido to the mountain barrier in the middle of Honshu.

It does not appear that we can project that conquest still farther back, through the Inland Sea area to Kyushu and the Nansei Islands. Ainu place names are missing from Western Japan, and we are faced there with an alternative hypothesis, which holds that the previous population of that area spoke Austronesian (also known as Malayo-Polynesian; see chap 2,A) rather than Ainu (Chew 1978, pp. 198–99). This hypothesis is based upon the presence of Austronesian-speaking aborigines in Taiwan, to the south of the Nansei Islands, and of Austronesian words in the Japanese language. It has even been argued that Japanese is a hybrid language, half Altaic and half Austronesian (Polivanov 1968).

The idea of a hybrid language runs counter to linguistic theory, which holds that each language has a basic structure, derived from a single ancestor. According to Miller (1980, pp. 157–67), the Austronesian elements in modern Japanese language are better regarded as loan words, resulting from intercommunication between Japanese and Austronesian speakers. Such intercommunication could have been taken place either in Western Japan or by travel back and forth between Taiwan and the Nansei Islands.

In summary, it would appear that Proto-Peninsular and Pelagic speakers moved from Korea to Kyushu Island sometime before 2500 B.C. and developed the Japanese language in relative isolation on that island. They were flanked there by emerging Korean speakers on the mainland, by Ainu speakers in Eastern Japan, and by Austronesians in Taiwan, if not also in the Nansei Islands. They began to expand northward into the other main islands before the time of Christ, to judge by the historical evidence that the Wa people spoke Japanese (sec. A, above), and moved southward into the Nansei Islands after that time, to judge by the glottochronological estimate for divergence of the Ryukyuan language.

If this reconstruction is correct, we should expect Japanese speakers to have developed Yayoi culture on Kyushu Island from a local form of Jomon culture. They would have carried their language and the new culture into the rest of Japan by means of population movement, advancing into Eastern Japan at the expense of Ainu speakers with a different form of Jomon culture and into the Nansei Islands at the expense of people who spoke Austronesian or local languages and who had local cultures.

Research in physical anthropology sheds additional light on this problem. According to Turner (1976), the teeth in the Bronze-Age burials of northeastern China resemble those of the modern Japanese, whereas the teeth of the Middle to Late Jomon skeletons in central Japan are like those of the modern Ainu. These facts support the linguistic hypothesis that the ancestors of the modern Japanese speech community arrived on Kyushu Island while ancestors of the Ainu speakers still inhabited Honshu Island. Study of the dental morphology on Kyushu Island is needed to determine when the arrival actually took place.

D. *Archeological Test*

In compiling my prehistoric chart (fig. 17), I have used the terminology and conventions described in chapter 1,B and figures 1–2. I have also made the following procedural changes from Japanese practice:

1. Archeologists in other parts of the world are accustomed to set up a single, overall chronological chart for each region studied, in order to be able to examine comparatively the relationships among the cultures within that region. Japanese archeologists have instead constructed separate chronological charts for the Preceramic, Jomon, Yayoi, and Kofun cultures (sec. B, above). I have brought the four together in a single chart, covering all of Japan during prehistoric and protohistoric time.
2. The Japanese place sets of general periods along the sides of their charts. These overlap at their ends when the charts are put together. I include the overlaps in both my historic and prehistoric charts (figs. 15, 17) and separate the contemporaneous periods with diagonal lines.
3. In discussing the historic developments (sec. A, above), I use the term *Japanoid* to refer to the cultures that appear to have developed into Japanese civilization or to have become acculturated to it. Hereafter,

83

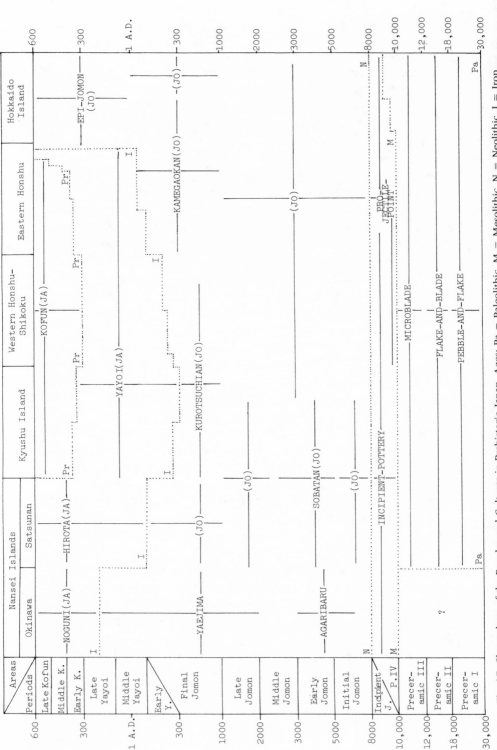

Fig. 17 Chronology of the Peoples and Cultures in Prehistoric Japan. Ages: Pa = Paleolithic, M = Mesolithic, N = Neolithic, I = Iron,

I shall formally treat these cultures, together with Japanese civilization, as members of a single, Japanoid series. The Yayoi and Kofun cultures are considered to be subseries within this series.

4. It seems highly unlikely that Jomon culture could have occupied most of Japan for nearly eight thousand years as a single monolithic entity. I therefore treat it as a series of cultures. I have rejected the alternative possibility of treating it as a subseries because Jomon differs more from Yayoi and Kofun than those two do from each other.

5. For the sake of consistency, I tried to divide the Jomonoid series into subseries, corresponding to Yayoi and Kofun within the Japanoid series (Rouse 1979). My overall classification is too tentative to use here, but I have inserted three of its units, Sobatan, Kurotsuchian, and Kamegaokan, in the figure because they are pertinent to my consideration of the evidence for and against the alternative hypotheses of invasion and internal development.

The Japanese have modeled their general periods and ages after those for the historic era (fig. 15). The names for these units vary from author to author. I have chosen to use the terminologies of Oda and Keally (1979) for the preceramic periods, of Aikens and Higuchi (1982) for the ceramic periods, and of Serizawa (1978) for the ages.

As in discussing Japanese history (sec. A, above), I shall proceed age by age, in terms of the divisions shown in figure 17. The first two ages, Paleolithic and Mesolithic, have been so recently discovered that the archeologists studying them have not yet been able to reach a consensus about how to categorize the constituent assemblages. In the following discussion, I shall use my own classification, drawn from the conflicting versions in the literature (especially Serizawa 1978 and Oda and Keally 1979). I shall simply call my units cultures, since we do not yet know enough about them to establish a hierarchy.

For the Paleolithic Age, I recognize four successive cultures, Crude-lithic, Pebble-and-flake, Flake-and-blade, and Microblade. The Crude-lithic culture is marked by chopper-shapped pebbles and by flakes which may have been used as knives or scrapers. They bear so few traces of workmanship and are so formless that many archeologists consider them to be natural stones. For this reason, I have omitted the Crude-lithic culture from figure 17. If and when the finds are proved to be artifacts, they will extend the occupation of Japan back to 130,000 B.C. (Aikens and Higuchi 1982, fig. 2.30, say 400,000, but that date exceeds the available evidence; Ikawa-Smith 1982, p. 146.)

While the subsequent Pebble-and-flake culture has similar specimens, they are more generally accepted as artifacts because they show clearer traces of manufacture according to cultural norms (chap. 1,B:1). Moreover, they occur in limited areas which can be recognized as places of human habitation because they contain concentrations of burnt stone and groups of cobblestones (Oda and Keally 1979, pp. 14–15). These camp sites are well dated between 30,000 and 18,000 B.C. They appear to be part of a cultural horizon that was widespread through East Asia at the time and that included Taiwan, which, like Japan, was then attached to the mainland (Sung 1981).

Oval axes chipped on both sides make their appearance midway through the culture. Some have been ground along their cutting edges, as in the contemporaneous assemblages of New Guinea and northern Australia (chap. 2,D). The two occurrences are probably independent, since there is nothing like them in the intervening areas (Oda and Keally 1979, p. 7). Thus, even at this early date the people of Japan were technologically ahead of their time; elsewhere in the world the grinding of stone axes did not develop until after 10,000 B.C., at the beginning of the Neolithic Age.

Around 18,000 B.C. a new Flake-and-blade culture arose in the Inland Sea area and spread to the rest of Japan. The artisans retained their previous types of choppers and axes but made significant improvements in their flake tools. They now began to vary the shapes of the cores from which they struck these tools in order to produce long, narrow blades as well as the shorter, more irregular flakes. They also learned to trim the proximal end of each tool steeply when they needed a scraper, or a side edge when they wanted to make a knife. This blunted the back of the knife so that it could more easily be held in the hand. They also created the first art object known from Japan, a crude stone figurine (Serizawa 1978, fig. 3).

The final, Microblade culture resembles that of the Paleo-Arctic subseries in the Eskimo area (chap. 3,D) and, like it, may be assigned to the Diuktoid series, centering on the Siberian mainland. It appears that the Diuktoid technique of striking microblades off wedge-shaped cores (called boat-shaped in Japan) spread from the mainland to Hokkaido and the northern part of Honshu, where it became diagnostic of the new culture. In the rest of Japan, on the other hand, the stone workers preferred to strike their microblades off miniature versions of the conical or prismatic cores they had previously used to produce large blades (Hayashi 1968).

By the end of the Microblade culture, the late-Pleistocene ice sheets had broken up, raising the sea level, separating Japan from the mainland, and causing the climate there to become more temperate. The local inhabitants responded to these events by advancing from the Paleolithic to the Mesolithic Age. The new age lasted from 10,000 to 8,000 B.C. and contained two overlapping cultures, Projectile-point in the east and north and Incipient-pottery in the west and south (fig. 17).

The artisans of the Projectile-point culture shifted wholly or in part from microblades, hafted on the sides of shafts, to bifacially chipped points, hafted on the ends. This change seems to be a local development, unrelated to the parallel sequence in the Arctic area (chap. 3,D); it began in the center of Japan and then spread northward. The Projectile-point people also developed more efficient types of axes, presumably in order to cope with the expansion of forests as the climate grew warmer (Serizawa 1978, fig. 2).

Production of projectile points did not reach Kyushu Island in the south. Microblades continued in use there, but they now became associated with the first pottery known anywhere in the world (Serizawa 1978, pls. I, II). Some authorities refer to the resultant culture as Incipient Jomon, since its pottery is ancestral to that of the Jomon series, but I prefer to call it Incipient-pottery in order to indicate that it is otherwise more closely related to the contemporaneous Paleolithic and Mesolithic cultures. Its peoples continued to live in camps and to obtain their food by hunting, to the apparent exclusion of fishing and the gathering of plant foods. Their original pottery was round bottomed, smooth surfaced, and decorated with short ridges pinched from the clay. We do not yet know enough about the situation on the mainland to be able to determine whether pottery-making was invented there or in Japan (Ikawa-Smith 1964, pp. 103–06).

Part way through the Mesolithic Age, the making of pottery diffused eastward from Kyushu Island through the Inland Sea and Kansai areas to the edge of the Kanto Plain, becoming associated in those areas with the local practices of making projectile points and stone adzes. Thus, two additional Jomon traits became coupled with it. Soon afterwards, the potters in the expansion area invented cord-marking, after which the series is named.

The rest of the series' diagnostics do not appear until the Neolithic Age, that is, until the Initial Jomon period (roughly 8000–5000 B.C.). Shell refuse indicating the consumption of seafood, stones used to grind plant food, and pit dwellings, which imply a more sedentary way of life, were developed early in Initial Jomon time. Intentional burial and clay figurines came somewhat later. The pots now had pointed bases and were successively decorated mainly by rolling sticks or cords on the wet clay, by shell impression, and finally by shell scraping.

The foregoing events indicate that the Jomonoid series originated in Japan, even though its pottery may have come from the mainland. Its diagnostic traits appear successively, some at the end of the Mesolithic Age and others at the start of the Neolithic Age, instead of beginning all at once, as would have been the case if a population movement had taken place. There is reason to believe that the final synthesis of the innovations to form the new series took place on or around the Kanto Plain (Kimio Suzuki, personal communication).

This brings me to the Early Jomon period (ca. 5000–3000 B.C.) and to the time when, if Miller's hypothesis is correct, the ancestors of the Japanese speech group entered the archipelago (chap. 4,D). I have so far been unable to cite clear evidence of population movement into Japan. What do the Early Jomon remains have to say?

To facilitate discussion of the problem, I shall postulate the existence of a Sobatan subseries within the Jomonoid series. This is uncertain, since the Japanese apply the term *Sobata* to a pottery type and I do not know whether its usage may appropriately be extended to include all the ceramic traits diagnostic of the population which produced that particular type. Neither is it known whether the other aspects of the population's culture, including its behavioral traits, were similar to or different from those elsewhere in Japan; too little research has been done in Sobatan sites to determine this. All we can say is that the presumed Sobatan subseries is limited to northern, western and southern Kyushu and the adjacent Satsunan part of the Nansei Islands (fig. 17), and that it is characterized by round-bottomed vessels incised rectilineally with a blunt tool (Kidder 1968, figs. 93, 94). These vessels contrast with the flat-bottomed, cord-stamped pottery prevalent in the rest of Japan at the time.

According to Kidder (1968, p. 51), "the distinctiveness of Sobatan pottery tends to...indicate that its fundamental affiliations are not within the Japanese sphere." He notes that it may be derived from the Comb-marked (Geometric) pottery of Korea, and he is followed in this by Miller (sec. D, above). However, their conclusion does not fit the results obtained by Sample (1978) from excavations at the site of Tongsamdong in southeastern Korea. She obtained a long sequence of occupations, the first three of which—Chodo, Mokto, and Pusan—can be considered contemporaneous with Sobatan culture in Japan because they have yielded trade sherds from there. Classic Comb-marked pottery does not appear at the Tongsamdong site until the fourth—Tudo—occupation, hence that pottery cannot be considered ancestral to Sobatan pottery, as Kidder and Miller thought. We must turn instead to the period in Korea immediately preceding the start of Sample's sequence, which has not yet been systematically investigated. Until it is, the idea that the Sobatans were responsible for introducing the proto-Japanese language into Japan will remain an untested hypothesis.

By Middle Jomon time (ca. 3000–2000 B.C.), the center of Jomon development had shifted from the Kanto plain to the mountains separating Western and Eastern Japan. This change was probably a response to the continued warming of the climate, which reached its peak during this period, providing the best conditions for mountain life (Kidder 1977, p. 26, chart). The local sites are unusually large and contain huge amounts of grinding, digging, and cutting tools, a fact which has led some authors to suggest the development of agriculture. It is more likely, however, that the local people were simply making effective use of the wealth of nuts, fruits, and wild vegetable foods available during the postglacial climatic optimum.

Pottery increased in quantity and variety. "For the first time it was made in shapes and sizes intended to serve a variety of purposes, some of which were ritual....The fact that the decoration was often so excessive as to interfere with the function of the pots must mean that it had more than simply esthetic value. Snakes and heads of animals or subhumans range from explicit to stylized. Other clay ritual objects are lamps or 'incense burners,' stands, and female figurines. Houses on mountain sites occasionally had platforms on one side, on which stood upright stones. Phallic symbols were widely made" (Kidder 1977, p. 28).

As the climate deteriorated during the subsequent Late Jomon period (ca. 2000–1000 B.C.) the center of development shifted to the Tohoku district in northern Honshu Island. Hunting, fishing, and the collection of shellfish reached their height there and were combined with the gathering of acorns, chestnuts, and other land foods in a seasonal round (Aikens and Higuchi 1982, fig. 3.67). While the pottery became simpler—it was mainly decorated with cord-marked zones outlined with incised lines—the other artifacts show increasing evidence of ceremonialism. Stone pavements and circles were now erected, figurines became more elaborate, and clay plaques and carved stone figures came into use. The dead continued to be placed in simple pit graves, but these were for the first time grouped into cemeteries. Differences in social status are indicated by variations in the grave goods.

These developments reached their climax during the Final Jomon period (ca. 1000–1 B.C. in the Tohoku district). The local culture was now so distinct that the Japanese have coined a name for it, Kamegaoka. I shall treat this culture as a subseries, adding the suffix -an to its name. It was distributed from the Chubu Mountains, on the boundary between Western and Eastern Japan, to the middle of Hokkaido Island (fig. 17).

According to Kidder (1977, p. 32), Kamegaokan culture "looks very much like an extension of Late Jomon but [is] increasingly ritualized. There are proportionately more carved wooden objects, ornamental bone and horn pieces, earrings and other accessories, phallic symbols, polished stone axes, all stereotyped in their own particular way." Increasing differentiation of social status is indicated by limitation of the finer pottery and figurines to certain parts of the sites.

Meanwhile, the inhabitants of Kyushu and the Satsunan Islands in Western Japan were following a different line of development. Except for an interval during Late Jomon time when they adopted the zoned incised cord-marking of proto-Kamegaokan culture, their pottery became increasingly plain and as a result began to approximate that of the subsequent Yayoi subseries. Jars and pedestaled bowls, both of which are typical Yayoi forms, made their appearance during the Late Jomon period. There was as yet no evidence of ritual development and social differentiation like those present in Eastern Japan at the time.

During the Final Jomon period, Western Japan was characterized by smooth-surfaced vessels decorated with horizontal ridges. I shall tentatively call this pottery and its associated culture Kurotsuchian in order to distinguish it from the Kamegaokan subseries of Eastern Japan (fig. 17). The finds resemble much more closely those of the Plain-pottery culture in Korea than those of the Kamegaokan subseries. The custom of burying in stone chambers diffused from Korea at this time, and the graves were now grouped into cemeteries. One site has yielded a large, ceremonial pit with a "stage" in its center, which may be considered a precursor to similar structures in Yayoi sites (Aikens and Higuchi 1982, pp. 180–82).

Recent excavations in the Kurotsuchian sites of northeastern Kyushu, closest to Korea, have also yielded evidences of agriculture in the form of rice paddies, the grain itself, and semilunar, ground-stone knives used to harvest it. They are accompanied by clay spindle whorls and by ground-stone copies of the metal projectile points being made in Korea at the time. The associated pottery was at first pure Kurotsuchian, then a mixture of Kurotsuchian and Yayoi, and finally pure Yayoi; the two are so much alike as to indicate local development, subject to influence from the plainware prevalent in Korea at the time.

This combination of local development with outside influence continued into Yayoi time. For example, bronze bells, imitating those on the mainland, first appeared during the Early Yayoi period and slag heaps indicative of iron working, during Middle Yayoi. Iron implements became dominant in Late Yayoi time. Bronze mirrors of Korean type were traded in during the Early period and Han-dynasty mirrors from China, during the Middle and Late periods.

The events just outlined—differentiation of the Kamegaokan and Kurotsuchian subseries within the Jomoid series and transformation of Kurotsuchian into Yayoi, the first Japanoid subseries—may be considered an example of divergent evolution, comparable to the rise of the Zapotec and Mixtec civilizations in Mesoamerica (Flannery and Marcus 1983). Whether or not the Early Jomon inhabitants of Kyushu Island came from Korea, as Miller's linguistic hypothesis presupposes, they certainly became increasingly different from their neighbors to the east and north as time passed. The divergence may at first have been due to the geographical separation of the two populations and to the contrast between their subtropical and temperate climates but, especially during the Final Jomon and Yayoi periods, the primary factor seems to have been interaction between the Kyshu islanders and the inhabitants of southeastern Korea.

Comparing the finds in these two areas at the beginning of Yayoi time, Kaneko (1968, pp. 3–4) concluded that they constitute a single, "nuclear Yayoi area," extending across the Korea and Tsushima Straits. She explained the existence of this area by postulating a migration of the Yayoi peoples across the straits, in accordance with the prevailing belief at the time. The subsequent finds, as summarized above, indicate instead that the area came into existence through diffusion across the straits. Kaneko's nuclear area must be considered an interaction sphere rather than a migration route (Pearson 1978b, pp. 184–85).

The Kurotsuchians who were becoming Yayois reacted to foreign influence in the same manner as their successors, the Kofun peoples, who developed Ancient Japanese civilization under Chinese influence, and the Modern Japanese, who have similarly absorbed elements of Western civilization. In all three cases, the local population retained its own cultural identity and appears to have been subject to little, if any, immigration from abroad. It changed through transculturation rather than acculturation or population movement (chap. 1,B:9, 11).

Let us now examine the spread of the Yayoi subseries from its place of origin in northwest Kyushyu Island. It expanded into the rest of that island shortly after its inception, but never continued south into the Nansei Islands (fig. 17). The inhabitants of the Satsunan group at the northern end of the chain did acquire a Japanoid culture, presumably through acculturation, but the sole Yayoi artifacts found further south are fragments of pottery, which appear to have been traded for shell bracelets (Pearson 1976, p. 319).

The main thrust of the Yayoi expansion was to the east and north, into Kurotsuchian territory around the Inland Sea and the Kamegaokan homeland across the mountains in Eastern Japan (fig. 17). The nature of the entry into Kurotsuchian territory is difficult to determine because that people's diagnostic complex differs so little from the subsequent Yayoi complex. The fact that no traces of a Kurotsuchian to Yayoi transition have been found in the Inland Sea area, as they have in Kyushu, suggests population movement. Indeed, the Yayoi ceramics of Kyushu Island and the Inland Sea area are so much alike that they have been categorized as a single Ongagawan complex (Bleed 1972, p. 10); and the culture of which Ongagawan pottery is a part has been termed a single Pioneer Yayoi culture (Aikens and Higuchi 1982, fig. 4.37). Nevertheless, the alternative possibility that the inhabitants of the Inland Sea area became Yayois through acculturation cannot be ruled out.

The change from Kamegaokan to Yayoi is more clear-cut. The two peoples' diagnostic complexes are almost completely different, the only major holdover from one to the other being in house type (fig. 18). There was, in other words, almost complete replacement of the Kamegaokan diagnostics by the Yayoi diagnostics. This indicates migration rather than acculturation.

To be sure, the Yayoi remains in the formerly Kamegaokan area are marked by Jomonoid traits (Aikens and Higuchi 1982, fig. 4.37), but these are superficial. The Yayoi pottery of the area, for example, has the typical material, surface finish, and shape of classic Yayoi pottery with elements of Jomon decoration imposed on them (fig. 19). Here again, as in Polynesia and the Eskimo area, we see in operation the principle that a people modifies its culture as it migrates (chap. 1,B:10).

The advent of the Yayoi people and culture is close enough to the historic period that we may reverse directions and, instead of following events from prehistory into history, may project historic conditions back into prehistory. During most of historic time, the Japanese and the Ainu were separated by a frontier, which was not broken until the Japanese extended their control over all of Hokkaido Island after the Meiji restoration (sec. A, above). Such a frontier is to be expected when one population expands at the expense of another, as Anglo-Americans are aware from their experience in moving westward at the expense of Native Americans.

During the Edo period, 1600–1868 A.D., the Japanese-Ainu frontier extended across the southwest part of Hokkaido Island (fig. 15). For a long period before that, between 50 B.C. and 1600 A.D., it had stood farther south across the northern end of Honshu Island. (See Aikens and Higuchi 1982, fig. 4.37, for a map of its precise position during this period.)

Possible earlier stands of the frontier still farther south are indicated by the jogs in the boundary between the Neolithic and Iron Ages depicted in figure 17: (1) on the Kanto Plain between 100 and 50 B.C., (2) in the central mountains between 200 and 100 B.C., (3) on the Kansai plain between 225 and 200 B.C., and (4) near the eastern end of the

Fig. 18. Comparison of the Yayoi (*a–h*) and Kamegaokan (*i–p*) Cultures: (*a*) pit house; (*b*) pedestaled bowl; (*c*) bronze bell; (*d*) burial jar; (*e*) stone reaping knife; (*f*) wooden hoe blade; (*g*) quadrangular stone ax, chisel, and adze; (*h*) stone arrowheads; (*i*) pit-house plan; (*j*) spouted pot, showing stylized animals in the upper part of the body design; (*k*) pottery figurine; (*l*) pit burial; (*m*) pecked stone "hammer"; (*n*) bone projectile point, harpoon, and fishhook; (*o*) stone ax-adzes; (*p*) stone projectile points. (After Beardsley 1955, figs. 2, 1)

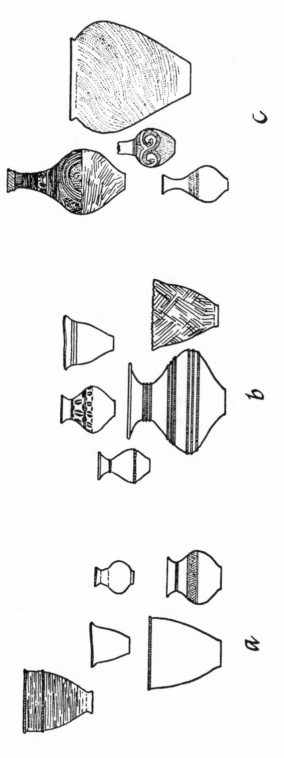

Fig. 19. Changes in Yayoi Pottery under Kamegaokan Influence: (*a*) earliest vessel types in Kyushu Island; (*b*) earliest vessel types in western Honshu Island; (*c*) earliest vessel types in eastern Honshu Island. (After fig. 30. *Japan before Buddhism* by J.E. Kidder, Jr. Copyright © 1959, 1966 by Frederick A. Praeger, Inc., Publishers; reprinted by permission of CBS College Publishing)

Inland Sea between 300 and 225 B.C. The last is the northern limit of the area in which Yayoi culture developed. Jogs 1 and 3 are so short that they may simply be artifices of our dating methods. Jog 2, however, appears to be a genuine halt at the mountains between western and eastern Japan; not only is it the longest jog but it also coincides with the principal natural and cultural boundary along the migration route. The Yayois finally breached this barrier by proceeding directly through the mountains instead of taking the easier route along the coast, where the Kamegaokans may have been strongly intrenched (Akazawa 1982, pp. 163–64).

What caused the newly developed Japanoids of the Yayoi subseries to expand so far and so rapidly between 225 and 50 B.C.? They had just acquired a new and more advanced agricultural economy, which may have given them an incentive to take advantage of the fertile land beyond their frontier (Kidder 1966, p. 130), as happened in the case of the pioneers who settled the American West. The metal weapons, superior fighting techniques, and possibly superior social organization they had borrowed from Korea gave them an advantage over the peoples beyond the frontier, again paralleling the situation in the American West. They seem to have expanded until they reached the limit of agriculture with the techniques available to them.

Their progress through Western Japan is unclear, as we have seen. In Eastern Japan, they probably absorbed elements of the previous population as they proceeded, but must also have driven some parts of it northward ahead of them. They imposed their own culture and language, put an end to Kamegaokan culture and, if the linguists are correct, substituted the Japanese language for Ainu. Since a people is defined by its culture (chap. 1,B:1), we can say that they repeopled Eastern Japan.

When they started to expand in the third century B.C. they faced Jomonoid peoples; and when they completed the movement in the nineteenth century, they did so at the expense of the Ainus. What is the relationship between these two groups? As figure 15 will indicate, the Epi-Jomon peoples who survived beyond the frontier on Hokkaido Island gave way about 800 A.D. to two peoples and cultures, Okhotsk and Satsumon. The Okhotsk people are clearly intrusive from the presently Russian islands to the north. The Satsumons, on the other hand, appear to be Jomonoids who had become partially acculturated to Japanoid culture. Their pottery shows Japanoid influence and they practiced some agriculture (Aikens and Higuchi 1982, pp. 304–20). They appear to have subsequently rejected these foreign traits, transforming themselves into the Ainus.

Parallels to this process can be cited from other parts of the world. For example, the Navahos and other Athapaskan-speaking Indians who invaded the American Southwest about 1500 A.D. at first copied the stone architecture and painted pottery of the Pueblo Indians they encountered there but later reverted to their native culture (Rouse 1962, pp. 44–45). And the peoples of Africa and the Indian subcontinent who were subjected to colonial rule during the nineteenth and early twentieth centuries have revived their own civilizations after independence, albeit in modified form.

Finally, let us examine the sequence of Japanoid subseries inside the frontier. Our review of the historical evidence indicated that the sequence developed locally, though under foreign influence (sec. A, above). Does the archeological evidence confirm this conclusion?

The earliest Yayoi sites show relatively few traces of social differentiation and ritual development. Theirs was a peasant culture, with a social structure and religion simpler than those of the contemporary Kamegaokans. The villages began to differ in size and presumably also in social complexity during the Middle Yayoi period. The more important ones were fortified with earthworks, palisades, and moats. Each village now had separate cemetery areas, which are believed to have been used by different corporate groups, as during historic time (Aikens and Higuchi 1982, pp. 212–46).

The Middle Yayoi graves on northwest Kyushu Island that have yielded large numbers of Han-style mirrors obtained by trade from the mainland have been identified as the burial places of the "kings" mentioned in the Chinese chronicles (Barnes 1981, p. 43). The first burial mounds also appear at that time in the site of Uriyudo on the Kansai plain (Aikens and Higuchi 1982, pp. 224–25). These consist of earth dug from bordering ditches, which foreshadow the moats that enclose the subsequent Kofun mounds. They recall the structure in which the chroniclers say that Queen Himiko was interred, supporting the hypothesis that she lived on the Kansai plain and bearing further witness to the development of an aristocracy that was to culminate during Kofun time in the foundation of the imperial dynasty.

The Middle and Late Yayoi periods are also marked by a number of isolated caches containing bronze bells and ceremonial weapons. These are believed to have been periodically unearthed by their owners for use in communal rites, probably to insure success in agriculture since they are situated on hilltops overlooking either agricultural terrain or sources of water for the irrigation of rice paddies. The weapons appear to have been made primarily in the northwest part of Kyushu and the southwest part of Honshu Islands, closest to Korea, while the bells were manufactured and distributed from the Kansai Plain. Between them were centers of salt production along the shore of the Inland Sea (Kidder 1977, pp. 47–52).

As a result of these developments, the interaction sphere that had extended from southeast Korea across the straits to northwest Kyushu Island during the Early Yayoi/Final Jomon period expanded in Middle Yayoi and Late Yayoi/Early Kofun times to include all of Kyushu, Shikoku, and Honshu Islands; and the center of the sphere shifted from northwest Kyushyu Island to the Kansai Plain (fig. 17). Both changes, of course, were rooted in and were undoubtedly facilitated by the spread of Yayoi culture. Southeast Korea remained in contact with the sphere but appears to have gradually become detached from it as it followed its own line of divergence.

Development from the Yayoi to the Kofun subseries took place within the enlarged sphere. The authorities agree that it was a local event, not the result of invasion. They identify the Kofun people and its culture by their distinctive burial complex, consisting of keyhole-shaped burial mounds surrounded by moats and furnished with artifacts such as the *haniwa* figures; they have traced the spread of the culture by plotting the distribution of that complex. It began on the Kansai Plain shortly before 300 A.D. and reached its maximum dispersal little more than a century later, presumably through acculturation caused by strong interaction within the sphere (fig. 17).

Most authorities distinguish three periods within the Kofun culture, Early, Middle, and Late, and consider the Middle period to be transitional between the other two. Egami (1962), on the contrary, recognizes only two periods, Early and Late. This enables him to say that horseback riding and its trappings appeared abruptly at the beginning of his Late Kofun period, and to conclude that "horse riders from northeastern Asia, bearing the culture of the northern equestrian tribes, came into

Japan via northern Kyushu and advanced along the Inland Sea to [the Kansai Plain]. They transferred their center of power to this area, and established what is known as the Yamato court, which succeeded in unifying most of Japan, with the exception of the lands of the Ezo in northern Honshu and Hokkaido" (Egami 1964, pp. 144–45).

If he is correct, archeologists should have found remains of "the culture of the northern equestrain tribes," including its burial complex, along the presumed route of migration. They have not done so. The indigenous complex persists in Japan through all the Kofun periods, with accretions appearing so gradually that they are better considered a result of the process of borrowing from Korea that had begun late in Jomon time and had continued throughout the Yayoi and Kofun periods (Edwards 1983, pp. 272–90).

Egami (1962, p. 12) bases his hypothesis of population movement on "the historico-mythological traditions about the origin of the imperial family." The historicity of traditions like these is open to question. Moreover, they provide an explanation for the origin of the Japanese state rather than its people and civilization, which is our concern here (sec. A, above). To account for the addition of horseback riding to the emerging Japanese civilization, we need only postulate the infiltration of equestrain specialists from Korea. This hypothesis of immigration—as opposed to population movement—can be inferred from the similarities in riding equipment between the mainland and Japan (fig. 20) and, since the specialists would have been assimilated in the local population, the hypothesis is not negated by the absence of a foreign burial complex. Alternatively, horseback riding may have diffused to Japan through some kind of two-way interaction.

Extensive research has also been undertaken on the earliest remains of full Japanese civilization, dating from the Asuka, Nara, and Heian periods (fig. 15). Here there is another sharp change in cultural diagnostics from burial mounds, which went out of use with the introduction of Buddhism and its burial practices, to palaces and temples, set in an urban rather than a rural environment (Yokohama 1978). Written history, which also began at the time, informs us that the Japanese obtained the innovations from China and Korea. Archeological evidence shows that the innovations were integrated into Japanese civilization on the Kansai Plain and spread out from there as the previously developed Japanese state extended its control over the surrounding territory (fig. 15).

99

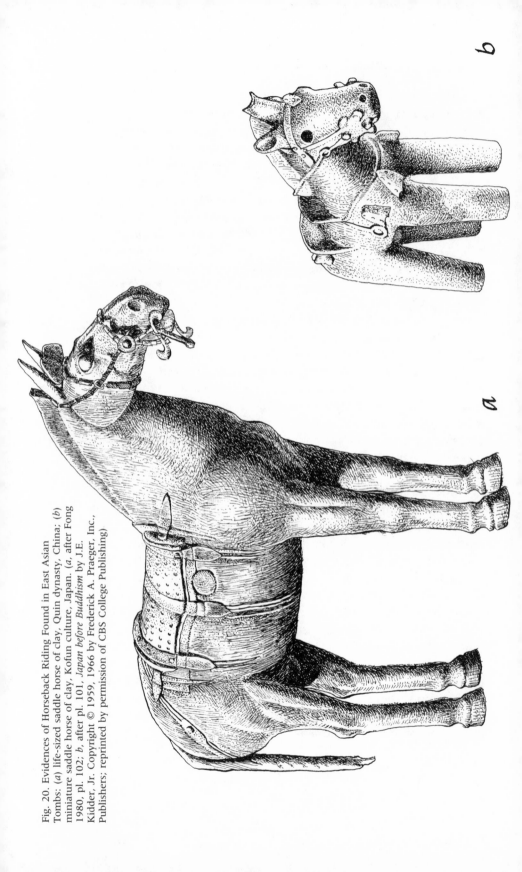

Fig. 20. Evidences of Horseback Riding Found in East Asian Tombs: (*a*) life-sized saddle horse of clay, Quin dynasty, China; (*b*) miniature saddle horse of clay, Kofun culture, Japan. (*a*, after Fong 1980, pl. 102; *b*, after pl. 101. *Japan before Buddhism* by J.E. Kidder, Jr. Copyright © 1959, 1966 by Frederick A. Praeger, Inc., Publishers; reprinted by permission of CBS College Publishing)

E. *Summary and Conclusions*

The linguistic, physical anthropological, and archeological tests all indicate that the traditional hypothesis of migration into Japan ca. 300 B.C. by a people who spoke the Japanese language and lived in the Yayoi culture is wrong. It is now clear that both the language and culture developed in situ on Kyushu Island at an earlier date and spread northeastward from there. The spread began during prehistory, shortly before the time of Christ, and continued through the Protohistoric, Ancient, Medieval, and Modern Ages (figs. 17, 15).

The hypothesis of population movement, cannot be completely abandoned. Historical and archeological research have both shown that it is still applicable to the terminal part of the spread, into Hokkaido Island, where it resulted in replacement of the Ainu language, culture, and race by the corresponding Japanese entities.

What happened in the intervening areas, that is, west and east of the central mountains on Honshu Island? The linguistic, physical anthropological, and archeological evidence reviewed above indicate that the spread from Kyushu Island into western Honshu may have been due either to population movement or to acculturation, but that the spread through the mountains into eastern Honshu has to be attributed to population movement because of the replacement there of Kamegaokan culture by Yayoi culture and the apparent shift from the Ainu to the Japanese language and dental morphology.

In the Polynesian and Eskimo cases, discrepancies between the linguistic and archeological conclusions did not have to be considered because they are minor and differences of detail are to be expected when comparing changes in two kinds of population groups (chap. 2,C). In the Japanese case, however, there is a major discrepancy that needs to be reconciled. The linguistic reconstruction indicates that Japanese speakers expanded from their Kyushuan base into the Nansei Islands after the development of Japanoid peoples and cultures, but the archeological evidence indicates that the movement took place before the rise of the Japanoids (Pearson 1976, pp. 319–21). Since the archeological evidence is stronger, we may provisionally accept the earlier date.

The results of the tests may be summarized as follows. Japan was settled during the latter part of the Pleistocene epoch, at a time when its islands were still attached to the mainland. The original settlers developed their own sequence of Paleolithic and Mesolithic cultures, which culminated in the introduction of microblades by transculturation from the Diuktoid series of northeast Asia about 12,000 B.C. (fig. 14). Pottery made its first appearance on Kyushu Island about 10,000 B.C., either through local development or by further transculturation from the mainland; and bifacially chipped projectile points began to be used in eastern Japan about the same time.

Pottery and bifacial points are but two of many innovations by which the authorities define the Jomonoid series of peoples and cultures, which occupied almost all of Japan during the ensuing Neolithic Age. Since the innovations follow each other in the archeological record, we have to conclude that the Jomonoid series developed locally, after the final retreat of the Pleistocene glaciers had severed the land bridge between Japan and the mainland and had improved the opportunities for hunting, fishing, and the gathering of wild plant foods.

Despite these evidences of local development, we must hypothesize a migration from Korea to Kyushu Island in order to account for the differentiation of the Korean and Japanese-Ryukyuan languages. Glottochronology suggests that the migration may have taken place during the Early Jomon period, ca. 5000 B.C., but we lack archeological confirmation, in part because too little is known about the situation at the time along the route from Korea to Kyushu Island and in part because the possibility that the Jomonoid series might then have been divided into several subseries has not yet been investigated. As in Melanesia and the Bering Strait region, we are dealing with segments of a migration that are too remote from its end points to be easily traced archeologically.

The population that is presumed to have developed the Japanese language and to have possessed a local form of Jomonoid culture continued to live on Kyushu Island throughout the Middle, Late, and Final Jomon periods. In Late Jomon time, it appears to have carried its language and major elements of its culture southward into the Nansei Islands, where it produced the Ryukyuan language and eventually became acculturated to Japanese civilization.

In Final Jomon time, the Jomonoids in northwest Kyushu developed Yayoi culture, thereby entering the Bronze-Iron Age and transforming themselves into the original Japanoids. They obtained metallurgy, agriculture, and the other distinctive Yayoi traits from the mainland by the process of transculturation. Soon after 300 B.C., they began to expand through the rest of Kyushu Island and into Honshu and Shikoku, introducing the Japanese language into the latter islands. West of the central Honshu mountains they absorbed or acculturated the Jomonoid population which I call Kurotsuchian. They seized the land east of the mountains from other Jomonoids whose culture was Kamegaokan and who may have spoken the Ainu language. Some of the Kamegaokans survived on Hokkaido Island, where they eventually became the Ainu people and were conquered by the Japanese.

Just as the Lapitoid migration was the source of Polynesian unity and the Thulean movement produced Eskimo uniformity, so the Yayoi expansion created the present homogeneity of language, culture, and race in Japan. Without it, the people of Japan would be much more diverse, like the present inhabitants of the Philippine Islands, for example.

The Yayoi expansion is not the only reason why the modern Japanese population is so homogeneous. Their ancestors might well have returned to diversity if they had not become organized into a single state during Kofun time. In effect, this state enlarged the scope of the local interaction sphere, first to include all of Kyushu, Shikoku, and Honshu Islands and most recently to incorporate Hokkaido and the Nansei Islands as well.

As in the case of the Polynesians and the Eskimos, we have been asking the wrong question about the Japanese people. Instead of searching for a foreign origin, we should have focused upon their present territory and have sought to delineate the movement or movements within that territory which have made them so homogeneous. Historical, linguistic, and archeological research all indicate that the answer lies in the origin of the Yayoi subseries in the part of Japan adjacent to Korea and its expansion from there during the first centuries B.C., facilitated by the innovations just acquired from the mainland.

Comparing the methodology used by Japanese archeologists with that used in the Polynesian and Eskimo areas, we may note that the Japanese have excelled in chronological research. They have worked out the distribution of pottery types and other artifactual traits in great detail, not only through time but also geographically within each time period, and are now engaged in doing the same for subsistence and other items of behavioral culture. (Some idea of the thoroughness of this research may be obtained from Kidder 1968; see especially his chronological chart on pp. 286–87 and the ten maps scattered through the volume.)

This is the principal reason for their success in demonstrating local development within their country.

Egami's attempt to show that warriors on horseback invaded Japan during Kofun time is a case in point. By making a gross distinction between Early and Late Kofun periods and contrasting the two of them, he creates the impression that there was an abrupt change from one period to another, which might well have been the result of migration. By distinguishing three periods, Early, Middle, and Late, and seeking the place as well as the time of first occurrence of each innovation within them, other archeologists have shown that the hypothesis of local development is more plausible.

One reason for the Japanese success is that they have gone beyond the periods just defined to establish subperiods, especially within the Yayoi and Kofun cultures where trade objects can be used to correlate local assemblages with historically known events on the mainland. The subperiods are designated by Roman numerals. They make it possible to date deposits within seventy-five-year intervals, that is, with greater accuracy than radiocarbon determinations, which normally have a bigger margin of error.

On the other hand, Japanese archeologists, like the local linguists, have lagged behind their colleagues in Polynesia and the Eskimo area in defining population groups and organizing them into cultural, as opposed to chronological, hierarchies. They did originally make a distinction between the Jomon people and their presumed descendants, the Ainus, on the one hand, and the Yayoi and Kofun peoples and their descendants, the Japanese, on the other hand, but they have taken this distinction for granted instead of treating it as a working hypothesis, to be tested by further comparative study, as I have attempted to do here.

It is only natural for investigators accustomed to the present homogeneity of the Japanese people to project that situation into the past. We should not assume, however, that the conditions which produced the present homogeneity also existed in the past. We need to conduct further comparative research to find out the true facts. Was the Jomonoid series of peoples a single entity or was it divided into a number of subseries, each with its own diagnostic complex of cultural traits?

The racial composition of the prehistoric Japanese population needs to be studied in the same way. Here too, much is known about the distribution of individual traits (Aikens and Higuchi 1982, pp. 3–7) but not about the co-occurrence of those traits in the form of complexes diagnostic of local populations. The study of dental morphologies appears to be most promising.

In a paper presented at the annual meeting of the Society for American Archaeology at Bal Harbour, Florida, in 1972, Kimio Suzuki attributed the Japanese archeologists' lack of interest in comparative research to the socio-political climate in his country while the militarists were in power. The climate inhibited freedom of thought about the Japanese state, its people, and their origins, and led to a focus upon non-controversial subjects such as the typology of artifacts and the refinement of chronology—which, as we have seen, has had advantages as well as disadvantages. Ikawa-Smith (1982b, p. 304) adds that the effect of the prevailing climate of thought was heightened by the isolation of Japanese scholars during and immediately after World War II. They missed a whole generation of thought in the West which laid the groundwork for the methods now being used to distinguish speech groups, peoples, and races in order to be able to study their languages, cultures, and gene pools respectively. I shall return to this subject in chapter 6.

5 THE TAINOS

The Tainos, also known as Arawaks, were the first people encountered by Christopher Columbus when he discovered the New World. The problem of this people's origins has long fascinated archeologists. When and where did the ancestors of the Tainos begin the long series of voyages that led to their meeting with Columbus in the West Indies?

Interest in this problem has been heightened by the geography of the West Indies. Its islands extend in a line along the eastern and northern edges of the Caribbean Basin, separating that basin from the Atlantic Ocean and the Gulf of Mexico (fig. 21). The islands form a series of stepping stones from the mouth of the Orinoco River in South America to the peninsulas of Yucatan in Middle America and Florida in North America. The gaps between the islands are so narrow that with three exceptions a traveler can always see the next island in the chain. Unlike Columbus, the Tainos did not have to cross vast expanses of open water to reach their rendezvous with him.

Many students of Taino origins have been lulled into a colonialist mentality by the ease of travel from island to island and the model of European conquest. Whenever these students encounter a new culture, they jump to the conclusion that it is the result of a migration from the mainland. It does not occur to them that the configuration of the islands is just as conducive to interaction as it is to migration, and that both

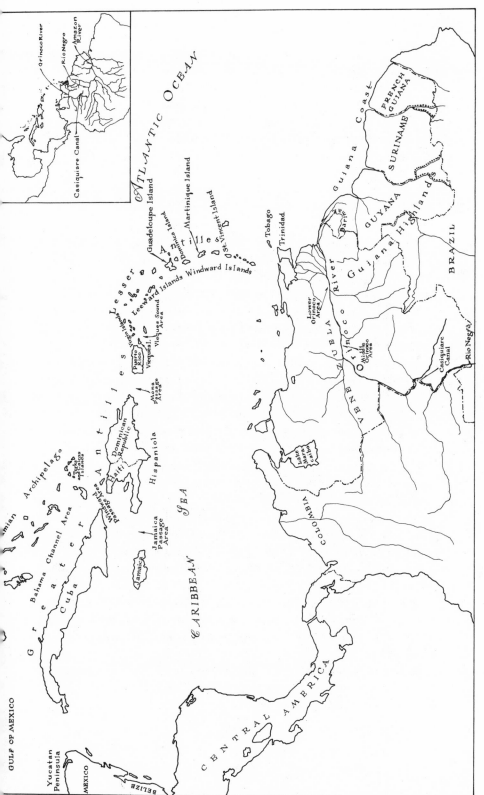

Fig. 21. Map of the Caribbean Area.

transculturation and acculturation are therefore strong possibilities. We must be careful when reviewing the evidence to give equal weight to all of these alternatives.

In length of human occupation, the West Indies fall midway between Polynesia, Japan, and the Eskimo homeland. Many of its islands were settled by 5000 B.C., early enough to complicate our efforts to learn about Taino origins.

A. *Setting*

Migrants or interactors who approached the West Indies from the interior of South America around 5000 B.C. would have been able to descend the Orinoco River almost to the edge of the continental shelf before reaching the sea. The postglacial rise of the water eventually detached two islands, Trinidad and Tobago, from the mainland, and they became the main points of entry into the West Indies, leading out not only from the Orinoco Valley but also from the Guiana coast to its east and the Venezuelan coast to its west.

Trinidad is situated within view of the Orinoco Delta, while Tobago lies farther out to sea. Beyond Tobago is one of the three breaks in sight from island to island, the other two being off Florida and Yucatan respectively, at the other end of the archipelago.

These breaks delimit the West Indies, as I shall use that term here. Omitting Trinidad, Tobago, and the other islands on the continental shelf, I shall include only the Lesser Antilles, the Greater Antilles, and the Bahamian Archipelago. They are the only oceanic islands, hence the only ones to have an impoverished fauna.

The Lesser Antilles consist of a series of almost completely submerged volcanic peaks, curving northwestward from Tobago to the Greater Antilles. Their southeastern half is known as the Windward Islands and their northwestern half as the Leeward Islands because one can sail before the trade winds from the former to the latter. The trades combine with the outpouring of floodwater from the Orinoco River to facilitate travel from South America, especially during the summer when that river is in flood. Travel during the summer and fall is dangerous, however, because of the threat of hurricanes (a word which comes from the Taino language).

At the entry into the Greater Antilles are a group of small, sedimentary islets known as the Virgins. Beyond them are four great land masses: Puerto Rica, Hispaniola—now divided into the Dominican Republic and Haiti—Jamaica, and Cuba. These islands are big enough to have supported a relatively large population, as they do today. Their long, indented shorelines facilitated fishing and the gathering of shellfish. There was a variety of wild plant foods, thanks to the diversity of the climate, which is moist on the leeward sides of the islands, dry on the windward sides, hot in the lowlands, and cool in the mountains. Agriculture is favored by the fertility of the soil.

The Bahamas and their sister islands, the Turks and Caicos, are composed of low coral islets with few natural resources except those of the sea. They cover a triangular area, bordered on the south by Haiti and Cuba and on the west by Florida. The apex of the triangle, adjacent to Florida, is the only part of the West Indies far enough north to have a subtropical climate (Sears and Sullivan 1978, pp. 19–20).

Overall, the islands offered a relatively broad range of resources, differing from place to place. By the time of Columbus, the Indians had developed an extensive trade network for the exchange of local products, taking advantage of the ease of interaction between islands (Rouse 1948, pp. 530–31).

Both the mainlanders and the islanders belonged to the American geographic race, which includes all the inhabitants of the New World except the Eskimos and the Aleuts (chap. 3,A). Since no significant variations within this race are known for the Caribbean area, we need not take biologically defined population groups into consideration in the following discussion.

Before considering the other two kinds of population groups—linguistic and cultural—we need to review the development of thought about them, in order to resolve problems of terminology. I shall proceed historically. When Columbus reached the Greater Antilles, its inhabitants told him that they were subject to raids by Carib Indians from the south. (Their name is the source of our word *Caribbean*.) Columbus sailed farther to the south during his second voyage in order to seek the raiders, and found them on Guadeloupe, the southernmost of the Leeward Islands (Sauer 1966, pp. 71–72).

Later explorers encountered other Indians who called themselves Caribs on the Windward Islands and the adjacent mainland, where they coexisted with people bearing different names, such as *Arawak* (e.g., Newson 1976, pp. 17–19). In effect, the islanders and the mainlanders had divided themselves into population groups, each with its own name.

It should not be assumed that population groups like these, which the natives themselves had created, coincide with those established by linguists through the study of languages and by archeologists through the study of cultural remains (Rouse 1983, p. 27). Lacking the concepts of language and culture, the natives used different criteria to define their groups—criteria which it is difficult if not impossible for modern researchers to understand because of the inadequacy of their data. Following the lead of Allaire (1977, pp. 18–20), I shall refer to the populations recognized by the natives as *ethnic groups*, in order to distinguish them from linguistically and archeologically defined groups.

An analogy may help to clarify this distinction. Terms such as *Arawak* and *Carib* designate differing populations of human beings in the same way that terms like *tiger* and *lily* denote contrasting populations of animals and plants. Both are names that local speakers apply to the organisms among whom they live—to human beings in the case of *Arawak* and *Carib* and to wildlife in the case of *tiger* and *lily*.

Natural scientists are accustomed to make a distinction between the popular names for animals and plants, such as *tiger* and *lily*, and the names formulated by means of Linnaean classification, such as *Panthera tigris*. Similarly, students of humankind ought to discriminate between the native names for human populations, such as *Arawak* and *Carib*, and the names formulated by means of scientific classification, that is, the names linguists have coined to refer to speech communities and their languages and those created by archeologists and ethnologists to refer to peoples and their cultures.

Archeologists and ethnologists apply the term *ethnoscience* to the study of the natives' own names for plants, animals, and other aspects of their natural environment (Rouse 1972, p. 167). This term and the kind of study it denotes are equally applicable to the ways in which the natives categorized their human environments, that is, to the ethnic groups into which they divided themselves.

In the last chapter (4,A), care was taken not to confuse population groups like these with social groups, especially with the Japanese state. This problem does not arise in the present chapter, since most societies in the Caribbean area were too small and underdeveloped to be mistaken for population groups. Here, the problem will be to discriminate ethnic groups, that is, the natives' own population groups, from the purely scientific groups formulated by linguists and archeologists.

I shall proceed geographically, noting the extent to which the three kinds of population groups cross-cut or coincided with each other. I shall start with the lower Orinoco Valley, the adjacent parts of the Guianan and Venezuelan coasts, and the islands of Trinidad and Tobago, off the Orinoco Delta (fig. 21), since they are the most likely source of the migration that brought the ancestors of the Tainos into the West Indies.

While the Arawaks and Caribs were not the only ethnic groups in these areas during the time of Columbus, they are the best known and have received the most attention because they were the most accessible to early explorers. The Arawaks were mainly in the Guianas and on Trinidad, and the Caribs in Venezuela, but the two overlapped. In the Guianas, they occasionally alternated from village to village (Rouse 1953a).

When linguists began to study the Arawaks and Caribs, they found that the two spoke languages belonging to different families. They named the families Arawakan and Cariban respectively, taking care to add the suffix -an to the ethnic names in order to avoid confusion between the natives' own groupings and the linguistic units. This convention is often ignored; some archeologists, for example, use the term *Arawak* interchangeably for both the ethnic group of that name and the linguistic family. They do so at their peril. Without the convention, one is likely to lose sight of the fact that most people who spoke Arawakan did not consider themselves to be Arawaks and that most Cariban speakers had never heard the word *Carib*.

Greenberg (1960, p. 794) subsequently grouped the Arawakan languages into an Equatorial subfamily within an Andean-Equatorial family and put the Cariban languages into a Macro-Cariban subfamily within a Ge-Pano-Carib family. It is still common practice, however, to speak of Arawakan and Cariban families (e.g., Durbin 1977) and I shall follow that practice here, treating the broader affiliations of the two as super-families and stocks respectively. (This is consistent with my handling of the Altaic family in chapter 4. Some authorities assign it to an Ural-Altaic stock, but I have not had occasion to do so in this book.)

Turning from speech communities and languages to peoples and cul-

111

tures, we find disagreement. Some authors, insensitive to the differences between ethnic (native), linguistic, and cultural groups, have simply assumed that the Arawaks and Caribs were separate peoples, each with its own culture. Other scholars have suggested the two shared a common culture and hence constituted a single people. The truth lies somewhere between these two extremes. Ellen Basso (1977, pp. 18–19) probably comes closest to it in a recent summary of the present status of "Carib ethnography" when she distinguishes three types of culture and notes that "each 'type' is not uniquely Carib[an], and in fact could include non-Carib[an] speaking tribes sharing many of the features that make the type distinctive for Carib[an] speakers. This suggests that many, if not most, lowland South American tribes should be considered as falling into general social and cultural groups that often encompass local groups of different language affiliation and history."

The tribes mentioned by Basso were the largest social groups or societies among the Arawaks and Caribs. Each tribe consisted of one or two villages, each with its own headman. Some headmen were more powerful than others, but there were no hierarchies as in Polynesia (chap. 2,A). No tribe, considered as a functioning unit, ever encompassed more than a portion of the people who called themselves Arawaks or Caribs, hence it would be a mistake to speak of the Arawak or Carib tribe.

A third ethnic group on the continent is pertinent to my review, the Waraos of the Orinoco Delta. They spoke a language originally considered independent but assigned by Greenberg (1960, p. 793) to his Paezan superfamily and Macro-Chibchan stock. They were also aberrant culturally; unlike the other local groups, they lacked pottery and agriculture and were organized into mobile bands rather than sedentary villages.

Moving from the continent into the West Indies, we come first to the Caribs discovered by Columbus. In his time, they occupied the Windward Islands, closest to South America, as well as Guadeloupe, at the southern end of the Leeward chain. Because they bore the same name as the continental Caribs, the authorities have until recently assumed that they, too, spoke a Cariban language (e.g., Steward and Faron 1959, p. 23). On the contrary, linguists have identified their language as Arawakan, while continuing to call it Island Carib (e.g., Taylor 1977a, pp. 26ff). There can be no better example than this of the need to distinguish between ethnic and linguistic groups!

Actually, the Island Caribs had two languages, one in general use and the other spoken only by the men. The general language, which is known as Island Carib, was typically Arawakan, while the men's language had a partially Arawakan grammar and a heavily Cariban vocabulary. These facts have led Taylor and Hoff (1980) to conclude that the latter was a pidgin language. It is sufficiently similar to a pidgin widely used by mainland Caribs "to accept some historical connection between them" (ibid., p. 302).

The Island Caribs reported that their territory had previously been occupied by a population known as Igneri, and that warriors from the south had conquered this population, killing off its men and marrying their women. Assuming that the conquerors were Cariban speakers from the mainland, as is implied by their name, Taylor and Hoff (1980, p. 312) conclude that the newcomers must have shifted to the Igneri language after arriving in the islands, but that they and their male descendants retained the secondary pidgin language as a symbol of their origin on the mainland.

In the time of Columbus, the inhabitants of the Windward Islands and Guadeloupe apparently shared a single culture in addition to the name *Carib* and the Igneri and pidgin languages. Consequently, most authorities apply the phrase *Island Carib* to the local people and their culture, as well as to their languages.

The Island Caribs presented two faces to the world. On the one hand they raided the Greater Antilles, stealing Taino women and, if the contemporary accounts are to be believed, consuming the flesh of captives. (Our word *cannibal* is a corruption of *Carib*). On the other hand, they appear to have been friendly to their neighbors on the continent and, at least in colonial time, they traded with them (Rouse 1948, p. 556). This well illustrates Lévi-Strauss's distinction between strong and weak interaction (chap. 1,B:11).

Most of our information about Island Carib culture comes from the French who colonized Guadeloupe and Martinique during the seventeenth century. They report that the adult males lived away from their families in a special men's house. Farming and fishing were well developed. Not surprisingly, the Island Caribs made pottery like that of their namesakes in the Guianas (Allaire 1984b). They were organized similarly, into independent villages with headmen whose status depended upon their own prowess. But they also had personal deities like those of the Tainos (Rouse 1948, pp. 555–56, 561–63).

Little is known about the historic inhabitants of the Leeward Islands north of Guadeloupe. By Columbus's time, that part of the Lesser Antilles seems to have become a no-man's land, through which the Island Caribs raided the Tainos.

The Indians encountered by Columbus in the Greater Antilles and the Bahamas lacked an overall name for themselves. The names *Taino* and *Arawak* were bestowed upon them by nineteenth-century scholars in order to fill this gap. *Taino* comes from an adjective meaning good or noble, which natives of the Greater Antilles used to explain to the Spaniards how they differed from the Caribs (Alegría 1981, p. 16). *Arawak* is derived from the discovery by Brinton (1871) that the natives spoke a language belonging to the Arawakan family.

Most of the inhabitants of the Greater Antilles and the Bahamian Archipelago in the time of Columbus must have belonged to a single speech community since Columbus was able to use the same interpreter almost everywhere he went. Modern linguists prefer to apply the term *Taino* to this speech community and its language in order to avoid confusion with the Arawak speech community and its language, which was present on the continent at the time (e.g., Loukoutka 1968, p. 126).

When used linguistically, the name *Taino* applies to the entire population of the Greater Antilles and the Bahamian Archipelago with three possible exceptions. The Island Caribs may have taken over the Virgin Islands as a base from which to raid the rest of the Greater Antilles; the so-called Ciguayos, of northeastern Hispaniola, are said to have spoken a different dialect or language, the nature of which is not known; and the Guanajatabeys, at the far end of Cuba, likewise had a different but unknown language. As we shall see later, Spanish accounts indicate that the Guanajatabeys were relics of an earlier population.

Ethnologists and archeologists divide the Taino speech community into two peoples and cultures: Taino proper, which I shall call Classic Taino, and Sub-Taino. The Classic Tainos inhabited Hispaniola and Puerto Rico; and the Sub-Tainos, the surrounding land: Jamaica, eastern and central Cuba, the Bahamas, and the Turks and Caicos Islands. Allaire (1984a) concludes from the archeological evidence that the pre-Carib inhabitants of the Virgin and Leeward Islands were also Sub-Taino.

The Classic Taino people differed markedly from their neighbors in the Lesser Antilles and on the mainland. They were organized hierarchically into chiefdoms rivaling those in Polynesia. (Our word *chief* and the Spanish *cacique* come from a Taino word.) There was also a class system, the units of which the Spaniards equated with their own nobles, commoners, and slaves.

Life revolved around the worship of household deities called *zemis*, which were carved in stone, wood, and other materials (Arrom 1975). Chiefs and priests derived political power and social status from their zemis. Important villages contained ceremonial plazas and ball courts, lined with embankments and sometimes bordered with stone pavements and/or lines of upright slabs engraved with figures of zemis. These deities were also worshiped in temples built of perishable materials and in cave shrines (Lovén 1935). Agricultural techniques were the most advanced in the Caribbean area; mounding and irrigation were used to increase the yield (Sturtevant 1961).

Possibly excepting the people who called themselves Ciguayos in northeastern Hispaniola, the Classic Tainos were peaceable and received the Spaniards hospitably until forced to defend themselves against attack. The residents of the eastern tip of Hispaniola are said to have visited Puerto Rico daily to socialize with their neighbors there (Casas 1951, 2:356). Trade was extensive, certain places being known for particular products (Rouse 1948, pp. 130–31).

Zemiism was less highly developed among the Sub-Tainos; and chiefdoms, social classes, plazas, and ball courts were simpler or lacking. The native population of the Bahamas had to rely more on sea food; their low, coral islands and the cool climate, in the north, were less suitable for the local form of agriculture.

Little is known about the non-Taino relict population of Guanajatabeys in western Cuba, because it became extinct too early to be recorded. It appears to have been composed of mobile bands, which lived by hunting, fishing, and gathering. Like the Waraos of the Orinoco Delta, the Guanajatabeys lacked both pottery and agriculture—even though the soil of western Cuba is exceedingly fertile. They formed a buffer group between the almost equally underdeveloped people of south Florida, the highly civilized Mayas in Yucatan, and the Sub-Tainos.

Persons who read about Caribbean ethnohistory are frequently confused by the practices of (1) calling the natives of the Lesser Antilles Caribs when in fact they spoke an Arawakan rather than a Cariban language, and (2) referring to the natives of the Greater Antilles as Arawaks, rather than Tainos, when in fact *Arawak* is the name of an ethnic group limited to the Guianas and Trinidad. To avoid such confusion, one must be careful when using a proper name such as *Island Carib* or *Taino* to specify whether it refers to an ethnic group, a speech community defined by its language, a people defined by its culture, some combination of these different kinds of population groups, or a social group.

Since the Tainos were the first Amerindians to interact closely with Europeans, they have provided us with a disproportionate number of the Native American words and cultural items we now use. The words *hurricane, cannibal, Caribbean,* and *chief* have already been mentioned. The cultural items include cassava—a root crop that was the Tainos' staple food and is widely used today throughout the tropics—canoes, hammocks, maize or corn, sweet potatoes, and tobacco. Our names for these items, too, come from the Taino language. In exchange, the Indians received not only the blessings of Western civilization but also its evils— especially diseases such as smallpox and measles, to which they had no immunity.

Crosby (1972, pp. 44–47) has called this process "the Columbian exchange." The Classic Tainos, among whom the Spanish first settled, bore the brunt of the exchange, and as a result they soon became extinct. Many of them succumbed to European diseases. Others starved to death because the Spaniards took them from their fields and forced them to labor in mines without making provision to feed them. Still others committed suicide or took refuge among their former enemies, the Island Caribs in the Windward Islands (Alegría, personal communication).

The Sub-Tainos suffered a similar fate except in Cuba, where Spanish settlement was aborted by the discovery of greater riches in Mexico and Peru. A few of the Cuban Sub-Tainos retained their separate identity until the nineteenth century, when they finally became assimilated into the Spanish-speaking population.

The Island Caribs remained free until the French colonized their principal islands during the seventeenth century. Some of them still live in a reservation on the formerly British island of Dominica, but they have lost their language and much of their native culture. Another group flourishes in Central America, to which the British transported them to make way for a colony of their own on the island of St. Vincent.

The group transported to Central America is known as Black Carib because, before being deported from St. Vincent, it had become racially African through intermarriage with escaped slaves (Taylor 1951). Yet it retained its Arawakan language and its Island Carib culture—another good example of the need to distinguish among the different kinds of population groups!

The Waraos have survived in the Orinoco Delta but the more advanced Indians on the mainland have mostly become assimilated, except in the Guianas, where descendants of the Arawakan and Cariban speakers still form separate parts of the ethnic mix. Their modern languages bear the names *Lokono* and *Kalina* respectively. Thus, we are able to supplement our knowledge about the virtually extinct population groups in the West Indies with information about living groups on the mainland.

B. *Hypotheses*

Most early students of the problem of Taino origins thought only in terms of the historic and modern groups just reviewed. For example, Sven Lovén (1935, p. 2) hypothesized "from historic sources" that the Guanajatabeys had migrated from Florida and that they had been followed by the "Island Arawaks," Ciguayos, and Island Caribs, coming successively from South America. He did not attempt to test these four migration hypotheses archeologically, nor could he have done so, since the groups to which he referred were defined by documentary evidence, which is not included among the archeological remains.

Had Lovén been able to trace the historic groups back into prehistory, he would presumably have found a very different situation than in Polynesia. There, the historic aborigines were able to retain their prehistoric identities because they were geographically isolated from each other and had organized themselves in terms of the roles played by their ancestors in the voyages of settlement. The native West Indians are more likely to have changed identities because they lived within sight of each other, interacted more intensely, and organized themselves in terms of their own prowess or their social relationships rather than the deeds of their ancestors (Wilson MS).

But this is beside the point. Neither in Polynesia nor in the West Indies did students of prehistoric migrations begin to make progress until they ceased to work with the population groups mentioned in the historic sources and began to formulate prehistoric groups based upon the kinds of empirical evidence in which they specialized: speech communities and their languages in the case of linguists and peoples and their cultures in the case of archeologists.

Linguists have concentrated on the two local speech communities that belong to the Arawakan family, Island Carib and Taino. Too little is known about the Guanajatabey language to be able to determine the origin of its speakers, and the Cariban family has been removed from consideration by the discovery that it was represented in the West Indies only by a pidgin language.

Arawakan specialists have reconstructed the proto-languages that preceded each modern and historic language, and through them they have been able to trace the family back to a homeland in the Amazon Basin. They have found that the speech communities in the line of development that culminated in the Tainos moved up the Río Negro, through the Casiquiare Canal, down the Orinoco Valley, and out into the West Indies (Stark 1977). According to the latest evidence, a speech community known as Proto-Northern originated in the Orinoco Valley and moved from there into the Guianas, Trinidad and Tobago, and the West Indies. The members of that community who reached the West Indies split into two spheres of intercommunication, one in the Lesser Antilles and the other in the Greater Antilles and the Bahamas Archipelago (fig. 21). The inhabitants of the Lesser Antillean sphere developed the Island Carib language and the inhabitants of the Greater Antillean-Bahamian sphere, the Taino language.

Like Heyerdahl in Polynesia (chap. 2,B), the pioneer West Indian archeologists worked only in terms of individual cultural traits. A Danish archeologist, Gudmund Hatt (1924, p. 33) introduced the concept of peoples and cultures in the 1920s. He classified the sites he dug in the Virgin Islands into three groups on the basis of their cultural content: Krum Bay, which lacked pottery; Coral Bay-Longford, which had yielded potsherds painted white on a red background; and Magens Bay-Salt River, which was marked by modeled and incised pottery. He concluded that the Krum Bay group of sites was the earliest because of the absence of pottery and that the Magens Bay-Salt River group was the latest because its modeled-incised designs resemble Taino artwork. This left Coral Bay-Longford in the middle of the sequence.

Since white-on-red pottery like that of the Coral Bay-Longford group was widespread in the Lesser Antilles and on the continental islands,

118

Hatt hypothesized that its makers had come from South America. He attributed its replacement by the modeled-incised pottery of the Magens Bay-Salt River assemblages to transculturation from the Classic Taino center in Hispaniola, where he had also done fieldwork.

In 1935–36, Froelich G. Rainey (1940) made a similar study of the peoples and cultures of Puerto Rico in his doctoral dissertation at Yale University. At three sites, he found a sequence of two ceramic deposits corresponding to Hatt's Coral Bay-Longford and Magens Bay-Salt River assemblages. He named his two units *Crab* and *Shell cultures* because his white-on-red pottery came from deposits full of crab jaws and his modeled-incised pottery from shell refuse. At all three sites, the Crab-culture remains underlay the Shell-culture remains, confirming Hatt's conclusion about their order. Rainey agreed with Hatt that the people who produced the white-on-red pottery must have migrated from South America, but the existence of a sharp break between most of his Crab- and Shell-culture strata led him to conclude, contrary to Hatt, that the people of the later culture had also come from South America.

Following up Rainey's research, I saw no reason to doubt his and Hatt's conclusion that the original, white-on-red pottery was the result of population movement from South America. Local development was ruled out by the absence in the previous population (by then known from many other sites besides Hatt's in the Virgin Islands) of pottery and such associated traits as agriculture and sedentary life. I was, however, faced with conflicting hypotheses about the origin of the later, modeled-incised pottery. Was it the product of a second migration from South America, as Rainey supposed, or of local development in the Greater Antilles, as Hatt thought?

In an attempt to reconcile these conflicting hypotheses, I made a study of the changes in ceramics from level to level within Rainey's Crab- and Shell-culture strata. I found a trend from white-on-red toward plain pottery as I proceeded from the bottom to the top levels within his Crab-culture strata and a reverse trend from modeled-incised towards plain pottery as I went from the top to the bottom levels within his Shell-culture strata. This led me to hypothesize a period of predominately plain pottery between his periods of white-on-red and modeled-incised pottery. I searched for, and found, deposits dating from such a period while in Puerto Rico during 1936–38 (Rouse 1952).

In hindsight, it is evident that the predominantly plain pottery fills a gap in our previous knowledge of the ceramic chronology within the Virgin Islands and Puerto Rico. The gap had arisen because the local collectors, upon whom we had relied for information about sites, were interested only in decorated potsherds. We now know that the ceramics had evolved through two periods of elaborate decoration separated by a period of relatively plain pottery. The shift in diet from crabs to shellfish also appears to have been a local phenomenon; it happened gradually and was limited to the parts of the Virgin Islands and Puerto Rico where those foods were readily available. And the sharp break encountered by Rainey between the Crab- and Shell-culture strata is now attributable to intra- rather than inter-island movement.

Recent archeological research in other parts of the West Indies supports these conclusions. Divergent ceramic sequences have been found throughout the region (Rouse, Allaire, and Boomert 1985). These sequences can all be traced back to the earliest white-on-red pottery and, through it, to the mainland of South America. The settlers who introduced the latter pottery, along with agriculture, appear to have separated into a number of interaction spheres, within which their pottery developed differently out of its common background.

The current linguistic and archeological hypotheses are thus compatible. The premise of a single movement of Arawakan speakers into the Antilles, followed by local development of the Island Carib and Taino languages within separate spheres of intercommunication, agrees nicely with the hypothesis of a single invasion of potters and farmers, followed by local development of ceramic styles and subsistence strategies within separate but smaller spheres of interaction.

It is not enough, however, simply to formulate linguistic and archeological hypotheses that are compatible. The validity of these hypotheses must also be established by testing them against the evidence and by satisfying ourselves that they are superior to all possible alternative hypotheses. The following two sections will be devoted to this task.

c. Linguistic and Physical Anthropological Tests

The still extant Warao language of the Orinoco Delta and the unknown Guanajatabey language of western Cuba are assumed to be relicts of the pre-Arawakan languages in the West Indies. It is thought that Arawakan-speaking invaders from South America pushed the remnants of the original population back into the peripheral positions they occupied in the time of Columbus, and that Cariban-speaking intruders subsequently mingled with the Arawakans who lived in the islands closest to the mainland. I shall examine these events in turn.

Julian Granberry (1971) has concluded that there are enough similarities between the Warao language and that of the Timucua Indians in the Florida peninsula to hypothesize a migration of ancestral Warao speakers northward through the West Indies from Venezuela to Florida. However, Floyd G. Lounsbury (personal communication) tells me that the similarities are neither numerous nor strong enough to eliminate the alternative hypotheses, independent invention and the transmission of linguistic norms from one local population to another through trade or other means of intercommunication. Granberry's find is inconclusive.

Linguists have achieved more success in studying the Arawakan languages. They began to classify them in the late 1700s and have had two centuries in which to refine their results. Kingsley Noble (1965, p. 108) has organized the languages into a phylogeny. I base my figure 22 on his diagram, but I have made several significant changes.

Noble arranged the Arawakan languages haphazardly across the top of his diagram, without regard either for geographical distribution or closeness of relationship. Following my practice throughout this book, I have grouped the historic languages geographically across the top of my diagram and have also added dates on the sides. These are taken from estimates which Noble (1965, pp. 107, 111) gives in his text. I have rounded off the middle three dates, which are based on glottochronology, to the nearest five hundred years. They are probably too young; as in the case of the Eskimo (chap. 3,c), the Caribbean speech communities were so close together that their rates of divergence must have been slowed by intercommunication.

Noble's diagram and mine begin with Proto-Equatorial, the original language in the superfamily of that name. Noble (1965, p. 107) located this language in the headwaters of the Amazon River but Lathrap (1970, pp. 70–79) and Stark (MS) have relocated it in the middle of the valley in order better to account for the distribution of the families that developed from it. Evidently, the Proto-Equatorial speech community split in two. One of its divisions spread downstream and to the south, giving rise to the Tupi-Guarani family. The other division moved upstream and to the north, producing the Arawakan family in its part of Amazonia.

So little is known about the Taino language that there is room for

121

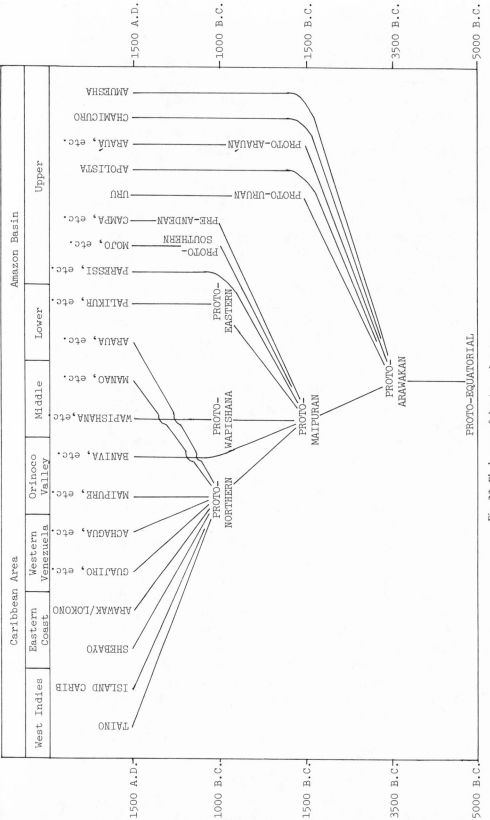

Fig. 22. Phylogeny of the Arawakan Languages.

disagreement about its place within the Arawakan family. Noble (1965, pp. 76–78) considered it a direct offshoot of Proto-Arawakan. Taylor (1977b, p. 60), who worked with a larger number of cognates, has instead derived Taino from Proto-Maipuran, a division of Proto-Arawakan, "if not" from Proto-Northern, a subdivision of Proto-Maipuran. José J. Arrom (personal communication) concludes that the Taino language is so much like the other languages of the Northern group that it, too, must have evolved from Proto-Northern.

I have chosen to use Arrom's placement in my chart, not only because Taylor, too, considered it to be a viable option but also because it is based on a greater range of data. Arrom has covered both the English and the Spanish literature, whereas Noble and, to a lesser extent, Taylor have not read widely in the Spanish sources. The pattern of distribution of the Arawak languages also favors Arrom's placement. If Taino had evolved directly from Proto-Arawak, as Noble thought, it would be the only direct offshoot of that speech community to have passed through the Casiquiare Canal into northeastern South America, at a time when the main thrust of Arawakan expansion was up the Amazon River (fig. 22). And if Taino had developed from Proto-Maipuran, it would have been the only direct offshoot of that speech community to have reached the Caribbean coast, at a time when all the other Maipuran languages were limited to the interior of the continent. Arrom's classification provides the most parsimonious solution to the problem of Taino ancestry.

The Shebayo language of Trinidad is even more poorly known than Taino. Noble derived it from Proto-Maipuran but I have instead made it an offshoot of Proto-Northern because this, too, better fits the pattern of distribution of the Arawakan languages.

The preceding paragraphs illustrate the need to follow up comparative (classificatory) research on languages with studies of geographical and chronological distributions. The two serve to check each other (chap. 1,c).

The following conclusions are to be drawn from the phylogenetic relationships and distributions shown in figure 22:

1. The Proto-Arawakan language appears to have arisen ca. 3500 B.C. around the junction of the Amazon River and its principal northern tributary, the Río Negro.
2. The people who talked Proto-Arawakan migrated up both streams,

and, as they did so, became differentiated into new speech communities. This happened during the third and second millennia B.C.

3. The speech community in the line of development leading to Taino is known as Proto-Maipuran. It appears to have originated on the Río Negro and to have expanded northward through the Casiquiare Canal into the Orinoco Basin. Correcting for the minimal bias of glottochronological dates, we may estimate that the Proto-Maipuran speakers reached the middle part of the Orinoco Basin towards the close of the second millennium B.C.

4. Back in its homeland on the Río Negro, the Proto-Maipuran speech community also moved down that river into the Amazon itself and descended to its mouth, evolving new languages as it went. Only one of them, Proto-Eastern, is relevant to our study. It appears to have originated in the lower Amazon Valley during the second millennium B.C.

5. The Proto-Eastern speech community expanded or was pushed through the Amazon Delta into the coastal lowlands of Brazilian Guiana, to the left of the Delta. There, it gave rise to several modern languages, of which Palikur is an example.

6. Meanwhile, the Proto-Maipuran inhabitants of the Río Negro and the Orinoco Valley had also diverged into new speech communities. A few of these communities managed to retain their separate identities in peripheral positions until the arrival of Europeans. They include Wapishana, on the border between Amazonia and the Guiana Highlands, and Baniva, on the Orinoco River just below its junction with the Casiquiare Canal.

7. The offshoot of the Proto-Maipuran language that ultimately led to Taino is known as Proto-Northern. If my phylogeny is correct, it originated about 1000 B.C. in the lower part of the Middle Orinoco Valley, downstream from the Proto-Maipuran-to-Baniva development. There, it gave rise to several historic languages, including Maipuran proper.

8. The speakers of Proto-Northern also radiated in various directions, as follows:

   a) Up the Orinoco River past the emergent Baniva speakers, through the Casiquiare Canal and down the Río Negro past the Proto-Wapishana speakers, and out onto the Middle Amazon River.

Manaus, the principal city in the latter area, bears the name of one of the resultant languages.

b) Down the mainstream of the Amazon River to its mouth, where the migrants produced the now-extinct Arauan languages.

c) Up the western tributaries of the Orinoco River to the base of the Columbian and Venezuelan Andes. There, it gave rise to the Achagua language, among others.

d) Up the northern tributaries of the Orinoco River to the west Venezuelan coast. Here, its best known and most remote offshoot is the Goajiro, on the peninsula of that name along the Venezuelan-Columbian border.

e) Down the Orinoco River to its Delta and thence southeastward along the Atlantic coast into Guyana and Suriname. The Arawak speech community and its modern descendant, Lokono, are products of this part of the radiation.

f) Past the Orinoco Delta to Trinidad, Tobago, and the West Indies. The Proto-Northerners who participated in this movement became differentiated into three speech communities, Shebayo on Trinidad, Island Carib in the Lesser Antilles, and Taino in the Greater Antilles. All three presumably came into existence early in the Christian era and survived until the time of Columbus.

In effect, the Proto-Maipuran speech community (3 above) and two of its offshoots, Proto-Eastern (4, 5) and Proto-Northern (7, 8, e) executed a pincer movement around the Guiana Highlands. Starting from their home base on the Río Negro, some Proto-Maipurans moved down that river and thence down the Amazon, becoming Proto-Easterners in the process. When they arrived in the Amazon Delta, they turned left onto the Brazilian coastal plain, which they occupied as far as the French Guianan border (fig. 21). On the other side of the pincer, Proto-Maipurans who were to become Proto-Northerners passed through the Casiquiare Canal, descended the Orinoco River to its delta, and turned right onto the Venezuelan coastal plain, whence they colonized the Atlantic seaboard of Guyana and Suriname. The people of the two pincers were separated in historic time by Cariban speakers in French Guiana. Interestingly, students of the Tupi-Guarani family have found evidences of a similar pincer movement around the East Brazilian Highlands, south of the Amazon River (Brochado 1984).

125

In the absence of a phylogeny of the Cariban languages, we can only speculate about the origin and spread of that family. It may have developed in the Guiana Highlands, where most of its present speech communities are concentrated, and have spread from there through the lower middle and lower parts of the Orinoco Valley to the Llanos (plains) of eastern Colombia, the Maracaibo Basin in western Venezuela, and the east Venezuelan coast. As we have seen (sec. A, above), Cariban speakers did not succeed in their attempt to impose their family upon the Island Caribs in the Lesser Antilles.

It would appear in conclusion that the ancestors of the Tainos participated in three successive radiations, each beginning at one of the nodes shown in figure 22. The original Proto-Arawakans, living in the middle of the Amazon Basin, moved upstream and onto the Río Negro, where they developed the Proto-Maipuran language. Some of the speakers of this language returned to the Amazon River while others forged ahead through the Casiquiare Canal into the middle of the Orinoco Valley, where they produced the Proto-Northern language. Some Proto-Northern speakers also moved back into Amazonia. Others turned to their left into western Venezuela and to their right onto the Guianan coastal plain. There was also a movement out into the West Indies, which produced the Carib and Taino languages. Internal pressure may have caused the first two radiations; the Cariban expansion surely had an effect on the third.

There has been relatively little physical-anthropological research in the Caribbean area, and to my knowledge it has not provided the information needed to test our migration hypotheses. The principal difference so far noted between the human skeletons of the preceramic and ceramic periods is that only the latter have cranial deformation. This is a cultural rather than a biological trait.

D. *Archeological Test*

In examining the archeological evidence pertinent to our initial hypotheses, we must limit ourselves to purely cultural evidence in order to avoid circular reasoning (chap. 1,c). We shall not compare the linguistic and archeological conclusions until we have learned what archeology per se has to tell us about the hypotheses.

Caribbean archeologists have unwittingly devised an approach to the study of migrations that is a mirror image of the linguistic approach.

We have seen that linguists began with comparative research and then checked it by studying the distribution of the resultant lines of development. Conversely, the archeologists have begun with chronological research, which is distributional, and have checked that research by comparing the composition of their distributional units.

In Puerto Rico, for example, I worked out sequences of local periods, which I named after typical sites (chap. 1,B,3). By synchronizing them with the local sequences that were becoming known from the other islands, I was able to set up a series of general periods (chap. 1,B,4) applicable to the Greater Antilles as a whole. I numbered these periods from *I* to *IV* and some of them into two parts, which need not concern us here (Rouse 1951).

While constructing a similar chronology in Venezuela, J. M. Cruxent and I noted that some local periods appeared to be culturally related. Assuming that each local period delimits a single people and culture (chap. 1,B,7), we grouped them into lines of development, which we called series (chap. 1,B,10). Subsequently, I introduced the concept of series into the West Indies. It has since come into general use throughout the Caribbean area, although not without causing some confusion. Many authors mistakenly view each series as a single people and culture, not as a line of development from one people and culture to another (e.g., Veloz Maggiolo et al. 1981).

The late Gary Vescelius (1980) pointed out the need for an intermediate hierarchical level—that of subseries—between the local peoples and cultures and the series to which they belong. He proposed that the suffix -*an* be used to distinguish the names of subseries from the names for series, which end in -*oid*. Thus arose the system of classification used here.

My hierarchy of peoples and cultures, subseries, and series parallels the linguistic hierarchy of speech communities and languages, subfamilies, and families. But I base my system upon studies of distribution, whereas linguists construct theirs before turning to distributional research; hence I produce chronological charts, whereas linguists work with phylogenies.

In accordance with practice in the areas previously reviewed, Caribbean archeologists have found it necessary to work back from the end point of the Taino migration. So far, they have not been able to trace the migration to its beginning in the Amazon Basin because too little is known about the chronology of that region. My chart, therefore, starts with the Orinoco Valley and the adjacent coasts in figure 23,*b* and continues with the West Indies in figures 23,*a*. It proceeds from right to left to left for the sake of consistency with the map of the Caribbean area (fig. 21).

All but one of the Greater Antillean areas, at the top of the chart, bear the names of passages between the islands rather than those of the islands themselves, in recognition of the fact that the ceramic finds on either side of each passage resemble each other more closely than they do the finds on the opposite ends of their own islands (Rouse 1982, p. 52, fig. 2). It would appear that the later inhabitants of the Greater Antilles preferred to travel by canoe rather than on foot, and that as a result they interacted more closely with their neighbors across the passages than with the other residents of their own islands. Each passage formed an interaction sphere, comparable to that between Korea and the Japanese island of Kyushu during the Final Jomon and Early Yayoi periods (chap. 4,D). This situation has been difficult for Caribbeanists to grasp because the present inhabitants of the Greater Antilles are oriented towards the land rather than the sea and as a result interact mostly within their own islands.

Figure 23 has been divided into two parts in order to illustrate another peculiarity of the Caribbean area: its general periods begin much later in the West Indies than on the mainland. I have placed the set of periods alongside each half of the figure in order to illustrate this point. Evidently, the ancestors of the Tainos paused for a long time in the Orinoco Valley before breaking through to the coast and for an equally long time on the coast before venturing into the West Indies. This recalls the halt of the Lapitan people at the entry into Polynesia (chap. 2,A).

Following Japanese practice, I include in the charts units of relative as well as absolute time, that is, ages as well as general periods (chap. 1,B,4). I have used different units than in Japan because the course of cultural development, which the ages reflect, was not the same in the Americas as in Eurasia. My terminology for these ages is taken from Willey and Phillips (1958, fig. 2), except that I have split their Formative Age into Ceramic and Formative in accordance with a distinction sometimes made between Village and Temple Formative. I shall proceed in terms of these ages.

The Lithic Age, with which the Willey-Phillips sequence begins, is characterized by the making of chipped stone tools. There is no ground stonework like that in the late Pleistocene cultures of Australia and Japan (chaps. 2,D; 4,D).

Human remains dating from the Lithic Age have yet to be found in the Orinoco Valley and the adjacent coastal area (fig. 23,b). They should be there, since they are known from the coastal lowlands to the west and from the Guiana Highlands to the east. Both the latter regions have yielded assemblages belonging to a Joboid series, which is marked by bifacially chipped, leaf-shaped stone tools, some large enough to have been used in woodworking and others so small and delicate that they must have been hafted in throwing spears. We know that these spears were used in hunting big game because they have been found among the bones of large, now extinct Pleistocene mammals. Toward the end of the Lithic Age, there was a shift from leaf-shaped to stemmed spearheads (Cruxent 1977, pp. 30–37).

A very different situation exists in the West Indies (fig. 23,a). There the Lithic Age is limited to the islands of Cuba and Hispaniola, with possible extensions into Jamaica and Puerto Rico. The earliest assemblages belong to Casimiran, the initial subseries in a Casimiroid series. It is characterized by massive chunks and flakes of flint, which were used as found or chipped into prismatic cores from which to strike off macroblades. The blades received no further treatment until the close of the Lithic Age, when the artisans began to trim them along their side edges. All appear to have been wood-working tools; there would have been relatively little incentive to make projectile points because of the absence of large land mammals in the West Indies.

The Casimiran Casimiroid flintwork's limitation to the western end of the Greater Antilles and the occurrence of similar artifacts in the adjacent parts of Middle America led Coe (1957) to postulate the flintwork's origin in that part of the mainland. Following up this lead, MacNeish (1982, pp. 38–48) has traced the Casimiroid tradition of flint chipping back to 7500 B.C. in Belize on the Yucatan Peninsula. Since this antedates the arrival of the tradition in the West Indies, we may hypothesize a population movement from Yucatan into Cuba and Hispaniola.

The Casimiran Casimiroid subseries has an intermittent distribution in figure 23,a because I have organized the figure around the passages between islands in conformity with the Ceramic Age settlement pattern, whereas the Lithic Age peoples lived separately on each island. Their settlements appear to have been oriented toward the land rather than the

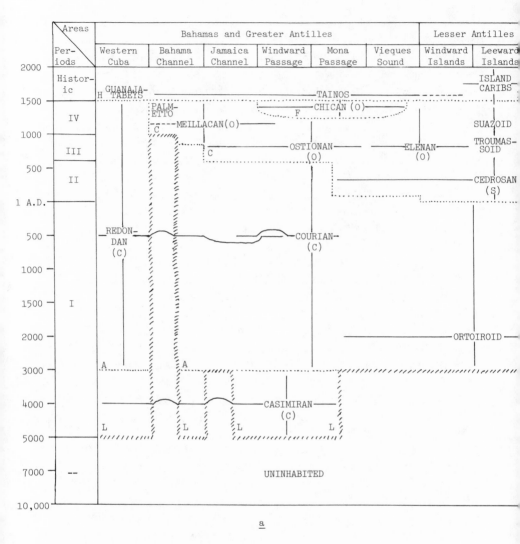

Fig. 23. Chronology of the Peoples and Cultures in the Caribbean Area: (*a*) West Indies; (*b*) Coast and Orinoco Valley. Ages: L = Lithic, A = Archaic, C = Ceramic, F = Formative, H = Historic. Series: (C) = Casimiroid, (S) = Saladoid, (B) = Barrancoid, (O) = Ostionoid, (D) = Dabajuroid.

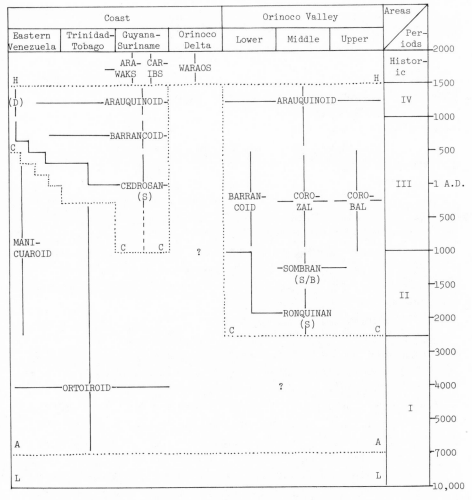

b

sea. In Belize, MacNeish (1982, pp. 38–39) has obtained evidence of movement up and down the local valleys in order to exploit inland food resources during the wet season and coastal resources during the dry season. The Casimiran Casimiroids may similarly have been divided into small bands that traveled seasonally from place to place, foraging for food as it became available (Kosłowski 1978), but this has not yet been demonstrated archeologically.

The ensuing Archaic Age is defined by the appearance of ground stone, bone, and shell tools. The classification of its assemblages is currently in dispute. I recognize two series, Ortoiroid and Casimiroid, and divide the latter into two subseries, Courian and Redondan (fig. 23,*a*).

The Ortoiroid series in known principally from the South American mainland and the continental islands. In it, the bifacially chipped stone tools of the preceding Joboid series are replaced by unformed chips and flakes, comparable to those of the Crude-lithic culture in Japan (chap. 4,D). Projectile points were now made of bone rather than stone. Shell refuse makes its appearance at favorable places along the coast, testifying to the beginning of an orientation towards the sea.

Scattered finds in the Lesser Antilles, the Virgin Islands, and Puerto Rico, extending as far as the Mona Passage area in figure 23,*a*, indicate an expansion of the Ortoiroid series in that direction (Veloz Maggiolo 1980). As its people proceeded, they learned to produce celts (leaf-shaped axes), first of shell and later of chipped and partially ground stone. The later sites on the island of Trinidad have also yielded single-bitted stone axes. These tools would have been useful in making dugout canoes for travel by sea.

Farther west along the Venezuelan coast, the Ortoiroid series was succeeded by a new Manicuaroid series, the origin of which is unclear. It is characterized by bipointed sling stones and shell hammers, to which were subsequently added gouges, ornaments, and projectile points, also made of shell (Rouse and Cruxent 1963, pp. 43–46). This was a peripheral development, which survived on the western edge of our study area long after the Archaic Age had given way to the Ceramic Age elsewhere, that is, into periods II and III of figure 23,*b*.

Turning to the West Indies, we find that the Casimiran Casimiroid peoples split during the Archaic Age into two subseries, Courian in Hispaniola and Redondan in Cuba. The Courian Casimiroids developed an elaborate array of ground stone and shell artifacts, including bowls, single- and double-bitted axes, beads, pendants, balls, and dagger-shaped ceremonial artifacts. Some of their bowls, axes, and ornaments are engraved with complex rectilinear designs. Ears reminiscent of those in a fleur-de-lis are also diagnostic; they were carved in the butts of stone axes and in the base of a shell pendant (Cruxent and Rouse 1969).

The Courian Casimiroid artisans also made improvements in their flint technology. They became sufficiently skilled in trimming macroblades to produce formal types of artifacts: stemmed spear points, knives whose back edges were dulled to make them easier to hold in the hands, and long scrapers, the ends of which were steeply trimmed. Trimming was never extended over the faces of the artifacts, as had been the case in the Joboid series of northern South America.

In the absence of large land mammals, it is assumed that the flint points were hafted in thrusting spears for use in hunting the manatee or sea cow. Nevertheless the Courian Casimiroid people were still oriented primarily towards the land. They and their Redondan Casimiroid neighbors continued to be distributed within islands—Hispaniola and Cuba respectively—rather than across the passages between them (fig. 23,a).

The Redondan Casimiroids did not participate in the Courian Casimiroid advanced in flint technology, nor did they have so great a range of ground stone tools. Most importantly, they chose to make and use shell gouges in place of the stone axes of the Courian Casimiroids. Clearly, they were peripheral to the latter.

A number of authors have derived the Redondan Casimiroid people and their culture from the Manicuaroid inhabitants of the east Venezuelan coast, because both of these peripheral peoples are characterized by shell gouges. The comparative (classificatory) research just reviewed has shown instead that the Redondan people and culture developed locally from Casimiran. Once again, we see the fallacy of relying upon similarities in individual types of artifacts taken out of the context of the cultures in which they occur.

The shell gouge could have spread from the Manicuaroid to the Redondan Casimiroid people by means of transculturation (chap. 1,B:11). The absence of true gouges among the intervening peoples precludes this, however, as does the appearance of gouges in Florida at an earlier date: 3500 B.C., as compared to 300 B.C. in Cuba and 2500 B.C. in

Venezuela (Rouse, Allaire, and Boomert 1985). We may conclude that the shell gouge diffused from Florida into Cuba, if it did not develop independently in the two places.

We come now to the Ceramic Age, during which the ancestors of the Tainos are presumed to have entered the West Indies. The beginning of this age appears on our charts not as a horizontal line but as a series of jogs, indicating a succession of relatively long-lived boundaries between Ceramic and Archaic Age populations. From the existence of the boundaries it can be inferred that Ceramic Age invaders from the Orinoco Valley halted at four prehistoric frontiers before reaching the one encountered by Columbus (fig. 24). I shall number the frontiers from 1 to 5. (For a previous version, see Rouse 1983.)

The earliest known ceramic series, Saladoid, is characterized by white-on-red painted pottery like that first encountered by Hatt in the Virgin Islands (sec. B, above). This series has now been traced back to the coastal plains of the Guianas and Venezuela and beyond them into the Orinoco Valley; it has also been followed forward through Puerto Rico onto the eastern tip of Hispaniola (fig. 23). It is the only kind of pottery made by the peoples who lived behind frontiers 1, 2, and 3 (fig. 24). It is accompanied by the first evidences of agriculture, settled villages, and, except behind frontier 1, the worship of zemis. These facts give us further reason to believe that we are dealing with a population movement.

By chance, the original Saladoid finds were made among peoples who lived directly on frontiers 1, 2, and 3 and who, as a result, were relatively impoverished. The decoration of these peoples' pottery is largely limited to the basic white-on-red painting, which contrasts strongly with the modeled-incised pottery of the Barrancoid and Ostionoid series that overlies it in many sites on the mainland and in the Greater Antilles respectively (fig. 23). Consequently, archeologists jumped to the conclusion that the Saladoid pottery was decorated only with white-on-red painting and that modeling-incision was a later innovation. Subsequent excavation in the centers of Saladoid development, where the pottery is more elaborate, has revealed as much modeling and incision as white-on-red painting. In its centers, Saladoid ceramics contains within itself most of the techniques, shapes, and decoration present in all subsequent series, a fact which indicates that it was ancestral to the later pottery.

The Saladoid series can be divided into three subseries, Ronquinan, Sombran, and Cedrosan, which evolved in that order (fig. 23,*b*). Ron-

134

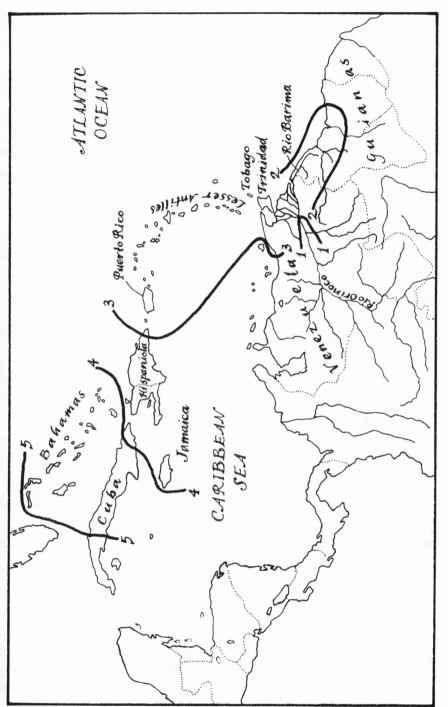

Fig. 24. Advance of the Ceramic-Archaic Age Frontier through the Caribbean Area.

quinan and Sombran Saladoid pottery occur only behind frontier 1, and Cedrosan Saladoid pottery only between frontiers 1 and 3.

More than fifty radiocarbon dates have been obtained for the Ronquinan and Sombrian Saladoid assemblages behind frontier 1. They are so variable that they can be used to support either a long or a short chronology. I have chosen to adopt the long chronology, because it better fits the general sequence of ceramically defined periods for the mainland areas. It gives the Saladoid series a beginning date of about 2500 B.C. (The short chronology would start it at 100 B.C., and would thus collapse period II of figure 18,b into period III.)

The earliest known assemblages of Ronquinan Saladoid pottery come from the Middle Orinoco area, around the town of Parmana (fig. 21). Their sherds are technologically poor—thin, soft, and friable—but surprisingly complex in both shape and decoration. They include bottles as well as bowls and modeled-incised as well as painted decoration (fig. 25,a,b). There are also flat clay griddles resembling the iron griddles on which the present population of the area bakes bread. (For a typical prehistoric griddle, see figure 26,d). Then as now, the bread was probably made from the roots of the cassava plant; no traces of corn have been found in Ronquinan Saladoid deposits (Roosevelt 1980).

Evidence of a Ronquinan Saladoid movement downstream has been found at the site of Saladero, after which the overall series is named, just above the Orinoco Delta. Here, J. M. Cruxent and I (1958–59, pp. 213–20) encountered a small assemblage of Ronquinan Saladoid refuse beneath a much larger deposit of Barrancoid remains. The Ronquinan Saladoid potsherd are technologically superior to their Barrancoid successors—thinner, finer, and harder. They come mainly from simple open bowls decorated with delicate white-on-red or red painted designs and with short, intermittent incised lines that contrast strongly with the areal painting and complex modeling-incision of the overlying Barrancoid assemblages (fig. 25,c,d). They are likewise simpler than their parent pottery in the middle Orinoco area. Overall, this assemblage gives the impression that it was laid down by a small, frontier community peripheral to a center of Saladoid development farther up the Orinoco River.

The Ronquinan Saladoids halted for at least a half millennium at frontier 1, just above the Orinoco Delta, before breaking through that ecological barrier (fig. 23,b). Originally, we sought evidence of their

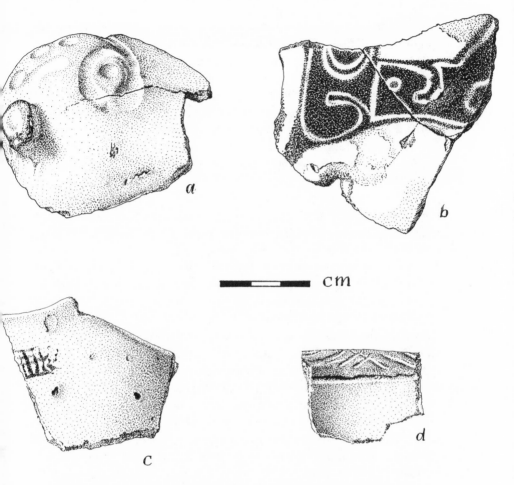

cm

Fig. 25. Earliest Ronquinan Saladoid Pottery: (*a*) modeled-incised design on vessel wall, La Gruta complex; (*b*) white-on-red painted sherd, La Gruta complex; (*c*) red-painted sherd, Saladero complex; (*d*) incised sherd, Saladero complex. (*a, b*, specimens in the Museum of the American Indian, Heye Foundation; *c, d*, Yale Peabody Museum specimens)

advance to the coast on the island of Trinidad and in eastern Venezuela, on the assumption that they had moved down the west side of the Delta. We failed and have had to turn to an alternative possibility. Aad Boomert (personal communication) has suggested that the Ronquinan potters moved down the east rather than the west side of the Delta and turned up the Río Barima onto the Guiana coastal plain, where they may have formed a new frontier (fig. 24,2) and have developed a new subseries, Cedrosan Saladoid. The land behind the presumed new frontier had previously been occupied by peoples who were still in the Archaic Age (fig. 23,a).

Boomert's hypothesis makes better sense ecologically than the one we had been testing. The Ronquinan Saladoid migrants would have been attracted to the Guiana coastal plain by the presence of large streams bordered by natural levees comparable to those on which they had lived in the Orinoco Valley. Such levees were not available to them on Trinidad or the east Venezuelan coast, where for the most part mountains come directly down to the sea.

What would have caused the Saladoid population of the Lower Orinoco area to break through the Delta and occupy the Guiana coast? For the answer to this question, we must return to the Middle Orinoco area and examine the fate of the Ronquinan Saladoids who remained there. As time passed, that people's pottery became thicker, firmer, and smoother; its shapes and designs grew larger, bolder, and more complex; and its modeling-incision began to overshadow its white-on-red painting. These changes ushered in the Sombran subseries which, while still Saladoid, was on the way to becoming Barrancoid (fig. 23,b).

The Ronquinan-Sombran development took place during period II in the mainland chronology, that is, during the second millennium B.C. if our interpretation of the radiocarbon dates is correct. During period III, that is, the first millennium B.C., the Sombran Saladoid people may have moved downstream, pushing the Ronquinan Saladoids who lived there out into the Guianas.

These events are presumed to have touched off a pair of developments, from Sombran Saladoid to Barrancoid pottery in the Lower Orinoco area and from Ronquinan Saladoid to Cedrosan Saladoid pottery in the Guianas. The former hypothesis is substantiated by the ceramic changes from bottom to top of the Barrancoid deposit at the site of Saladero (Rouse 1978). The latter hypothesis needs to be tested by searching in the Guianas for evidences of a Ronquinan-Cedrosan transition. So far, only one purely Saladoid assemblage has been found there, at Wonotobo Falls in Suriname, and it is fully developed Cedrosan (Boomert 1983). It is radiocarbon dated around the time of Christ, which is not quite early enough for it to have served as a source of the subsequent Cedrosan Saladoid movements (fig. 23,*b*).

At several sites on the Guiana coast and in Trinidad, including Wonotobo Falls, Cedrosan Saladoid assemblages are overlaid by mixed Saladoid-Barrancoid assemblages. This indicates that Barrancoid people followed the Saladoids onto the coastal plain and the adjacent islands. Either they traded pottery with the local inhabitants or they settled down among them.

The Cedrosan Saladoids retained many of the ceramic customs of their Ronquinan predecessors but added distinctive new traits, such as turtle effigy bowls with flippers along their sides and, on occasion, modeled heads and tails at either end (as in fig. 26,*b*). Zoned incised crosshatching is also diagnostic; it replaces the red-painted crosshatching of the Ronquinan potters (cf. fig. 26,*b* and 25,*c*).

The Cedrosan Saladoid population radiated out of the Guianas around the time of Christ. This movement is well documented by a series of detailed chronological charts. They show that the expansion through Trinidad to the coast of Venezuela was relatively slow and short (fig. 23,*b*). The migrants in this direction may have been put off by the absence of large flood plains, natural levees, and gallery forests, to which they had become accustomed in the Orinoco Valley and on the Guiana coast.

The advance into the West Indies proceeded much more rapidly. The Cedrosan Saladoids swept through the Lesser Antilles, the Virgin Islands, and Puerto Rico within a century or two, coming to a halt at frontier 3 on the eastern tip of Hispaniola (fig. 23,*a*). There they remained stationary for four centuries, either because they needed time to adapt themselves to such a large land mass or because they found it difficult to conquer its relatively large Archaic Age population.

The Cedrosan migrants settled first on the banks of the largest streams, a short distance inland, and relied on land rather than sea food, as if they were still in the Guianas (Barrau and Montbrun 1978). They subsequently expanded to the coast and began to move farther into the interiors of the large islands. While colonizing the Windward Islands,

139

Fig. 26. Typical Cedrosan Saladoid Vessels and Utensils: (*a*) white-on-red painted pot, Puerto Rico; (*b*) modeled-incised pot, Guadeloupe; (*c*) incense burner, Martinique; (*d*) clay griddle, Martinique. (*a*, Yale Peabody Museum specimen; *b–d*, after Mattioni and Nicolas 1972, pls. 20, 39, 84)

they acquired the taste for land crabs that had so intrigued Rainey (Allaire, personal communication), but they did not begin to exploit the full range of shellfish until after they had completed their movement, possibly because they had by then exhausted the local supplies of crabs (Goodwin 1979).

Early on, they began to decorate their pottery with polychrome designs and to produce a variety of religious paraphernalia. These include incense burners (fig. 26,c); bowls furnished with tubes which are believed to have been inserted in the nostrils for the purpose of sniffing *cahoba* (tobacco or another narcotic); small mound-shaped, three-pointed objects of clay, stone, or shell (e.g., fig. 27,b); and elaborate carved stone pendants (fig. 27,a). All these types of artifacts except the incense burners are known to have been used by the Tainos for the worship of zemis (sec. A, above), and hence we may say that the Cedrosan Saladoids introduced zemiism into the Antilles.

Chanlatte (1979) has found a concentration of the religious objects at La Hueca on Vieques Island, accompanied by the modeled-incised component of Cedrosan Saladoid pottery but not by its white-on-red and polychrome painting. Adjoining this site is another one, Sorcé, which contains a full range of Cedrosan Saladoid pottery but fewer and simpler religious artifacts. Chanlatte accounts for these differences in content by postulating two migrations from South America, the first of which he calls Huecoid and the second Saladoid. However, the La Hueca and Sorcé sites have yielded equally early radiocarbon dates, and their artifactual traits overlap enough to indicate that both are products of the Cedrosan Saladoid movement into the Antilles.

The La Hueca site may have been settled by an advance party of Cedrosan Saladoid potters and Sorcé, by later immigrants who brought an overlapping share of the total culture. If so, the two finds would be an example of the founders' effect, that is, of the principle that small groups of colonists introduce limited sets of traits (chap. 1,B,10). In Polynesia, where this effect has been recognized for some time, the original settlers are presumed to have developed in relative isolation (Vayda and Rappaport 1963, pp. 133–36). In the West Indies, however, there must have been interaction among successive groups of immigrants (sec. A, above).

Alternatively, the La Hueca site may have served as a place of residence for elite members of the Cedrosan Saladoid population, like those pres-

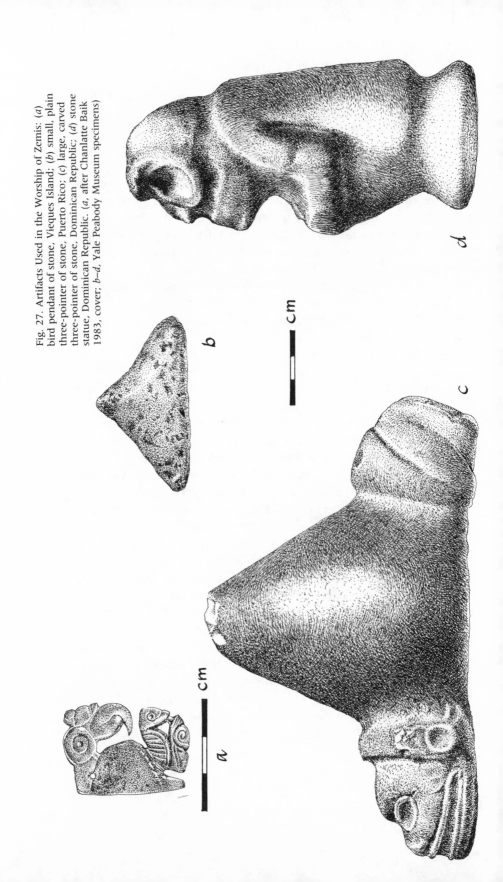

Fig. 27. Artifacts Used in the Worship of Zemis: (a) bird pendant of stone, Vieques Island; (b) small, plain three-pointer of stone, Puerto Rico; (c) large, carved three-pointer of stone, Dominican Republic; (d) stone statue, Dominican Republic. (a, after Chanlatte Baik 1983, cover; b–d, Yale Peabody Museum specimens)

ent among the Tainos in the time of Columbus, or else the two sites may have been inhabited by different descent groups. These various possibilities need to be systematically investigated in accordance with the principle of multiple working hypotheses (chap. 1,A).

Elsewhere (Rouse MS), I have noted that the modeled-incised pottery of La Hueca and the painted pottery that accompanies it at Sorcé constitute separate wares, like chinaware and stoneware in our own civilization, and have compared this ceramic duality to the duality of languages among the Island Caribs (sec. A, above). Just as Carib war parties appear to have brought both a Cariban and a pidgin language into the Lesser Antilles, losing the former to the local Igneri (Arawakan) language, so the Cedrosan Saladoid potters may be said to have brought two wares with them, one derived from Ronquinan Saladoid pottery and the other, which is isolated at the La Hueca, from an unknown source.

Cedrosan Saladoid culture reached its climax at the La Hueca and Sorcé sites, after which it began to decline. First it lost its Huecan component, that is, the modeled-incised pottery and accompanying paraphernalia that had led Chanlatte to postulate a Huecoid series. Next polychrome painting was abandoned and finally white-painted designs. At this point, the Cedrosan subseries and the Saladoid series of which it was a part may be said to have come to an end.

Originally, I classified the post-Saladoid pottery of the Greater Antilles into three series, Ostionoid, Meillacoid, and Chicoid (Rouse 1964). Later, I separated off a fourth series, Elenoid, from Ostionoid (Rouse 1982a). With the introduction of the concept of subseries, I find it advisable to treat all four of these units as subseries within a single Ostionoid series, and to rename them Elenan Ostionoid, Ostionan Ostionoid, Meillacan Ostionoid, and Chican Ostionoid respectively. This brings me back to a dual succession of Ceramic Age series in the Greater Antilles, corresponding to Hatt's Coral Bay-Longford/Magens Bay-Salt River sequence and Rainey's sequence of Crab and Shell cultures (sec. B, above).

At the beginning of period III, midway through the first millennium A.D., Cedrosan Saladoid pottery gave rise to the first two Ostionoid subseries, Elenan in the Leeward Islands and the Vieques Sound area and Ostionan in the Mona Passage area (fig. 23,a). Both new subseries retained the technology and shapes of the final Cedrosan pottery, as well as its tabular lugs, on which modeled-incised figures had previously been placed, and its red-painted areas, on which the earlier potters had

143

painted white designs. Neither the first Elenan nor the first Ostionan potters added other kinds of decoration, and as a result they produced the largely plain pottery that is characteristic of period III in the overall sequence (sec. B, above).

The Elenan Ostionoid artisans gradually made their pottery thicker, coarser, and rougher and simplified its shapes. The Ostionan Ostionoid potters were more conservative. They continued to produce relatively thin, fine, and smooth pottery and retained all the previous shapes (fig. 28,b,c). They gradually extended red paint over the entire surface of the vessel, converting that paint into a red slip and frequently polishing it.

As time passed, both the Elenan and Ostionan Ostionoid potters revived the practices of modeling and incision and used them to make human and animal adornos resembling the zemis worshiped by the historic Taino Indians. The figures that have been found in the Elenan area are simpler and cruder than those in the Ostionan assemblages. Religious objects carved in stone, bone, and shell also reappear; they, too, are simpler and less frequent in the Elenan area. In the Ostionan area, these religious objects include bowls provided with snuffing tubes, small three-pointers like those made in the previous period (fig. 27,b), and new types of pendants carved in stone, bone, and shell. The incense burners produced by the Cedrosan Saladoid potters during the early part of period II did not reappear. Consequently, we may say that zemiism was revived in modified form during the latter part of period III.

So far as is known, the Elenan Ostionoid population remained stationary throughout its existence. The Ostionan Ostionoids recommenced the previous Cedrosan Saladoid movement, expanding westward at the expense of the Courian Casimiroid people of the Archaic Age (fig. 23,a). Some Ostionan Ostionoids proceeded by sea along the south shore of Hispaniola into the Jamaican channel area (Rouse and Moore 1984). Others went primarily by land through the great northern valleys of Hispaniola into the Windward Passage area (Veloz Maggiolo, Ortega, and Caba Fuentes 1981).

In effect, the Ostionan Ostionoids moved the Ceramic-Archaic Age frontier forward through Hispaniola and Jamaica to a fourth position on the eastern end of the next island, Cuba (fig. 24,4). This parallels the Japanoid advance through the eastern part of Honshu Island to the southern tip of Hokkaido Island at the expense of the Jomonoids (fig.

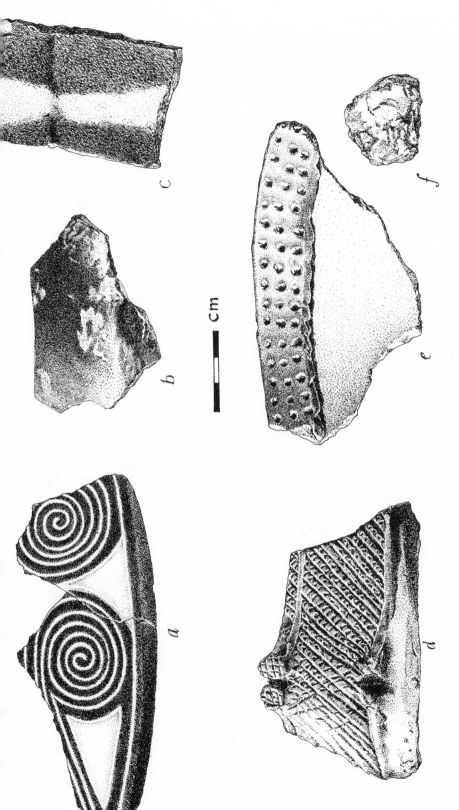

Fig. 28. Markers for the Ceramic Age Repeopling of the Greater Antilles: (*a*) Cedrosan Saladoid pottery, Puerto Rico; (*b, c*) Ostionan Ostionoid pottery, Puerto Rico, Dominican Republic; (*d, e*) Meillacan Ostionoid pottery, Haiti; (*f*) Palmetto ware, Bahamas. (Yale Peabody Museum specimens)

15). Both populations remained stationary for some time behind their new frontiers.

Towards the end of period III, about 800 A.D., the Ostionan Ostionoids living along frontier 4 developed a new form of pottery and thereby transformed themselves into Meillacan Ostionoids (fig. 23,a). Their new pottery was unchanged in material and shape but its surfaces were now left unpolished. Red painting disappeared and was replaced by designs that were incised and punctated into clay or applied as strips and dots to the vessel surfaces. The edges of the incisions were made jagged and the applied strips were left unsmoothed, as if to emphasize the roughness of the vessel surfaces (fig. 28,d,e).

The designs produced by means of incision consist primarily of obliquely hatched lines inclined in different directions. They resemble the designs incised on stone vessels and other kinds of decorated artifacts by the Archaic Age artisans of Haiti (Rouse 1982b, pls. 1, 2, figs. 1, 2). It would appear that Meillacan Ostionoid potters borrowed these designs from the Courian Casimiroids whom they encountered on frontier 4, just as the Yayoi potters of the Japanoid series borrowed decoration from the Jomonoid artisans whom they replaced in the eastern half of Honshu Island (fig. 19).

The potters living on frontier 4 also reproduced Archaic Age designs in appliqué-work. They further used this technique to fashion human and animal lugs like the ones that were developing at the time among the Elenan and the Ostionan Ostionoid potters back from the Ceramic-Archaic frontier. The appearance of these lugs among the Meillacan Ostionoids indicates that they, too, participated in the late period III revival of zemiism.

Despite these evidences of local development, Veloz Maggiolo, Ortega, and Caba Fuentes (1981) argue that migrants from South America brought Meillacan Ostionoid ceramics into the West Indies. They base their argument on similarities between its decoration and that of historic Indian pottery in the Guyana highlands, but they acknowledge a lack of distributional data connecting these two remote and disparate occurrences. Zucchi (MS) has countered by hypothesizing that Arauquinoid potters from the Venezuelan Llanos introduced Meillacan Ostionoid pottery into the Greater Antilles. Her hypothesis, too, suffers from a lack of distributional support. And neither hypothesis takes into consideration the comparative evidence that Meillacan pottery is classifiable within the Ostionoid series.

The reasoning behind the two migration hypotheses resembles that used to "prove" that the Eskimos are descendants of the Magdalenian people of late Pleistocene time in Europe (chap. 3,B) and is equally unconvincing. Similarities by themselves mean nothing, since there is always a chance that they are the result of transculturation, independent development, or inheritance from common ancestors rather than migration. Such alternatives can only be eliminated by subjecting migration hypotheses based upon similarities to distributional and classificatory (i.e., developmental) tests. The hypotheses that derive Meillacan Ostionoid pottery from South America do not meet these tests.

On the other hand, the Meillacan Ostionoid potters did expand locally from their presumed place of origin in the Windward Passage and Jamaica Channel areas into the Bahama Channel area (fig. 23,a). In other words, they continued to maintain the orientation toward the sea that had characterized their Cedrosan Saladoid and Ostionan Ostionoid predecessors, and they advanced the Ceramic-Archaic age frontier from its period III position to the position it occupied in the time of Columbus (fig. 25,5).

After the Meillacan Ostionoids entered the Bahamas, their pottery degenerated, presumably for lack of good clay, and they created a new ware, known as Palmetto. The new pottery is thick, coarse, plain, and crumbly (fig. 28,f). If the Spaniards had not arrived when they did, the Palmetto potters might well have abandoned ceramics entirely, as the ancestors of the Polynesians and the Eskimos did during the course of their migrations (chaps. 2,D; 3,D).

Reviewing the evidence for repeopling of the Greater Antilles during the Ceramic Age, that is, in the first and second millennia A.D., we may say that it consists not of overall similarities in the archeological record but of a pattern of change from Cedrosan Saladoid through Ostionan and Meillacan Ostionoid pottery to Palmetto ware (fig. 28). Each of these ceramic units developed on a frontier, 3 in the case of Ostionan Ostionoid, 4 in the case of Meillacan Ostionoid, and 5 in the case of Palmetto were (fig. 24).

While Meillacan Ostionoid pottery was emerging on frontier 4 and Palmetto ware on frontier 5, the Ostionan Ostionoid potters back from these frontiers in the Mona Passage area were following their own line of development. They became increasingly preoccupied with the worship of zemis, and by the beginning of period IV had developed it into a specialized activity characterized, as in historic time, by priests, temples, and idols. When this happened, we may say that they had advanced from the Ceramic into the Formative Age (the Temple Formative of some authors. See fig. 23,*a*).

At the beginning of period IV, about 1200 A.D., the Ostionan Ostionoids in the eastern half of the Dominican Republic transformed themselves into Chican Ostionoids by developing a new form of pottery, which was the most advanced of its time in the Caribbean area. If we consider Cedrosan Saladoid pottery, as represented at La Hueca and Sorcé, to be classic, then Chican Ostionoid may be termed post-classic. It constitutes a second climax of ceramic art, following the decline during period III (Rouse 1982a). Its vessels are smooth, fine, and have a variety of shapes, including collared bowls and effigy bottles. They lack the painting of the previous periods, but are elaborately decorated with modeled-incised designs, many of which appear to have been revived from Cedrosan Saladoid pottery.

Before the discovery of classic Cedrosan Saladoid pottery with its elaborate modeling and incision, it was thought that Barrancoid potters from the mainland had introduced modeling and incision into the Greater Antilles and were therefore responsible for the rise of Chican Ostionoid pottery. Now it is clear that Barrancoid and Chican Ostionoid pottery are parallel developments from a common Saladoid ancestry. Indeed, the Barrancoid series had become extinct during period III, prior to the rise of the Chican Ostionoid subseries, and hence could not have been ancestral to that kind of pottery (cf. fig. 23,*b* and *a*).

During the course of period IV, the manufacture of Chican Ostionoid pottery spread westward into the Windward Passage area and eastward through Puerto Rico into the Vieques Sound area. Its entry into Puerto Rico has been particularly well documented. Two sites in the middle of the south coast of that island have yielded pottery of the Boca Chica complex, which is native to the southeast coast of Hispaniola. Evidently, immigration—as opposed to a population movement—carried this complex from Santo Domingo to the boundary between the Mona Passage and Vieques Sound areas. The potters on either side of the boundary adopted most of the new complex's diagnostic traits, while retaining many of their own, and as a result became acculturated to the Chican Ostionoid series (fig. 29).

Ball courts and dance plazas originated in the Mona Passage area during period III and accompanied Chican Ostionoid pottery in its spread from that area during period IV. The game itself is assumed to have come from South America, but it was not played on earth- or stone-lined courts and with belts of stone until it reached the Mona Passage area. Alegría (1983) has suggested that these innovations are the result of transculturation from Middle America.

Within the Mona Passage area, too, the small, plain three-pointed stones of periods II and III increased in size during period IV and began to be carved with figures of zemis (fig. 26,c). Different kinds of carved stone figures developed in the other passage areas (fig. 26,d).

Chican Ostionoid pottery and the associated ball courts and ceremonial paraphernalia can be ascribed to the Classic Taino Indians. These remains are stylistically similar to artifacts obtained by the conquistadors from the Taino Indians and to finds in sites where the Spanish settlers first interacted with the Indians, at La Navidad in northern Haiti and Isabela on the north coast of the Dominican Republic (Deegan and Williams MS; Palms 1945, p. 303).

Meillacan Ostionoid pottery can similarly be correlated with the western group of Sub-Taino Indians. Examples of it have been found at the first Spanish settlement in the territory of that group, at Redon on the southwestern peninsula of Haiti (Moore MS). The nature of the pottery made by the eastern group of Sub-Tainos, that is, the period IV inhabitants of the Leeward Islands north of the Island Carib base on the island of Guadeloupe, remains to be determined; that pottery may or may not have been Elenan.

Finally, let us turn to the situation in the Windward Islands, farther south. The initial, Cedrosan Saladoid pottery of these islands developed successively through two new series, Troumassoid and Suazoid (fig. 23,a). Neither of them resembles any of the pottery we have just discussed, as it should if the hypotheses of Meillacan and Chican Ostionoid migration from South America we have considered above were correct. This is another reason for concluding that all the Ostionoid subseries developed in relative isolation in the Greater Antilles.

The earlier, Troumassoid series is obviously a local development from Cedrosan Saladoid. Opinion differs about the Suazoid series. Some ar-

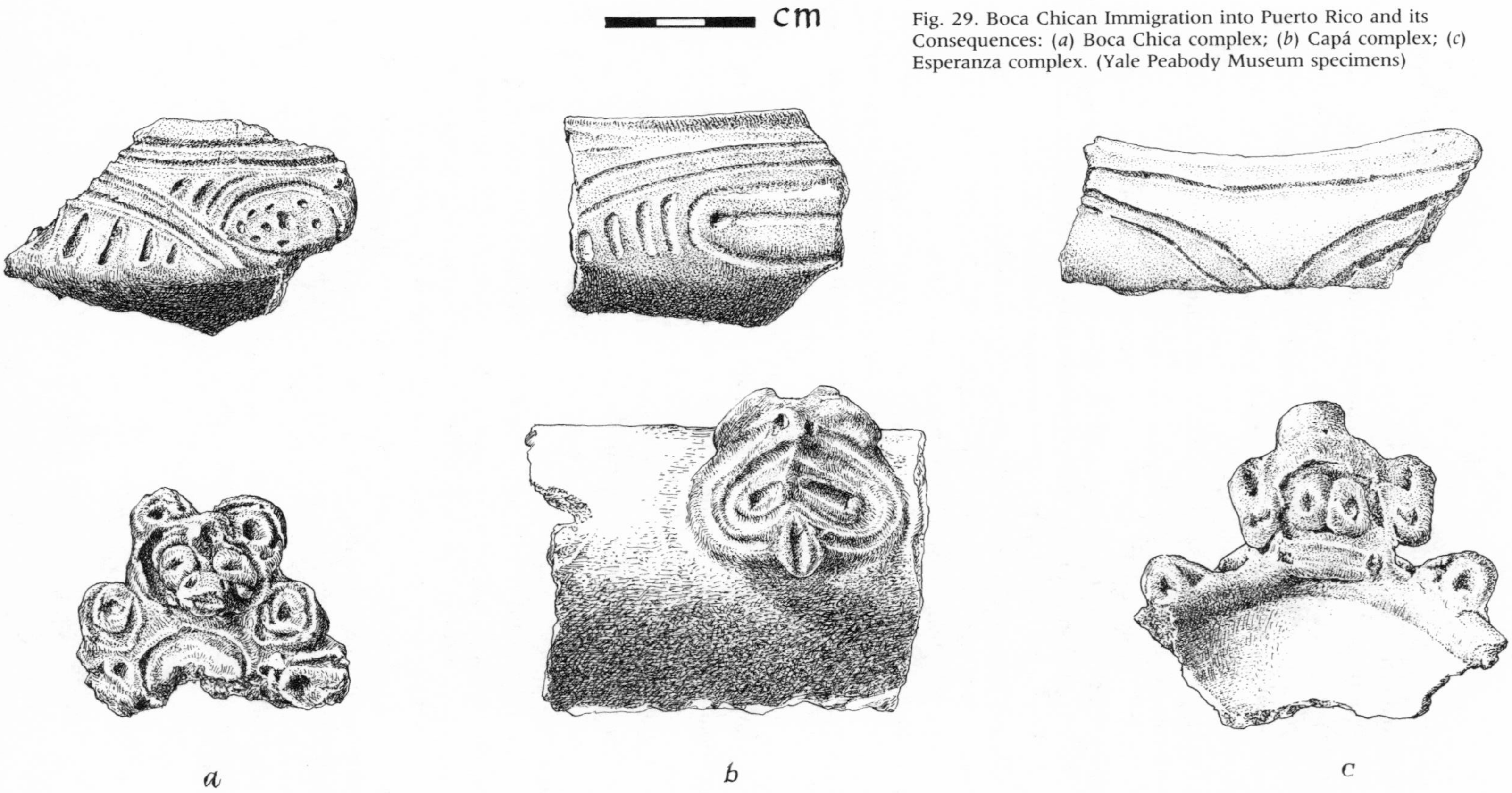

Fig. 29. Boca Chican Immigration into Puerto Rico and its Consequences: (*a*) Boca Chica complex; (*b*) Capá complex; (*c*) Esperanza complex. (Yale Peabody Museum specimens)

cheologists (e.g., Haag 1965, p. 244) have concluded that it too was a local development. Others (e.g., Bullen and Bullen 1976) consider it the result of population movement from South America.

Allaire (1977) has tested these two possibilities on the island of Martinique. His analysis of trends in the local ceramic sequence, which he has worked out in relatively great detail, indicates local development. Moreover, he has been unable to find any potential antecedent for Suazoid pottery in South America. He therefore correlates that pottery with the Igneri Indians, who preceded the Island Caribs in the Lesser Antilles.

But what, then, was the nature of Island Carib pottery? Searching the literature for an answer to this question, Allaire (1984b) has found that the Island Caribs of French colonial time made and used plainware similar in material and shape to that of contemporary Cariban speaking groups in the Guianas. Studying the prehistoric collections in Island Carib territory, Boomert (MS) has identified a Cayo ceramic complex, which resembles Koriabo, a complex in the Guianas dating from 1000 to 1500 A.D. (Neither complex is shown in figure 23 because they have not yet been formally classified into series.) Boomert hypothesizes that people who made Koriabo pottery and called themselves Caribs invaded the Windward Islands during the first half of the second millennium A.D. and there developed the Cayo complex, which subsequently devolved into the plainware.

Boomert's hypotheses are consistent with the native tradition that war parties from the south invaded the Windward Islands and settled down among its native Igneri Indians, and with the linguists' conclusion that these immigrants adopted the Igneri language while imposing their name and some of their customs upon the native population (sec. B above). Nevertheless, both Boomert and Allaire are inclined to doubt the historicity of the native tradition and to assume that Arawakan-speaking Caribs from the mainland replaced the previous Igneri population. Further chronological and comparative (classificatory) research is needed to resolve this difference of opinion and to test the validity of the various hypotheses.

E. *Summary and Conclusions*

Caribbeanists have come a long way in searching for the origin and development of the Taino Indians since Lovén (1935) stated it as a fact that they had migrated from South America bringing their culture with them. We now realize that peoples mentioned in historical documents, such as the Tainos and the Igneris, cannot be traced back into prehistory—we must work instead with population groups defined by the two kinds of evidence about prehistory currently available, linguistic and archeological. We use the linguistic evidence to formulate and trace speech communities in terms of their languages and the archeological evidence to formulate and trace peoples in terms of their cultures. (Races and their biological traits offer another approach to the problem that has not yet been tried in the Caribbean area.)

Caribbean linguists and archeologists have processed separately the information about their respective kinds of population groups, using contrary strategies designed to take advantage of the unique qualities of their evidence. The linguists have begun with comparative (classificatory) research, after which they have studied the distribution of the resultant units. They have been able to follow this strategy because languages are structurally integrated systems of communication, which develop one from another in a manner that is relatively easy to trace.

Caribbean archeologists, on the contrary, have started with distributional study and have used it to formulate their population groups. They construct chronologies, each unit of which delimits a local culture (chap. 1,B:6), and learn as much as possible about stone-working, pottery-making, and other activities within the limits thus established. They use the resultant information to classify the local cultures into subseries and series and thereby to establish lines of development, comparable to those with which the linguists begin their strategy (Chap. 1,B,10).

Archeologists must follow this procedure because cultures are not integrated systems like languages; rather, they are bundles of activities which can, and often do, have different histories. Consequently, investigators must acquire their knowledge of each culture by studying the co-occurrence of its various activities within the units of their chronologies. They begin with the best documented activities, which are stone-chipping in the case of the Lithic Age, stone grinding in the case of the Archaic Age, pottery-making in the case of the Ceramic Age, and religion in the case of the Formative Age, and use their knowledge of these activities as a framework upon which to build a picture of other activities, such as subsistence and residential pattern.

Fortunately, both linguistic and archeological research are relatively well developed in the Caribbean area, and we have been careful to keep the two approaches completely separate so as to prevent the conclusions reached through one of them from biasing the conclusions reached through the other one. For example, at an intermediate stage in the search for Taino origins, Taylor and Rouse (1955) compared the results of their respective linguistic and archeological research and found them to be incompatible. Instead of attempting to reconcile them, we continued to pursue independent lines of research, based upon the strategies of linguistics and archeology respectively.

The agreement between the current results of linguistic and archeological research, which I have just reviewed, is more convincing because of this. Both indicate that the Island Carib and Taino Indians developed in situ as the result of a single population movement from South America around the time of Christ. The linguists have shown that the Proto-Northern speech community entered the West Indies about that time and eventually pushed the previous inhabitants back into the western end of Cuba, where Columbus encountered them. The newcomers diverged into two new speech communities, Island Carib in the Lesser Antilles and Taino in the Greater Antilles and the Bahamas.

Archeologists have found that the Cedrosan division of the Saladoid series of peoples reached the West Indies about the same time, introducing pottery, agriculture, and the worship of zemis. The Cedrosan Saladoids displaced two previous populations, Casimiroid, which had invaded Cuba and Hispaniola from Middle America, and Ortoiroid, which appears to have come from South America. In the Windward Islands, closest to South America, the Cedrosans developed successively into two new series, Troumassoid and Suazoid, and in the rest of the islands, they diverged into a third, Ostionoid.

The Ostionoid series began as a pair of subseries, Elenan in the Leeward Islands and the Vieques Sound area and Ostionan in the Mona Passage area. Elenan may have survived until historic time in the Windward Islands, where it is probably to be correlated with the eastern group of Sub-Taino Indians with whom the Island Caribs interacted in that area. Ostionan, on the contrary, gave rise to two new subseries, Chican in the Mona Passage area and Meillacan in the Windward Passage and Jamaica Channel areas. Elenan Ostionoid culture is that of the eastern group of Sub-Taino Indians; Chican Ostionoid, that of the Classic Taino Indians; and Meillacan Ostionoid, that of the western group of Sub-Tainos.

This is not to say that the West Indies became isolated from the adjacent mainland after the colonization of the islands by Ceramic Age peoples. There must have been frequent intercommunication, resulting in the spread of loan words from continental speech communities to the emerging Island Carib and Taino communities. There must also have been weak interaction, resulting in transculturation and immigration from island to island. But neither linguistic nor archeological research has revealed convincing evidence of a period of strong interaction, resulting in acculturation or population movement.

The spread of the South American ball game into the West Indies during period II or III is a possible example of transculturation, as is the presumed diffusion of ball-court structures and paraphernalia from Middle America during period III or IV. The Island Carib invasion of the Windward Islands and Guadeloupe may be an example of immigration. Fortunately for us, this movement took place late enough in prehistoric time to be remembered in the traditional history of the area and to be reflected in the linguistic structure of the historic Indians by a pidgin language and in their social structure by a dual pattern of residence (Rouse MS). Yet even this conclusion cannot be taken for granted; it needs to be subjected to further linguistic and archeological tests.

Turning now from the West Indies to the source of its Ceramic-Age inhabitants on the continental islands and the mainland of South America, we find a state of flux. The migration hypotheses proposed for this part of the world in the 1950s and 1960s have been discredited and the alternatives suggested to take their place are still controversial. This should not surprise us; the findings in our previous case studies have also become less reliable the farther back each people has been traced from its historic terminus.

From a geographical point of view, the ancestors of the Tainos could have entered the West Indies via either the east coast of Venezuela, Trinidad, or the Guianas. The historic evidence favors Trinidad and the Guianas; Arawakan speakers were concentrated there during the Historic Age. Nevertheless, archeologists and, to a lesser extent, linguists have focused upon Trinidad and the east coast of Venezuela in tracing the ancestors of the Tainos back to the mainland. Having failed in this endeavor, they are now turning their attention to the Guianas.

My fellow archeologists and I are in the same position here that Heyerdahl was in when he demonstrated by the voyage of the Kon Tiki that the Polynesians could have come from Peru (Chap. 2,B). We have become aware that the ancestral Tainos may have entered the West Indies via the Guianas but have not yet tested this hypothesis by means of systematic fieldwork along that potential migration route.

Why did we originally overlook the possibility of movement out of the Guianas? In part, we were victims of historical accident. Saladoid pottery was first found on the continental islands and we traced it back from there into the Orinoco Valley and onto the east coast of Venezuela. This led us to hypothesize that the ancestors of the Tainos had come from some combination of the three places, and we began to search for them there, not realizing that it is a mistake to limit oneself to the areas indicated by the available evidence. One should always take into consideration all potential migration routes and design one's research accordingly.

We were also misled by the present situation in the Caribbean area. The Guianas are now peripheral to the Caribbean Basin, and we assumed that this was also true during the Ceramic Age. Douglas Taylor's linguistic fieldwork in the Guianas in 1967–69 and excavations by Aad Boomert and other locally based archeologists have indicated that we were wrong. We should have expanded our range of multiple working hypotheses to include the possibility of movement into the Antilles via that region.

A third event that has brought the Guianas to our attention is the rise of interest among archeologists in residential and subsistence patterns, that is, the places where people have chosen to live and the manner in which they have exploited the food resources available in each place. Studies of these subjects indicate that, as the ancestors of the Tainos entered the West Indies, they headed for the major streams, settled along their banks some distance from their mouths, and exploited the resources in the surrounding forests, paying relatively little attention to seafood. The only places in northeastern South America where they could have acquired these preferences are in the Orinoco Valley and on the Guiana coastal plain.

At the end of chapter 3, I contrasted the role of structuralism and functionalism in the study of migrations, noting that the structural approach provides evidence of movement along potential routes while the functional approach enables us to determine how and why each population group adapted to the differing conditions it encountered along the routes established by structural research. The foregoing experience indicates a need to qualify that statement. The fact that the peoples of a single series who inhabited adjacent areas chose to live under similar conditions may be considered evidence in favor of population movement; we may assume that the people of the first area developed a preference for conditions there and carried it into the second area. This, however, will only be confirming evidence; the existence of the migration must be established by distributional and structural analysis before the functional evidence of population movement can be fully accepted.

In the present instance, the fact that the first Cedrosan Saladoid settlers in the Antilles had residential and subsistence patterns similar to those of the Ronquinan Saladoid people in the Orinoco Valley and the Cedrosan Saladoid people in the Guianas is not sufficient to establish the existence of a population movement along that route. We need to test this hypothesis by searching for assemblages in the Guianas that are transitional between the Ronquinan and Cedrosan subseries and are early enough to document a migration from the Orinoco Valley into the Guianas.

_ 6 GENERAL CONCLUSIONS _

In chapter 1, I considered the nature of migration hypotheses and the methods of forming them. Chapters 2–5 were devoted to four cases in which archeologists, with the help of linguists and physical anthropologists, have more or less successfully tested migration hypotheses. The testing methods remain to be discussed.

The migrants in my case studies—Polynesians, Eskimos, Japanese, Tainos, and their immediate ancestors—range from food gatherers through simple farmers to peoples with the complex superstructure of professional activities that we call civilization. They do not include peoples who raised cattle. I had originally intended to add a chapter on the Bantu movements from West into East and South Africa in order to remedy this deficiency, but I found that research on Bantu prehistory has not yet progressed far enough to be considered a success story. While linguists and historic archeologists have made considerable headway in studying the expansion of Bantu speech communities and Bantu societies respectively, prehistoric archeologists have only reached the stage of formulating alternative hypotheses about the movements of Bantu peoples (Ehret and Posnansky 1982). Prehistoric archeologists have not yet worked out enough sequences of local periods to be able to test their hypotheses and to decide among them (Huffman 1979).

Nevertheless, it is reasonable to assume that the methods used in my case studies are equally applicable to cattle herders. Some may argue that fully mobile pastoralists leave too few remains to be studied by the procedures illustrated here. Pastoralists, however, should be no more difficult to handle than specialized hunters like Eskimos, who are included among the case studies. Both kinds of people were seasonal migrants; both had to develop complex equipment with which to sustain their mobility; and, in both cases, their technological virtuosity compensates for the paucity of their remains by providing a greater variety of artifacts through which to trace their movements.

Three of the migrations in the sample—Eskimo, Japanese, and Taino—were still under way at the beginning of history in their respective regions and the fourth—Polynesian—had been completed only a few centuries earlier. Consequently, the archeologists studying all four migrations have been able to work back from history into prehistory and to correlate their research with that undertaken by linguists, physical anthropologists, and other users of the so-called direct historical approach. Archeologists who investigate earlier peoples lack this advantage but in recompense are able to collaborate with stratigraphers, paleontologists, biogeographers, and others who study past environments (e.g., Cherry 1981).

The rest of the procedures used in my case studies apply equally well to earlier time frames; for example, they have been successfully employed to trace the expansion of the Danubian peoples in central Europe (Alexander 1978). Conversely, research on the peopling of the New World has suffered from a failure to follow my cases' practice of beginning at the end of a migration. Students of the movement into the New World have started with the arrival of the first settlers in the United States and Canada, where the data are poor, instead of commencing with the end of the migration in South America, where much more information has survived and the historic Indians have retained a way of life like that of the first settlers (Rouse 1976, Dillehay 1984).

A. Role of the Disciplines in Testing Hypotheses

The earlier and less successful participants in the case studies were generalists, who tested their migration hypotheses against the same broad range of data they had used to formulate them. For example, Heyerdahl made no distinction between archeological, linguistic, physical anthropological, ethnological, and historical data in compiling a list of traits in support of his Ruling Theory that the Polynesians came from America (chap. 2,B), nor did Lovén when he placed the origin of the Tainos in South America (chap. 5,B).

The more successful contributors have acted as specialists while testing their hypotheses. Each has worked entirely within the discipline of his or her choice, focusing on its peculiar kinds of data and utilizing its body of method and theory. Each has also followed the discipline's research strategy, as advocated by Platt in his discussion of strong inference (chap. 1,A).

Among the case studies, this development is best illustrated by the differences between linguistic and archeological tests. The linguists have focused upon speech communities, each consisting of all persons who were able to communicate in the same language. They have analyzed the languages in both their spoken and written forms and have utilized the results of their analyses to classify them into families. As that term implies, the languages of a family are presumed to have descended from a common ancestor.

Linguists work back from the known languages of a family to their unknown predecessors by comparing cognate sounds and words and reconstructing the manner in which they changed from language to language. This makes it possible to set up a tree or phylogeny, showing the family's lines of development. Each line delimits a subfamily, containing the speech communities most closely related to each other. Linguists infer the movements of the speech communities from their positions within the phylogeny.

The archeologists in the case studies have focused upon peoples rather than speech communities. Each people consists of all persons who, through interaction rather than intercommunication, have come to share the same artifacts and activities, that is, the same culture. Archeologists have excavated to obtain artifacts, food remains, and other products of the people's activities, have analyzed their finds, and have used the results of their analyses to set up chronological charts, composed of sequences of local periods tied together by devices such as ages and traditions. Each local period delimits a people and culture, that is, a local population and its artifactual and behavioral norms.

The successful archeologists have then used a comparative approach analogous to that of the linguists. They have more or less formally classified their cultures into series and subseries, corresponding to the families and subfamilies of languages, and have regarded the subseries as lines of development within the series. Instead of putting these lines into family trees, however, they have plotted them on their chronological charts and have inferred migrations from the distributions on the charts.

The essential difference between the two strategies is that linguists work primarily with the development of languages, which they diagram on their phylogenies, and archeologists with the occurrences of cultures, which they plot on their chronological charts (Chap. 5,D). Once phylogenies have been set up, time-space units can be added to them, as has been done in this book and, once chronologies have been prepared, lines of development can be inserted in them, as has been accomplished here through use of the concepts of series and subseries (Chap. 1:B,10). The end result is the same in both cases, but it is reached by different strategies.

There is good reason for the difference. Languages have overall structures, which they pass on to their successors. Linguists are able to use these structures as base lines along which to follow the changes within a family back from its most recent languages to the common ancestor. Cultures, on the contrary, are loose aggregates of different kinds of artifacts, activities, and beliefs that can, and often do, develop independently (Rouse 1972, fig. 14). Archaeologists must therefore identify cultures and trace their histories in terms of the co-occurrences of artifactual traits and their behavioral correlates.

To be sure, individual artifacts do have identifiable structures, built into them through the activity of manufacture. Some of these structures are technological and others stylistic. Archeologists use either or both kinds of structure to set up the lines of development we are calling series. (Eskimo archeology exemplifies the use of stone technology for this purpose and Caribbean archeology, the use of ceramic style; see chaps. 3,D and 5,D.) Unfortunately, series are not inclusive enough or long-lasting enough to be organized into phylogenies in the linguistic manner. All attempts to do so have failed. (Compare, e.g., MacNeish 1952, fig. 23 and Wright 1972, diagram 4.)

The successful contributors to the case studies have resolved this problem by relying primarily on the structure of sites rather than the structure of artifacts, that is, on the co-occurrences of the artifacts within assemblages and on the contextual relationships of the assemblages. Just as the structures of languages enable linguists to set up phylogenies, so also do the structures of sites—especially stratigraphies—make it possible for archeologists to establish chronologies.

Both linguists and archeologists check the inferences about migrations they draw from phylogenies and chronologies by comparing the contents of the languages and cultures plotted there. Miller, for example, has been able to corroborate his inference that the Proto-Tungusic speech community, from which the Korean and Japanese communities are descended, moved eastward to the north of the Proto-Mongols by noting that the Proto-Tungusic language contains words for subsistence patterns adapted to the northern forests rather than the Mongolian steppes (chap. 4,c). This approach has been most extensively used in Indo-European linguistics and Eurasian archeology (e.g., Friedrich 1970).

Physical anthropologists have played a significant role only in the first two case studies. They have tested the prevailing hypotheses about Polynesian and Eskimo migrations by comparing local populations in terms of their biological—as opposed to their linguistic or cultural—traits, and by studying the relationships among the racial groups thus established. In the Polynesian example, they have measured the relative frequency of leukocyte antigens within selected population groups throughout Oceania and have constructed a phylogeny of the groups by calculating the degree of similarity and difference among them. Having thus followed a strategy similar to that in linguistics, they have found that their data produces similar results (chap. 2,c). The Eskimo specialists have instead formulated skeletally defined races, which can be identified among human remains, and have traced the distribution of these races. Their strategy has therefore been archeological; they have studied past occurrences instead of using present resemblances to reconstruct the past (chap. 3,c).

The strategy used in Eskimo archeology is also applicable to the Japanese and Taino cases. Limited success has already been achieved in the former case by comparing the structure of Japanese, Ainu, and Jomon teeth (chap. 4,c). A similar comparison needs to be made of Ceramic- and Archaic-Age teeth in the West Indies (chap. 5,c).

While sociocultural anthropologists have contributed to the formation of migration hypotheses in all four of the case studies, they have been unable to test the hypotheses for the following reasons:

161

1. They obtain their data by observing peoples' behavior, by questioning them about the past, and by reading historical records when they are available. Their observations are reliable, but they can never be sure that the oral traditions and written records they study are not mythological or else biased by religious or political considerations. The Polynesian migration traditions (chap. 2,E) and the historical references to the origin of the imperial dynasty in Japan (chap. 4,E) are cases in point.

2. Sociocultural anthropologists, as their name implies, concentrate on immigration rather than population movement (chap. 2,B:9). They study the movements of individuals, families, or work parties, not the cumulative result of many such movements in the form of changes in whole populations. Accordingly, they have little interest in the process that concerns us here, the peopling or repeopling of an area. They focus on events like the conquest of the Windward Islands by Carib war parties rather than the displacement of the preceramic population of those islands by Ceramic-Age invaders from South America (chap. 5,B–D).

3. Insofar as sociocultural anthropologists do study populations, they work in terms of ethnic classifications made by the persons they study instead of developing their own scientific classifications, as linguists, archeologists, and physical anthropologists do. Ethnic groups cannot be followed back into prehistory because it is impossible to identify them archeologically, as we saw in the case of the Tainos (chap. 5,B,E).

4. Sociocultural anthropologists are able to trace the movements of societies on maps, which lack time depth, because such movements take place almost instantaneously. If and when they do try to apply this procedure to population movements, which happen over a period of time, they are doomed to failure. To succeed, they would in effect have to convert themselves into linguists, archeologists, or physical anthropologists and shift from maps to phylogenies or charts in order to delimit the populations in time as well as in space and to trace their movements in both dimensions (e.g., Rouse 1985).

Given these conditions, it is not surprising that Adams, Van Gerven, and Levy omitted sociocultural anthropology from their survey of *The Retreat from Migrationism* (1978). They recognized that the methods of studying the movement of societies cannot be used to test hypotheses about the movement of peoples.

B. *Strategy of Archeological Tests*

Since my book is primarily concerned with the inference of population movement within the discipline of archeology, rather than linguistics or physical anthropology, I shall go further into the archeological procedures. How have the participants in the case studies been able to show that population movement is more likely than local development or acculturation, the two alternatives noted in chapter 1, section C? And how have they ruled out immigration, common heritage, adaptation to similar conditions of the environment, and other processes that may also have affected the nature of archeological remains?

When I entered the discipline of archeology fifty years ago, no one was aware of these problems. Archeologists were accustomed to describe their finds in some detail and then to give brief opinions about the origin and meaning of the finds in a concluding chapter. This was true, for example, of Rainey's monograph *Porto Rican Archaeology* (1940; chap. 5,B).

Midway through my career, interest shifted from the remains themselves to the conclusions to be drawn from them, and formal procedures were developed to generate hypotheses and test them against the remains (e.g. Watson, Le Blanc, and Redman 1984). Some archeologists have treated each hypothesis separately, but most have weighed them against one or more alternative hypotheses, such as those noted at the beginning of this section, in accordance with Chamberlain's principle of multiple working hypotheses (chap. 1,A).

Logically, the next methodological advance ought to be development of a linear branching strategy, covering the whole range of hypotheses and making it possible to eliminate the less likely ones systematically in accordance with Platt's method of strong inference (chap. 1,A). The participants in my case studies are trending in this direction, and it is a major reason for their success.

My understanding of their strategy is diagrammed in figure 30 (for a previous version, see Rouse 1977, table 1). It consists of four ascending levels of inference, listed in the first column of the figure, which are numbered from 1 to 4.

It is important to note that no single contributor has worked through

163

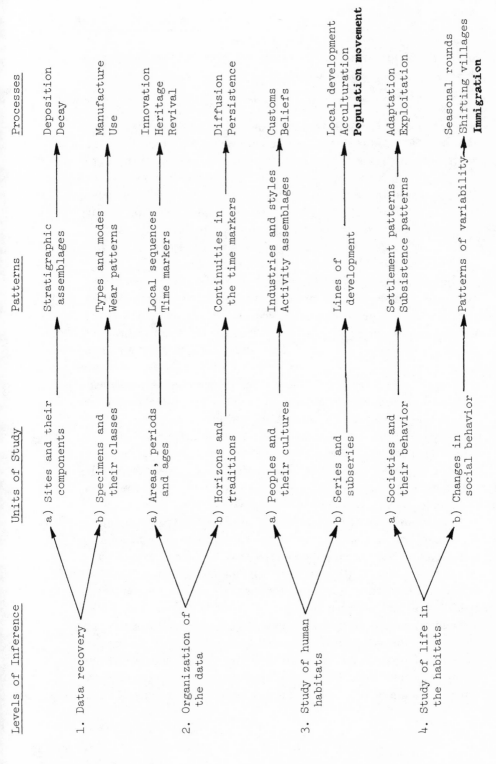

Fig. 30. Strategy for Testing Hypotheses of Prehistoric Migration. (The last two columns contain examples only.)

every part of the strategy. Each of them has specialized in one or more of its parts, but the range of their specialties has been so great that, among them, they have covered the whole range. More importantly, they continue to make advances in all parts of the strategy, contrary to the situation in other regions, where certain approaches, such as chronology, are thought to be outmoded.

Like every science, archeology is a cooperative enterprise, to which each person contributes in accordance with his or her interests and the nature of the available information. Research on the four levels of the strategy is becoming so complex and so sophisticated that each of them is on the verge of being recognized as a subdiscipline within archeology, as follows:

Level 1. The participants in my case studies have begun by collecting and processing the human remains needed to test their migration hypotheses. While research on this level is commonly called *field archeology,* it also includes the analysis of specimens in the laboratory, as a glance at the *Journal of Field Archeology* will illustrate.

Level 2. The objects and information obtained on the first level have had to be organized chronologically rather than topically, for the reasons given in the previous section. *Chronological archeology* is not, however, the final goal, as assumed by some of the archeologists involved in the case studies; rather, it serves to delimit the samples needed to test hypotheses on higher levels of inference.

Level 3. Chronological charts make it possible to narrow one's research to a particular point in time and space, that is, to a single local period. The study of such a period requires cooperative research: archeologists investigate its culture; linguists, the languages spoken at the time; physical anthropologists, its human biology; and geologists and biologists, its natural conditions. Their joint aim is to reconstruct the environment of the local period in all of its aspects, human as well as natural.

From this point of view, a culture may be regarded as a habitat, into which the inhabitants of a local period—the people who "possess" the culture—are born and which they pass on to their descendants. It is thus a part of their heritage, together with the linguistic, racial, and natural conditions under which they live; and they face the same problem whether to conserve or to modify it that they do with respect to the rest of their environment. Archeological study of the conflict between

165

conservation of a cultural habitat and its development used to be called *culture history*, but the term *cultural archeology* is now preferred (Trigger 1978, pp. 100–02). *Developmental* or *evolutionary archeology* would be a better expression of the final aim of research on this level (Rouse 1982).

Level 4. Inferences about human behavior within each cultural habitat constitutes the final level of the strategy. Here, archeologists focus upon the individuals who occupied the habitat and upon their use of its cultural, linguistic, racial, and natural resources. Since individuals act as members of societies, this approach is often called *social archeology* (Renfrew 1984). *Ecological archeology* would be more appropriate, for the aim is to explore individuals' and societies' relationships to their human and natural environments.

The products of research on the four levels are listed across the top of figure 30. First, the participants in my examples have formed units of study by classifying their remains. Next, they have searched the re-mains assigned to each class for a pattern that can be used to define and to identify that class. Finally, they have inferred the behavioral processes that are most likely to have produced each pattern. Their units and examples of their patterns and processes are listed in the second, third, and fourth columns of the figure respectively.

Each level has two sets of units. These serve to divide it into sublevels, which are lettered *a* and *b* in the figure. The arrows connecting the levels, sublevels, and divisions of the sublevels are intended to show the order of the strategy, starting with the recovery and organization of the data on levels 1 and 2 respectively and continuing through the testing of hypotheses of population movement on sublevel 3b and of immigration on sublevel 4b.

The specialists in each step of the strategy have hypothesized a set of alternative units, patterns, or processes, as the case may be, and have eliminated all but the most probable ones. They have then used the surviving hypotheses in their test of the next set of alternative working hypotheses. Thus, they have collectively progressed from the left to the right side of the figure, from the top to the bottom, and from one validated hypothesis to another. Each validated hypothesis explains and justifies the preceding one, and for this reason the entire procedure has been termed *archeological explanation* (Watson, Le Blanc, and Redman 1984). Let us consider the steps in turn:

1a. *Sites.* The strategy begins with the study of sites rather than specimens because, as I discussed in the previous section, sites provide the overall structural information that enables one to attribute finds to particular periods, cultures, and societies and, through the last two categories, to trace the course of population movement and immigration respectively.

Archeologists begin to make inferences as soon as they identify a site, and sometimes they are wrong. I once started to dig a deposit of shells in Puerto Rico under the mistaken impression that it was a place of human habitation, only to find that it had been laid down by natural agencies and, as a result, was unsuitable for use as a unit of archeological research (fig. 30, 1a, col. 2).

When excavating human sites, one is often able to divide them into components, each containing a different assemblage of remains. Stratigraphic sequences are examples; they contain assemblages lying on top of, or alongside, each other. Such sequence constitute patterns, which have been produced by processes of deposition and modified by processes of decay (fig. 30, 1a, cols. 3, 4).

The nineteenth-century archeologists involved in our case studies were only able to operate at the beginning of sublevel 1a. They identified sites and occasionally divided them into components, but did not investigate the patterning of assemblages within the sites nor the processes that had produced the patterns. Consequently, they were unable to move on to higher levels of inference, where knowledge of these patterns and processes is essential. When they tried to do so, they were forced to resort to unfounded speculation, that is, to science fiction rather than scientific inference.

Many avocational archeologists, such as Barry Fell (1976, 1978), still make this mistake. They draw conclusions from artifacts whose context is not known, either because these artifacts were found in isolation or because their finders took them from the ground without recording their relationship to the other parts of their assemblages. Such artifacts tell us nothing about migrations because we cannot determine empirically who produced, used, and deposited them. We are no better off in studying them than in interpreting the Crude-lithic finds of Japan, which lost their context during prehistoric time as the result of geological action (chap. 4,D).

1b. *Specimens*. The simple act of calling an object an artifact is an inference. We take that inference for granted when we find an object that has been heavily modified through human action. We cannot do so, however, when a specimen has been only slightly worked. In that case, we must consider and eliminate the possibility that it was produced by natural agency (fig. 30, 1b, cols. 2,4).

Archeologists are increasingly being asked to distinguish real artifacts from fakes made for sale to collectors, and this is becoming harder to do as the falsifiers improve their skills. The decision whether artifacts are authentic is made by comparing them with artifacts known to be real and determining whether they have like patterns of attributes (fig. 30, 1b, col. 3).

The same procedure is used to classify artifacts. The ones that look alike are grouped together as a class, and the class is defined by noting its pattern of shared attributes. Such patterns are called *types* if they are inferred from entire buildings or portable artifacts, or *modes* if they are inferred from features of the structures or artifacts (Rouse 1972, pp. 300–01, 283). The two kinds of patterns have been built into the objects by the processes of manufacture, performed in accordance with custom and belief (fig. 30, 1b, col. 4).

The archeologists who initiated the case studies were only able to identify artifacts and assign them to classes. They never thought to define the classes by determining their diagnostic patterns of attributes or to explain the patterns by studying processes of manufacture. This is another reason why they were only able to produce science fiction when they tried to move on to higher levels of inference.

2a. *Areas, periods, and ages.* The successful contributors to my case studies have used chronological charts to order their data on level 2 and to trace migrations on levels 3 and 4. Construction of the charts constitutes sublevel 2a in the strategy.

Polynesian and Arctic archeologists have only established sequences of local periods, one for each of the areas marked off across the tops of their charts. Japanologists and Caribbeanists have added general periods along the sides of their charts and have inserted ages into the bodies of the charts (fig. 30, 2a, col. 2).

The local periods function as pigeonholes, to which new sites and specimens may be assigned as they are found. The areas, general periods, and ages serve as indexing devices, through which to organize the pigeonholes. Polynesian and Arctic archeologists have used only areal indices, eschewing both general periods and ages, but I have found it convenient to add a set of general periods to my summary of Arctic research (chap. 3,E), basing it upon Birket-Smith's outmoded classification of Eskimo peoples and cultures. Japanologists and Caribbeanists, on the other hand, have formulated all three kinds of indices. They combine them in various ways for the purposes of conserving sites, curating specimens, and computerizing the information about both of them. Museum exhibits and storage containers, for example, are often arranged by areas and general periods (e.g., Rouse 1984).

The participants in the case studies have inferred their sequences of local periods from the assemblages discovered in their study of sites on sublevel 1a and from the sites' patterns deposition and decay. They have defined each local period by determining which of the types and/or modes formulated through the study of specimens on sublevel 1b are diagnostic. These types and modes are often called *time-markers* (Rouse 1972, p. 299). They are equivalent to index fossils in paleontology. The markers for each local period constitute a pattern, some parts of which are the result of heritage from the previous period and others, of innovation or revival during the period being defined (fig. 30, 2a, cols. 3,4).

General periods and ages have been inferred from the trends common to the sequences of local periods. They, too, are defined by their artifactual content. With the advent of radiocarbon analysis in the 1940s and 1950s it also became possible to determine their calendric limits. Specialists in chronological charts (sublevel 2a) went back to their sites (1a) in order to collect organic materials, and to their specimens (1b) to have these materials analyzed in radiocarbon laboratories. They used the results to test the validity of their charts and, after making the necessary modifications, added dates to the sides of the charts, where they provide a measure of elapsed time, equivalent to latitude and longitude on a map.

Radiocarbon analysis and the other methods of metric dating that have become available in recent years have not obviated the need for the previous kinds of chronological research. Just as historians and historical geologists still find it necessary to organize their data in terms of areas, periods, and ages as well as distances and dates, so the successful archeologists continue to work with all of these categories, using distances and dates to quantify areas, periods, and ages.

Some chronologists (e.g., Ford 1962) have been so preoccupied with the study of traditions on the next higher sublevel of inference that they have ignored or slighted the concept of period. These experts overlook the fact that by definition a tradition has to be a time-marker. Unless and until one has demonstrated that a given type, mode, or combination of them actually does recur from assemblage to assemblage within a single local period and hence is a product of the process of innovation within that period, of heritage from the previous period, or of revival from a still earlier period, one is not justified in treating it as part of a tradition.

2b. *Horizons and traditions.* In defining the units of a chronological chart on the previous sublevel, one will have contrasted them and noted their differences. Now one must redress the balance by noting their similarities. If these extend from area to area within one general period, they are known as *horizons* (fig. 1,b). If instead they extend from period to period within a single area, they are called *local traditions* (fig. 1,b). The term *tradition* is also used more generally to refer to similarities that extend diagonally from one unit of a chronological chart to another, cutting across both its general periods and its areas (fig. 30, 2b, col. 2).

Willey and Phillips (1948, pp. 29–40) refer to horizons and traditions as *integrative units* because the two entities serve to tie together the local periods that form the body of a chronological chart. They also function as a second set of indexing devices, complementing the areas, periods, and ages set up on the previous sublevel (2a). Like the latter, they are used to organize museum exhibits and books on local prehistory, to enter information into a computer, and to retrieve it.

Horizons and traditions are formed by recording the occurrences, or else the frequencies, of time-markers on chronological charts (Ford 1962). If a marker has a long and continuous distribution and changes in a regular pattern, one may consider it to be a valid horizon or tradition and may proceed to determine how it spread, whether by diffusion through space, persistence through time, or some combination of the two processes (fig. 30, 2b, cols. 3,4).

If the distributions are discontinuous or change irregularly in frequency, one must go back through the previous sublevels and check the results there. By modifying them, one may be able to eliminate or reduce the discontinuities and irregularities. If not, one must conclude that the markers in question are not valid horizons or traditions and hence cannot function as indexing devices.

The concepts of horizon and tradition should not be overused. Many prehistorians, forgetting that their purpose is to order data, also employ them as units of study on higher levels of inference. When they do so, they end up tracing the diffusion of their time-markers rather than the migration of peoples or societies. This error has been a major reason for the failures documented by Adams, Van Gerven, and Levy in *Retreat from Migrationism* (1978). The successful participants in my case studies have consciously avoided it (Bellwood 1983).

3a. *Peoples and cultures.* Specialists in this stage of the strategy turn their attention from the remains themselves to the population groups, or peoples, who produced the remains and to the cultural habitats, or cultures, in which the peoples lived. Their aim is to reconstruct each people's culture and to correlate it with the knowledge of other aspects of the people's environment acquired by natural historians, linguists, and physical anthropologists (fig. 30, 3a, col. 1).

The focus here is on a people's activities. One seeks to learn the kinds of activities carried out, the locations where each took place, and the effect each had on the natural landscape. The Japanese excavations in rice paddies, burial mounds, and imperial palaces illustrate this type of research (chap. 4,D). One also wants to know the types of artifacts and forms of thought employed in each activity. The study of Taino cere-monial plazas and of the accompanying worship of zemis is an example (chap. 5,D). The range of a people's culture thus extends from ecological to cognitive information (Renfrew 1983).

The local periods established on sublevel 2a are the key to research on peoples and cultures (3a). Since each period is by definition culturally homogeneous—except for the differences in culture among its social groups, which are the subject of study on level 4—each period delimits the bounds of a local culture and of its inhabitants. Interaction among the people who live within the bounds perpetuates the local culture and, as the period draws to a close, produces a new culture (fig. 30, 3a, col. 2).

When archeologists begin their research on sublevel 3a, their only knowledge of the content of each local culture consists of the complex of time-markers used to define it as a local period. Within a stone age, this many be a lithic industry; in the presence of pottery, a ceramic style; and in the case of civilization, a style of architecture used to house professional specialists. Industries and styles are patterns, from which

171

can be inferred behavioral processes, that is, the customs and beliefs to which the artisans conformed while producing their buildings and artifacts (fig. 30, 3a, cols. 3,4).

The successful participants in my case studies have expanded this skeletal knowledge by returning to the body of data accumulated about a particular local period on level 1 and retrieving from it information about additional kinds of artifacts, beyond the time-markers. They have also investigated non-artifactual remains, such as the remnants of food. Most important of all, they have examined the co-occurrences of artifacts and non-artifactual remains in assemblages, each indicative of one or more of the local people's activities and of the customs and beliefs to which the people conformed in carrying out those activities. Here again, we see the need to study the structure as well as the content of sites (fig. 30, 3a, cols. 3,4).

The broadened picture is vital to the success of migration studies. Too many archeologists trace population movements only in terms of time-markers and, as a result, produce conclusions based narrowly on technological or stylistic details rather than on the totality of each culture. Japanese archeology is an example. The political and intellectual climate in that country before, during, and immediately after World War II inhibited the study of peoples and cultures by Japanese archeologists (chap. 5,E).

Several aspects of the broadened picture are particularly important in tracing population movements. One is knowledge about a people's ability to travel from place to place. The Polynesian specialists have had the greatest success in studying this aspect of the problem (chap. 2,E). Another aspect is the changes which migrants make in the natural environment of their new homeland. Edgar Anderson (1952, pp. 8–15) has applied the phrase *transported landscape* to this phenomenon, which includes the crops, weeds, and diseases that migrants may bring with them. A third important kind of information is the nature and location of the migrants' settlements, which are often overlooked by students of migration. As we have seen in the case of the Eskimos and Tainos (chaps. 3,E; 5,E), continuity in the nature and placement of settlements provides evidence about population movement but discontinuities are not necessarily significant, since the migrants may have chosen to adapt to new conditions instead of seeking out their old ones.

3b. *Series and subseries.* The next step in the strategy is to classify the local cultures and the peoples defined by them. The resultant units are plotted on one's chronological charts, where they depict lines of development, comparable to those which in phylogenies delineate subfamilies and families of languages and species and genera of hominids (fig. 30, 3b, col. 2).

In discussing the case studies, my interest in these procedures has led me to reformulate the horizons and local traditions established on sublevel 2b. I have followed out these horizontal and vertical continuities in whatever other directions they take on chronological charts and have examined their patterns of change from one local period to another. Thus, I have been able to distinguish the patterns of continuity and change that I call subseries and series of local cultures and to insert them in my chronologies (fig. 30, 3b, col. 3).

It is from such patterns of continuity and change that the successful participants in my case studies have inferred population movements. They have also considered and rejected the alternative processes of independent development and acculturation, in accordance with the principle of multiple working hypotheses (fig. 30, 3b, col. 4).

4a. *Societies and their behavior.* After learning as much as possible about the cultural habitats demarcated upon chronologies and about their development, prehistoric archeologists are finally in a position to study life within the habitats. For this purpose they shift from the cultures that had been their primary units of study on level 3 to the individuals who inhabited the cultures. They view the individuals as members of societies, that is, as members of social groups that perform collective behavior, and they study that behavior per se instead of viewing it from the standpoint of cultural norms (fig. 30, 4a, col. 2).

Individuals are organized into three kinds of societies: residential units, such as households, villages, and states; activity units, formed to accomplish specific tasks such as hunting, trade or burial; and relational units, to which individuals belong because of such criteria as age, descent, and status (Rouse 1972, table 6). Most of these units are limited to a single people and culture but some, like trade networks, may extend across cultural boundaries.

Archeologists who proceed to study social units must again go back into their pool of data for information they have not yet had occasion to use and, where necessary, enlarge the pool by further research on level 1. In the case of sites (1a), they focus on settlement patterns,

173

especially the manner in which each of a people's societies was distributed over the landscape. In the case of artifacts (1b), it is necessary to shift from the structure of these objects, which had been the main concern in studying peoples and cultures (level 3), to their use. One determines use partially by observing the positions of the artifacts in the settlement pattern—another reason why the structure of sites is so important—and partially by studying patterns of wear on the artifacts. Here, we see why studies of structure and function have to be considered complementary (chaps. 3,E; 5,E). Structural patterns are basic to research on level 3 and functional patterns, to research on level 4 (fig. 30, 4a, col. 3).

From settlement patterns, wear patterns, and other evidences of social behavior, specialists in social archeology are able to infer such processes as adaptation and exploitation. They seek to determine how the members of particular social groups met their needs and why they were able to succeed in the struggle for survival (fig. 30, 4a, col. 4).

4b. *Changes in social behavior.* Finally, the specialists investigate the changes that have taken place in the composition and behavior of the societies. They study behavioral variability and the manner in which it is patterned, insofar as the data permit them to do so. From the patterns they infer the processes whereby the societies adjusted to changes in their cultural, natural, linguistic, and racial conditions (fig. 30, 4b, cols. 2–4).

This is the part of the strategy in which to consider immigration, that is, movement of the social groups distinguished on the previous sublevel. The shifting of villages from one locality to another is an example. If the villagers crossed a cultural boundary, one may detect their movement by finding sites containing a foreign cultural complex intrusive among sites which have the local complex and may then proceed to examine the effect of the intrusive complex on the native behavior (see, e.g., fig. 29). To this extent, the concepts and procedures used in the study of cultural change (sublevel 3b) are also applicable to the study of social change (sublevel 4b). When, however, specialists in social change study intra-areal movement, they must shift to different concepts and different techniques, which focus upon function rather than origins and hence are beyond the scope of this book.

On sublevel 4b, it is important to take into consideration not only one-way but also two-way movements of social groups, such as seasonal rounds and trading expeditions. These, too, may extend across cultural boundaries, in which case they are detectable by identifying the presence of foreign-made artifacts in local assemblages; or they may be limited to single areas, in which case it is necessary to use other concepts and techniques peculiar to level 4.

Some archeologists have become so preoccupied with the study of societies and their behavior that they proceed directly from the evidence and its organization to level 4, overlooking the need to take into consideration the knowledge of peoples and their culture available as a result of research on level 3. This is justifiable when working with one's own culture, in which one has been educated, but it is a mistake when studying a culture different from one's own. One cannot expect to be able to determine a society's adaptation to its environment when one knows only the natural and not the cultural component of that environment (to say nothing of its linguistic and racial components).

It is equally poor practice for a specialist in level 3 of the strategy to ignore either the potentialities or the results of research on level 4. Rainey committed this error when he jumped to the conclusion that the sharp break between the Crab- and Shell-culture strata in his Puerto Rican sites had resulted from population movement, without stopping to consider the alternative possibility that it was due to the movement of villagers from one locality to another (chap. 5,B).

In reality, archeologists need to consider two kinds of alternative hypotheses: those limited to a single part of the strategy, such as population movement, independent development, and acculturation; and those situated in different parts of the strategy, such as the movement of populations and villages. Research on both kinds of alternatives is equally important, despite the fact that the two are studied on different levels of the strategy. Unless both are kept in mind, one will not be able to consider all possible explanations of one's finds and to make all necessary eliminations in accordance with the principle of multiple working hypotheses and the method of strong inference.

c. *Population Movement vs. Immigration*

While the four cases have been examined in order to shed light on the methods of studying population movement, they also tell us something about the nature of the process, its consequences, and its causes. Let us consider these subjects in the final two sections.

Comparison of population movement with immigration is an appropriate way to start, since the two of them have been confused in several of the case studies. We have already seen that population movement is a macroprocess, which takes place over such a long period of time that we only experience parts of it, whereas immigration is a microprocess, which goes on around us all the time (sec. A, above). We must be careful not to read attributes of the process we experience fully into the process with which we are not so familiar.

Populations occupy areas, which are delimited by boundaries and frontiers (chap. 5,D). Immigrants must cross these boundaries and frontiers in order to penetrate the areas (Green and Perlman 1985).

Population movement may be defined as the original peopling of an area or, if humans already lived there, as the repeopling that takes place when a foreign population enters the area and displaces or absorbs its native inhabitants. The invading population must bring with it a new language, culture, and/or morphology and impose them on the natives. (By *morphology* is meant the population's bodily traits, including its genes; Rouse 1972, fig. 11.) Otherwise, the invaders will not change the local way of life and we cannot say that a population movement has taken place.

Immigration is the intrusion of individual settlers into an already populated area. The intruders usually travel as members of a family, war party, or some other kind of social group. If the group speaks the same language as the local people, comes from a similar culture, and belongs to the same race, it will simply lose itself in the local population. If it differs in one or more of these respects and if additional immigrants do not arrive to support it in maintaining its way of life, it will eventually be assimilated into the local population and the immigration will have come to an end.

If, on the other hand, the immigrants arrive in large enough numbers to dominate the entire area, if they bring along a different language, culture, morphology, or some combination of the three, and if they are able to keep them intact, a population movement will have commenced. In effect, a foreign speech community, people, and/or race will have colonized the local area. The colonists will probably live alongside the native inhabitants, retaining their own language, culture, and/or morphology, as the case may be. They may eventually abort the movement

176

by withdrawing to their former homeland, or they may complete it by absorbing or expelling the native inhabitants of their new homeland.

A population movement then, is more than the cumulative result of immigration. The migrants must take over an entire area and cause an overall change in its human conditions. This is the reason prehistorians have to study the process in the environmental part of their strategy, on level 3, instead of handling it with the behavior of immigration, on level 4.

The European colonization of North America is a typical example of population movement. Over a period of four centuries the colonists destroyed or absorbed most, but not all, of the American Indian population. A few Indians, especially in the southwestern part of the United States, have retained their separate languages, cultures, and race, creating a situation of plurality (Spicer and Thompson 1972).

The linguists' version of the Island Carib conquest of the Windward Islands (chap. 5,A) provides a good example of immigration. The Island Carib warriors who settled among the previous Igneris were able to segregate themselves and their descendants in separate men's houses and to preserve their pidgin speech there. They also imposed their own name on the local population, but they did not change the domestic aspects of the local culture, expect possibly for its pottery, nor did they replace the Igneri language with their own. Like the Normans whom William the Conqueror led into Britain and the artisans whom the Moors brought into Spain, the Island Carib warriors were eventually absorbed by the Igneri population.

A population movement resembles the passage of a wave of water, which proceeds only in one direction and along a broad front. Populations, like waves, advance areally rather than lineally. Just as a wave of water deposits its flotsam on the shore, disturbing and eventually destroying the debris left there by previous waves, so also a population movement brings with it one or more languages, cultures, and morphologies, which disturb and may eventually replace those of the previous population. And just as a wave may increase the variety of debris along the shore, so also a population movement may expand the number of speech communities, peoples, and/or races, creating a plurality of whole languages, cultures, and/or morphologies (Smith 1965).

Waves eventually cease, and the water becomes calm. Population

177

movements also come to an end. They are followed by periods of stability, in which the migrants are connected with their previous homeland, if at all, only by long-distance interaction. They then begin to diverge from their parent population. They interact, intercommunicate, and interbreed primarily among themselves, and as a result they develop differently. They are also faced with different natural, linguistic, cultural, and morphological conditions in their new homeland; they adapt to them; and this, too, makes them more divergent.

J. M. Cruxent (personal communication) has likened immigration to travel on a train, which runs up and down a track and, as a result, penetrates a new area only in one place. The train leaves the surrounding natural and human landscapes intact. Nevertheless, the immigrants among its passengers bring with them new linguistic, cultural, and/or morphological traits, and pass them on to receptive members of the local population, creating a plurality of traits along the tracks. As a result, the local way of life and that from which the immigrants have come begin to converge. The convergence increases as the train turns around and returns to its place of origin, carrying emigrants and their linguistic, cultural, and morphological baggage in the opposite direction, and as other trains move up and down the tracks.

Population movement thus leads to divergence and immigration to convergence. A population that occupies a new area is affected by its natural and human conditions, tends to form its own line of development, and as a result becomes increasingly different from its parent population. Immigrants exchange linguistic, cultural, and biological traits with their hosts, causing the latter to become more like their own parent population.

The full extent of the divergence resulting from population movement did not become apparent to me until I had completed my study of the cases. I was surprised to find that, in at least three of them, the migrants had reached a higher level of development than the inhabitants of their original homelands. The Eastern Polynesian people possessed more complex chiefdoms, more advanced architecture and art, and more elaborate religious practices than the Western Polynesians. The Tainos of the Greater Antilles surpassed the Igneris of the Lesser Antilles and the latter's Island Carib successors in the same three respects. And it was not the Japanoids of Kyushu Islands who produced the Japanese state and civilization; these developments originated in western Honshu and eventually reached

178

their climax among the people who migrated into eastern Honshu. Even in the case of Thulean Eskimos, it can be argued that those who moved from Alaska across northern Canada into Greenland developed an unequaled ability to adapt to variations in the Arctic climate, as is evidenced by the fact that they were able to survive the advent of the Little Ice Age, when the adjacent Norse population died out. Now the Greenland Eskimos are on the way to becoming the first Native American nation since the Spaniards destroyed those in Mexico and Peru.

There is no reason to believe that the advancing peoples also developed more complex languages and morphologies. Cultures, languages, and morphologies are independent units, which change differently. Cultures tend to be more variable than the other two because of their lack of an overall structure and their adaptability to differences in the environment.

The foregoing analysis explains why the successful participants in my case studies, whether archeologists, linguists, or physical anthropologists, have all used some form of developmental classification to reconstruct patterns of change and have traced population movements in terms of these patterns of change, instead of working with similarities in cultural, linguistic, or morphological traits. Patterns of change are indicative of the divergence that takes place during population movement, while similarities, if they have not resulted from independent invention or trade, are an indication of the convergence caused by immigration.

Heyerdahl's attempt to demonstrate that the native population of Polynesia came from America is a case in point. He failed in this attempt because he studied the similarities between the two regions instead of seeking patterns of change in language, culture, and morphology that would link the Polynesians with the inhabitants of a neighboring area. Had he worked with patterns of change, he would have found that they led him to Melanesia rather than to the Americas. If, on the contrary, he had formulated a hypothesis of immigration or trade and had tested it against the similarities, as others have done in studying the origin of the sweet potato, he would indeed have established a connection with the Americas (chap. 2,B).

In selecting sites and artifacts with which to illustrate the Polynesian, Eskimo, Japanese, and Taino movements (figs. 6–8; 12–13; 18–19; 25–28), I have had to include differences as well as similarities along the

179

migration routes, in order to do justice to the patterns of change by means of which the experts have traced the movements. Conversely, my illustrations of the diffusion of horseback riding into Japan (fig. 20) and the immigration of Boca Chica potters into Puerto Rico (fig. 29) focus upon similarities.

D. *Peopling, Repeopling, and Their Causes*

When prehistorians study the peopling of an area, they can be sure that all of its original settlers came from abroad. When, however, they turn to the repeopling of an area, they cannot know exactly how many of the new people are foreigners. The number will depend upon which of the three alternatives—population movement, acculturation, or indepedent development—has taken place. In population movement, invading people become the majority; in acculturation, the natives prevail; while in independent development there is little, if any, change. These differences come about because *people* is a derivative concept. Peoples are defined by their cultures, not by any inherent characteristics.

The distinction between the peopling and repeopling of an area must be taken into consideration in examining the causes of population movement. Peoples who move into virgin territory encounter different conditions than peoples who have to contend with previous populations.

One might suppose that the Lapitan potters and their offshoots, who peopled Polynesia, had an easy time of it, since they were unopposed. Yet they halted on the western side of Polynesia for over two thousand years (fig. 5). Presumably, it took them all that time to develop adequate equipment and techniques with which to travel the much longer distances between islands in the Polynesian triangle. Their task might have been easier if Polynesia had been previously inhabited. They could have learned from the people they encountered there how to travel the long distance between islands.

The populations that repeopled the Arctic American coast, eastern and northern Japan, and the West Indies did have to overcome the resistance of previous inhabitants. It is probably no accident that, like the Europeans who colonized the New World, all three of these populations were more highly developed than the peoples whom they replaced. The Thule Eskimos were better able than their Dorset predecessors to adapt to changes in their natural environment. The Yayoi people, who are presumed to have expanded into eastern Japan, had advanced from food gathering to agriculture, had adopted a new technology, metal working, and had acquired superior weapons, which must have made it easier for them to handle the previous inhabitants. The ancestors of the Tainos were likewise agriculturalists entering the territory of food gatherers. While they introduced pottery, there is no evidence that they had superior weapons. This may explain why they were slow to go beyond the entry into the Greater Antilles, where they encountered the first large body of previous settlers (figs. 23,*a*; 24).

There has been some hypothesizing about the reasons for the movements. The migrants into Polynesia appear to have responded to the pressure of overpopulation. For the most part, they lived on tiny islands, which could not support much of an increase in the number of inhabitants. They would have had to spread to other islands in order to survive.

The Thule Eskimos, too, may have been affected by overpopulation, but a more important stimulus for them seems to have been the climatic change that led to the opening up of the central and eastern Arctic to the hunting of sea mammals, their specialty. Overhunting of the mammals in their old homeland may also have been a factor (chap. 3,D).

It has been suggested that the Japanoid peoples expanded at the expense of the Jomonoids in order to take advantage of agricultural opportunities in the areas to which they moved (chap. 4,D). Overpopulation was probably not much of a factor in the earlier part of their movement, from western to eastern Honshu Island; they moved so rapidly that there would hardly have been time for pressure to build up (fig. 17). Their delay in continuing into Hokkaido Island may be attributed to the need to adapt the growing of rice to the cooler northern climate. When they resumed their movement, they were also inspired by the opportunities to trade with the Ainus and later by the need to forestall a Russian threat to the rest of Hokkaido Island (chap. 4,A).

The progenitors of the Saladoid potters who settled in the Orinoco Valley may have been attracted there by its opportunities for agriculture, if they were not also impelled by overpopulation in their former homeland. The Saladoid peoples themselves appear to have been motivated to continue onto the less fertile coast and into the Lesser Antilles by the pressure of populations that were expanding behind them, first the Barrancoids and later the Arauquinoids (fig. 23,*b*). They responded to external rather than internal conditions.

Population pressure appears to have played little, if any, role in the spread of the Ostionoid successors to the Saladoids through the Greater Antilles into the Bahamian Archipelago. These peoples were too remote from the mainland to have experienced external pressure. The Island Caribs were a threat to them but do not seem to have developed early enough to have affected their expansion. And overpopulation can be ruled out for three reasons: The Ostionoids were moving into ever larger islands (the Bahamas excepted); they show no evidence of the militarism that might be expected to accompany competition for scarce land; and, most important of all, they had not yet completed their occupation of the Greater Antilles when the Spaniards arrived. Some of the best agricultural land—now world-renowned as the source of Cuban tobacco—was still in the hands of the previous food-gathering population.

It is interesting to compare the movements into Polynesia and the Antilles. The proto-Polynesians advanced from one small island to another, seeking to avoid the consequences of overpopulation and developing increasingly elaborate chiefdoms to cope with the scarcity of land. The proto-Tainos moved from small islands to large ones, where they had more land than they could use, and yet they, too, produced hierarchical chiefdoms. There is obviously more than one route towards complex societies.

So too, there is more than one reason for the peopling or repeopling of an area. The migrants may have responded to their own overpopulation or to pressure from neighboring populations. Alternatively or in addition, they may have been attracted by more favorable conditions in their new homeland. And they may also have been affected by changes in the natural and/or human components of either their old or their new environments.

REFERENCES

Adams, William Y., Dennis P. Van Gerven, and Richard S. Levy. 1978. The Retreat from Migrationism. In *Annual Review of Anthropology*, vol. 7, pp. 483–532. Palo Alto: Annual Reviews.

Aikens, C. Melvin, and Takayasu Higuchi. 1982. *Prehistory of Japan*. New York: Academic Press.

Akazawa, Takeru. 1982. Cultural Change in Prehistoric Japan: Receptivity to Rice Agriculture in the Japanese Archipelago. In *Advances in World Archaeology*, vol. 1, pp. 151–211. New York: Academic Press.

Alegría, Ricardo E. 1981. *El uso de la terminología etnohistórica para designar las culturas aborígenes de las Antillas*. Cuadernos Prehispánicos. Valladolid: Seminario de Historia de América, Universidad de Valladolid.

——— 1983. *Ball Courts and Ceremonial Plazas in the West Indies*. Yale University Publications in Anthropology, no. 79. New Haven.

Alexander, J. 1978. Frontier Studies and the Earliest Farmers in Europe. In *Social Organization and Settlement*, ed. D. Green, C. Hasselgrove, and M. Spriggs, pp. 13–29. British Archaeological Reports, International Series, no. 47. Oxford.

Allaire, Louis. 1977. *Later Prehistory in Martinique and the Island Caribs: Problems in Ethnic Identification*. Ph.D. diss. Yale University. Ann Arbor: University Microfilms.

———. 1980. On the Historicity of Carib Migrations in the Lesser Antilles. *American Antiquity*, 45 (no. 2): 238–45.

———. 1984a. Archéologie des Antilles. In *Encyclopaedia Universalis*, in press. Paris.

———. 1984b. A Reconstruction of Early Historical Island Carib Pottery. *Southeastern Archaeology*, 3 (no. 2): 121–33.

Amakasu, Ken. 1973. Aspects of Yayoi and Tumulus Art. In *The Beginnings of Japanese Art*, by Namio Egami, pp. 166–78. Vol. 2 of *The Heibonsha Survey of Japanese Art*. New York and Tokyo: Weatherhill/Heibonsha.

Anderson, Edgar. 1952. *Plants, Man and Life*. Boston: Little, Brown.

Arrom, José J. 1975. *Mitología y artes prehispánicas de las Antillas*. Mexico City: Siglo Veintiuno Editores.

Bandi, Hans-Georg. 1969. *Eskimo Prehistory*. London: Methuen.

Barnes, Gina. 1981. Early Japanese Bronzemaking. *Archaeology*, 34 (no. 3): 38–46.

Barrau, Jacques, and Christian Montbrun. 1978. La mangrove et l'insertion humaine dans les écosystèmes insulaires des Petites Antilles: Le cas de la Martinique et de la Guadeloupe. *Social Science Information*, 17 (no. 6): 897–919.

Basso, Ellen B. 1977. Introduction: The Status of Carib Ethnology. In *Carib-speaking Indians: Culture, Society and Language*, ed. Ellen B. Basso, pp. 8–22. Anthropological Papers of the University of Arizona, no. 28. Tucson.

Beardsley, Richard K. 1955. Japan before History: A Survey of the Archaeological Record. *The Far Eastern Quarterly*, 14 (no. 3): 317–46.

Bellwood, Peter. 1978. *The Polynesians: Prehistory of an Island People*. London: Thames and Hudson.

———. 1979. *Man's Conquest of the Pacific: The Prehistory of Southeast Asia and Oceania*. New York: Oxford University Press.

———. 1983. On "Diffusionists" and Legitimate Aims in Polynesian Prehistory. *Asian Perspectives*, 23 (no. 2): 323–35.

Birket-Smith, Kaj. 1929. *The Caribou Eskimos: Material and Social Life and Their Cultural Position*. Vol. 5, *Report of the Fifth Thule Expedition, 1921–24*, pts. 1–2. Copenhagen: Gyldendal.

———. 1930. The Question of the Origin of Eskimo Culture: A Rejoinder. *American Anthropologist*, 32 (no. 4): 508–25.

Bleed, Peter. 1972. Yayoi Cultures of Japan: An Interpretative Summary. *Arctic Anthropology*, 9 (no. 2): 1–23.

Boas, Franz. 1888. The Eskimo. *Proceedings and Transactions of the Royal Society of Canada*, 5 (sec. 2): 35–39.

Boomert, Aad. 1983. The Saladoid Occupation of Wonotobo Falls, Western Surinam. In *Proceedings of the Ninth International Congress for the Study of Pre-Columbian Cultures of the Lesser Antilles*, held in the Dominican Republic, August 2–8, 1981, pp. 97–120. Montreal: Centre de Recherches Caraïbes, Université de Montréal.

———. MS. The Cayo Complex of St. Vincent and Its Mainland Origin. Paper read at the Eleventh International Congress for Caribbean Archeology, San Juan, Puerto Rico, July 28 to August 3, 1985.

Brinton, Daniel Garrison. 1871. The Arawack Language of Guiana in Its Linguistic and Ethnological Relations. *Transactions of the American Philosophical Society*, n.s. 14 (art. 4): 427–44.

Brochado, José Jaoquim Justiniano Proenza. 1984. An Ecological Model of the Spread of Pottery and Agriculture into Eastern South America. Ph.D. diss. University of Illinois, Urbana.

Buck, Sir Peter. 1954. *Vikings of the Sunrise*. Christchurch: Whitcombe and Tombs.

Bullen, Ripley P., and Adelaide K. 1976. Culture Areas and Climaxes in Antillean

Prehistory. In *Proceedings of the Sixth International Congress for the Study of Pre-Columbian Cultures of the Lesser Antilles*, Pointe à Pitre, Guadeloupe, July 6–12, 1975, pp. 1–10. Gainesville: Florida State Museum.

Caldwell, Joseph R. 1964. Interaction Spheres in Prehistory. In *Hopewellian Studies*, no. 6, pp. 133–43. Illinois State Museum Scientific Papers, vol. 12. Springfield.

Casas, Bartolomé de las. 1951. *Historia de las Indias*. 3 vols. Ed. Agustín Millares Carlo. Mexico City: Fondo de Cultura Económica.

Chamberlin, Thomas C. 1890. The Method of Multiple Working Hypotheses. *Science*, o.s. 15 (no. 366): 92–96. (This article has been reprinted a number of times and in several editions. The latest, most authoritative reprint is in *Science*, 148 [no. 3671]: 754–59, 1965.)

Chang, Kwang-chih, 1977. *The Archaeology of Ancient China*, 3d ed. New Haven: Yale University Press.

Chanlatte Baik, Luis A. 1979. Excavaciones arqueológicas en Vieques. *Revista del Museo de Antropología, Historia y Arte de la Universidad de Puerto Rico* (no. 1): 55–59. Río Piedras.

———. 1983. *Catálogo arqueología de Vieques: Exposición del 13 del Marzo al 22 de Abril de 1983*. Río Piedras: Museo de Antropología, Historia y Arte, Universidad de Puerto Rico.

Chard, Chester. 1974. *Northeast Asia in Prehistory*. Madison: University of Wisconsin Press.

Cherry, John. 1981. Pattern and Process in the Earliest Colonization of the Mediterranean Islands. In *Proceedings of the Prehistoric Society*, vol. 47, pp. 41–68. Cambridge, Eng.

Chew, J. J. 1978. The Prehistory of the Japanese Language in the Light of Evidence from the Structures of Japanese and Korean. *Asian Perspectives*, 19 (no. 1): 190–200.

Clark, Grahame. 1966. The Invasion Hypothesis in British Archaeology. *Antiquity*, 40 (no. 159): 172–89.

Clark, Jeffrey T., and John Terrell. 1978. Archaeology in Oceania. In *Annual Review of Anthropology*, vol. 7, pp. 293–319. Palo Alto: Annual Reviews.

Coe, W. R., II. 1957. A Distinctive Artifact Common to Haiti and Central America. *American Antiquity*, 22 (no. 3): 280–82.

Colton, Harold Sellers, and Lyndon Lane Hargrave. 1937. *Handbook of Northern Arizona Pottery Wares*. Museum of Northern Arizona, Bulletin 11. Flagstaff.

Cranz, D. 1967. *The History of Greenland: Containing a Description of the Country and Its Inhabitants*, trans. John Gambold. London: Brethern's Society.

Creel, Herrlee Glessner. 1937. *The Birth of China: A Study of the Formative Period of Chinese Civilization*. New York: Reynal and Hitchcock.

Crosby, Alfred W., Jr. 1972. *The Columbian Exchange: Biological and Cultural Consequences of 1492*. Contributions in American Studies, no. 2. Westport, Conn.: Greenwood Press.

Cruxent, José M. 1977. Apuntes sobre arqueología Venezolana. In *Arte Prehis-*

pánico de Venezuela, by Miguel G. Arroyo C., J. M. Cruxent, and Sagrario Perez Soto de Atencio, 2d ed., pp. 19–59. Caracas: Fundación Eugenio Mendoza.

Cruxent, Jose M., and Irving Rouse. 1958–59. *An Archeological Chronology of Venezuela.* 2 vols. Pan American Union, Social Science Monographs, no. 6. Washington, D.C.

———. 1969. Early Man in the West Indies. *Scientific American,* 221 (no. 5): 42–52.

Dawkins, William Boyd. 1874. *Cave Hunting: Researches on the Evidence of Caves Respecting the Early Inhabitants of Europe.* London: Macmillan.

Deegan, Kathleen, and Maurice Williams. MS. The Search for La Navidad in a Contact Period Arawakan Village. Paper read at the Eleventh International Congress for Caribbean Archeology, San Juan, Puerto Rico, July 28 to August 3, 1985.

Dillehay, Tom D. 1984. A Late Ice-Age Settlement in Southern Chile. *Scientific American,* 251 (no. 4): 106–17.

Duff, Roger. 1950. *The Moa-hunter Period of Maori Culture.* Wellington, N.Z.: Dept. of Internal Affairs.

Dumond, Don E. 1977. *The Eskimos and Aleuts.* Ancient Peoples and Places, vol. 87. London: Thames and Hudson.

———. 1980. The Archaeology of Alaska and the Peopling of America. *Science,* 209 (no. 4460): 984–91.

———. 1982. Trends and Traditions in Alaskan Prehistory: The Place of Norton Culture. *Arctic Anthropology,* 19 (no. 2): 39–51.

Durbin, Marshall. 1977. A Survey of the Carib Language Family. In *Carib-speaking Indians: Culture, Society and Language,* ed. Ellen B. Basso, pp. 23–38. Anthropological Papers of the University of Arizona, no. 28. Tucson.

Dyen, Isidore. 1956. Language Distribution and Migration Theory. *Language,* 32 (no. 4): 611–26.

Edwards, Walter. 1983. Event and Process in the Founding of Japan: The Horse-rider Theory in Archeological Perspective. *The Journal of Japanese Studies,* 9 (no. 2): 265–95.

Egami, Namio. 1962. Light on Japanese Cultural Origins from Historical Archeology and Legend. In *Japanese Culture: Its Development and Characteristics,* ed. Robert J. Smith and Richard K. Beardsley, pp. 11–16. Viking Fund Publications in Anthropology, no. 34. New York: Wenner-Gren Foundation for Anthropological Research.

———. 1964. *The Formation of the People and the Origin of the State in Japan.* Memoirs of the Research Department of the Tokyo Bunko, no. 23. Tokyo.

Ehret, Christopher, and Merrick Posnansky, eds. 1982. *The Archaeological and Linguistic Reconstruction of African History.* Berkeley and Los Angeles: University of California Press.

Emory, Kenneth P. 1959. Origin of the Hawaiians. *Journal of the Polynesian Society,* 68 (no. 1): 29–35.

———. 1979. The Societies. In *The Prehistory of Polynesia,* ed. Jesse D. Jennings, pp. 200–21. Cambridge: Harvard University Press.

Fairservis, Walter A., Jr. 1975. *The Roots of Ancient India: The Archaeology of Early Indian Civilization*, 2d ed. Chicago: University of Chicago Press.

Fell, Barry. 1976. *America B.C.* New York: Times Books.

———. 1980. *Saga America.* New York: Times Books.

Finney, Ben R. 1985. Anomalous Westerlies, El Niño, and the Colonization of Polynesia. *American Anthropologist*, 87 (no. 1): 9–26.

Flannery, Kent V., and Joyce Marcus, eds. 1983. *The Cloud People: Divergent Evolution of the Zapotec and Mixtec Civilizations.* New York: Academic Press.

Fong, Wen, ed. 1980. *The Great Bronze Age of China: An Exhibition from the People's Republic of China.* New York: Metropolitan Museum of Art, Alfred A. Knopf.

Ford, James A. 1962. *A Quantitative Method for Deriving Cultural Chronology.* Pan American Union, Technical Manual, no. 1. Washington, D.C.

Friedrich, Paul. 1970. *Proto-Indo-European Trees: The Arboreal System of a Prehistoric People.* Chicago: University of Chicago Press.

Garn, Stanley M. 1965. *Human Races*, 2d ed. Springfield, Ill: Charles C. Thomas.

Geist, Otto W., and Froelich G. Rainey. 1936. *Archaeological Excavations at Kukulik, St. Lawrence Island, Alaska.* Miscellaneous Publications of the University of Alaska, vol. 2. Washington, D.C.: G.P.O.

Giddings, J. Louis, Jr. 1952. Ancient Bering Strait and Population Spread. In *Science in Alaska*, ed. Henry B. Collins, pp. 85–102. Arctic Institute of North America Special Publication no. 1. Washington, D.C.

———. 1967. *Ancient Men of the Arctic.* New York: Alfred A. Knopf.

Golson, J. 1971. Lapita Ware and Its Transformations. In *Studies in Oceanic Culture History*, ed. R. C. Green and Marion Kelly, vol. 2, pp. 67–76. Pacific Anthropological Records, vol. 12. Honolulu: Bernice Pauahi Bishop Museum.

Goodwin, R. Christopher, 1979. The Prehistoric Cultural Ecology of St. Kitts, West Indies: A Case Study in Island Archeology. Ph.D. diss., Arizona State University, Tempe.

Granberry, Julian. 1971. Report—Final Collection of Texts, Vocabulary Lists, Grammar, of Timucua for Publication. In *Yearbook of the American Philosophical Society for 1970*, pp. 606–07. Philadelphia.

Green, Roger C. 1979. Lapita. In *The Prehistory of Polynesia*, ed. Jesse D. Jennings, pp. 27–60. Cambridge: Harvard University Press.

———. 1981. Location of the Polynesian Homeland: A Continuing Problem. In *Studies in Pacific Languages and Cultures in Honor of Bruce Biggs*, ed. J. Hollyman and A. Pawley, pp. 133–58. Auckland: Linguistic Society of New Zealand.

Green, Stanton W., and Stephen W. Perlman. 1985. *The Archaeology of Frontiers and Boundaries.* New York: Academic Press.

Greenberg, Joseph H. 1960. The General Classification of Central and South American Languages. In *Men and Cultures: Selected Papers of the 5th International Congress of Anthropological and Ethnological Sciences*, ed. A. F. C. Wallace, pp. 793–94. Philadelphia: University of Pennsylvania Press.

Groot, Gerard J. 1951. *The Prehistory of Japan*, ed. Bertram S. Kraus. New York: Columbia University Press.

187

Haag, William G. 1965. Pottery Typology in Certain Lesser Antilles. *American Antiquity*, 31 (no. 2): 242–45.

Hall, John W. 1970. *Japan from Prehistory to Modern Times*. Tokyo and Rutland, Vt.: Tuttle.

Haniwara, Kazuo, Masakazu Yoshizaki, et al. 1968. *The Ainu, Their Origin, and Their Culture* [in Japanese]. Sapporo: Hokkaido University Press.

Hatt, Gudmund. 1924. Archaeology of the Virgin Islands. In *Proceedings of the 21st International Congress of Americanists*, pt. 1, pp. 29–42. The Hague.

———. 1953. Early Intrusion of Agriculture in the North Atlantic Subarctic Region. *Anthropological Papers of the University of Alaska*, 2 (no. 1): 51–108.

Hayashi, Kensaku. 1968. The Fukui Microblade Technology and Its Relationships in Northeast Asia and North America. *Arctic Anthropology*, 5 (no. 1): 128–90.

Heyerdahl, Thor. 1950. *Kon-Tiki: Across the Pacific by Raft*. Chicago: Rand McNally.

———. 1953. *American Indians in the Pacific: The Theory Behind the Kon-Tiki Expedition*. Chicago: Rand McNally.

Heyerdahl, Thor, and Edwin N. Ferdon, Jr., eds. 1961–65. *Reports of the Norwegian Archaeological Expedition to Easter Island and the East Pacific*. Vol. 1, *Archaeology of Easter Island*; Vol. 2, *Miscellaneous Reports*. Monographs of the School of American Research and the University of New Mexico, no. 24, pts. 1–2. Santa Fe.

Heyerdahl, Thor, and Arne Skjölsvold. 1956. *Archaeological Evidence of Pre-Spanish Visits to the Galápagos Islands*. Memoirs of the Society for American Archaeology, no. 12. Salt Lake City.

Howells, W. W. 1970. Anthropometric Grouping Analysis of Pacific Peoples. *Archaeology and Physical Anthropology in Oceania*, 5 (no. 3): 192–217.

Huffman, T. N. 1979. African Origins: Review of "The Later Prehistory of Eastern and Southern Africa" by D. W. Phillipson. *South African Journal of Science*, 75 (no. 5): 233–37.

Ikawa-Smith, Fumiko. 1964. The Continuity of Non-Ceramic to Ceramic Cultures in Japan. *Arctic Anthropology*, 2 (no. 2): 95–119.

———. 1982a. Co-traditions in Japanese Archaeology. *World Archaeology*, 13 (no. 3): 296–309.

———. 1982b. Far Eastern Archeology: Review of "Prehistory of Japan" by C. Melvin Aikens and Takayasu Higuchi. *Science*, 217 (no. 4555): 146–48.

Jeffreys, Harold. 1937. *Scientific Inference*, 2d ed. Cambridge: Cambridge University Press.

Johnson, Allen. 1982. Reductionism in Cultural Ecology: The Amazon Case. *Current Anthropology*, 23 (no. 4): 413–28.

Kamaki, Yoshimasa. 1965. Overview of Jomon Culture. In *Jomon Period* [in Japanese]. Vol. 2, *Archeology of Japan*, pp. 1–28. Tokyo: Kawade Shobo Shinsa.

Kaneko, Erika. 1968. Japan: A Review of Yayoi Period Burial Practices. *Asian Perspectives*, 9: 1–26.

Kidder, J. Edward, Jr. 1966. *Japan Before Buddhism*, rev. ed. Ancient Peoples and Places, vol. 10. New York: Praeger.

———. 1968. *Prehistoric Japanese Arts: Jomon Pottery.* Tokyo and Palo Alto: Kodansha International.

———. 1977. *Ancient Japan.* Oxford: Elsevier-Phaidon.

Kim, Jeong-Hak. 1978. *The Prehistory of Korea*, trans. and ed. Richard J. Pearson and Kazue Pearson. Honolulu: University Press of Hawaii.

Kirch, Patrick V. 1978. The Lapitoid Period in West Polynesia: Excavations and Survey in Niuatoputapu, Tonga. *Journal of Field Archaeology*, 5 (no. 1): 1–13.

———. 1980. Polynesian Prehistory: Cultural Adaptation in Island Ecosystems. *American Scientist*, 68 (no. 1): 39–48.

———. 1982. Ecology and the Adaptation of Polynesian Agricultural Systems. In "Plants and People," ed. Jocelyn Powell and J. Peter White, pp. 1–6. *Archaeology in Oceania*, 17 (no. 1).

Kosłowski, Janusz K. 1978. In Search of the Evolution Pattern of the Preceramic Cultures of the Caribbean. *Boletín del Museo del Hombre Dominicana*, no. 13, pp. 61–79.

Koyama, Shuzo. 1978. Jomon Subsistence and Population. In *Senri Ethnological Studies*, no. 2, pp. 1–65. Senri, Osaka: National Museum of Ethnology.

Kroeber, A. L., 1948. *Anthropology: Race, Language, Culture, Psychology, Prehistory*, new ed. New York: Harcourt, Brace.

———. 1962. *A Roster of Civilizations and Culture.* Viking Fund Publications in Anthropology, no. 33. New York: Wenner-Gren Foundation for Anthropological Research.

Kroeber, A. L., and Talcott Parsons. 1958. The Concepts of Culture and of Social System. *American Sociological Review*, 23 (no. 5): 582–83.

Lathrap, Donald W. 1970. *The Upper Amazon.* Ancient Peoples and Places, vol. 70. New York: Praeger.

Leach, Edmund. 1973. Concluding Address. In *The Explanation of Culture Change: Models in Prehistory*, ed. Colin Renfrew, pp. 761–71. Pittsburgh: University of Pittsburgh Press.

Levinson, Michael, R. Gerard Ward, and John W. Webb. 1973. *The Settlement of Polynesia, a Computer Simulation.* Minneapolis: University of Minnesota Press.

Lévi-Strauss, Claude. 1971. El tiempo del mito. *Plural: Crítica y Literatura*, no. 1, pp. 1–4. Mexico City: Excelsior.

Loukotka, Čestmír, 1968. *Classification of South American Indian Languages.* UCLA Latin American Center, Reference Series, vol. 7. Los Angeles.

Lovén, Sven. 1935. *Origins of the Tainan Culture, West Indies.* Göteborg: Elanders Bokfryckeri Äkfiebolag.

MacArthur, R. H., and E. O. Wilson. 1967. *The Theory of Island Biogeography.* Monographs in Population Biology, no. 1. Princeton: Princeton University Press.

MacNeish, R. S. 1952. *Iroquois Pottery Types: A Technique for the Study of Iroquois Prehistory.* National Museum of Canada, Bulletin no. 124. Ottawa.

———. 1959. A Speculative Framework of Northern North American Prehistory as of April 1959. *Anthropologica*, n.s. 1: 1–17.

———. 1964. *Investigations in Southwest Yukon: Archaeological Excavations, Com-*

parisons and Speculations. Papers of the Robert S. Peabody Foundation for Archaeology, vol. 6, no. 2. Andover: Phillips Academy.

————. 1982. *Third Annual Report of the Belize Archaic Archaeological Reconnaissance.* Andover: Phillips Academy.

Malinowski, Bronislaw. 1947. Introduction to *Cuban Counterpoint: Tobacco and Sugar,* by Fernando Ortiz, pp. ix–xiii. New York: Alfred A. Knopf.

Mathiassen, Therkel. 1927. *Archeology of the Central Eskimos.* Vol. 4, *Report of the Fifth Thule Expedition, 1921–24.* Copenhagen: Gyldendal.

————. 1930, The Question of the Origin of Eskimo Culture. *American Anthropologist,* 32 (no. 4): 591–607.

Mattioni, M., and M. Nicolas. 1972. *Art précolombien de la Martinique.* Fort-de-France: Musée Départemental de la Martinique.

Maxwell, Moreau S. 1980. Archaeology of the Arctic and Subarctic Zones. In *Annual Review of Anthropology,* vol. 9, pp. 161–85. Palo Alto: Annual Reviews.

Miller, Roy A. 1967. *The Japanese Language.* Chicago: University of Chicago Press.

————. 1971. *Japanese and Other Altaic Languages.* Chicago: University of Chicago Press.

————. 1980. *Origins of the Japanese Language: Lectures in Japan during the Academic Year 1977–78.* Seattle: University of Washington Press.

Moore, Clark. MS. Redon: Preliminary Report of a Spanish-Indian Contact Site on the Southern Peninsula of Haiti. Manuscript in the Peabody Museum of Natural History, New Haven.

Morse, E. S. 1879. *Shell Mounds of Omori.* Memoirs of the Science Department, University of Tokyo, vol. 1, pt. 1. Tokyo.

Murdock, George Peter. 1959. *Africa: Its Peoples and Their Culture History.* New York: McGraw-Hill.

Newson, Linda A. 1976. *Aboriginal and Spanish Colonial Trinidad: A Study in Culture Contact.* London: Academic Press.

Noble, G. Kingsley. 1965. *Proto-Arawakan and Its Descendants.* Indiana University Publications in Anthropology and Linguistics, no. 38. Bloomington.

Oda, Shizuo, and Charles T. Keally. 1979. *Japanese Paleolithic Cultural Chronology.* Paper presented to the XIVth Pacific Science Congress held in Khabarovsk, U.S.S.R., August 20 to September 5, 1979. Tokyo: Archaeology Research Center, International Christian University.

Oliver, Roland, and Brian M. Fagan. 1975. *Africa in the Iron Age: c. 500 B.C. to A.D. 1400.* Cambridge: Cambridge University Press.

Olsen, Fred. 1974. *On the Trail of the Arawaks.* Norman: University of Oklahoma Press.

Ortiz, Fernando. 1947. *Cuban Counterpoint: Tobacco and Sugar,* trans. Harriet de Onís. New York: Alfred A. Knopf.

Oswald, Wendell H. 1967. *Alaskan Eskimos.* San Francisco: Chandler Publishing.

Palms, Erwin Walter. 1945. Excavations of La Isabela, White Man's First Town in the Americas. *Acta Americana,* 3 (no. 4): 298–303.

Pearson, Richard J. 1969. *Archaeology of the Ryukyu Islands: A Regional Chronology from 3000 B.C. to the Historic Period.* Honolulu: University of Hawaii Press.

———. 1976. The Contribution of Archaeology to Japanese Studies. *The Journal of Japanese Studies,* 2 (no. 2): 305–34.

———. 1978a. Lolang and the Rise of Korean States and Chiefdoms. *Journal of the Hong Kong Archaeological Society,* 7: 77–90.

———. 1978b. The Problem of Defining Continuities. *Asian Perspectives,* 19 (no. 1): 176–89.

Platt, John R. 1964. Strong Inference. *Science,* 146 (no. 3642): 347–53.

Polivanov, E. D. 1968. *Selected Works. Articles on General Linguistics.* Trans. Daniel Armstrong. Vol. 72, *Janua Linguarum, Series Major.* The Hague.

Rainey, Froelich G. 1940. *Porto Rican Archaeology.* In *The New York Academy of Sciences, Scientific Survey of Porto Rico and the Virgin Islands,* vol. 18, pt. 1. New York.

Reischauer, Edwin O., and John K. Fairbanks. 1958. *East Asia: The Great Civilization.* Vol. 1, *A History of East Asian Civilization.* Boston: Houghton Mifflin.

Renfrew, Colin. 1973. *Before Civilization: The Radiocarbon Revolution and Prehistoric Europe.* New York: Alfred A. Knopf.

———. 1983. Divided We Stand: Aspects of Archaeology and Information. *American Antiquity,* 48 (no. 1): 3–16.

———. 1984. *Approaches to Social Archaeology.* Cambridge: Harvard University Press.

Rink, Henry. 1887. *The Eskimo Tribes.* Meddelser om Gronland, vol. 11. Copenhagen and London: C. A. Reitzels Forlag.

Roosevelt, Anna Curtenius. 1980. *Parmana: Prehistoric Maize and Manioc Subsistence along the Amazon and Orinoco.* New York: Academic Press.

Rosendahl, Paul, and D. E. Yen. 1971. Fossil Sweet Potato Remains from Hawaii. *Journal of the Polynesian Society,* 80 (no. 3): 379–85.

Rouse, Irving. 1948. The Arawak. In *Handbook of South American Indians,* ed. Julian H. Steward, vol. 4, pp. 507–46. Bulletin of the Bureau of American Ethnology, no. 143. Washington, D.C.

———. 1951. Areas and Periods of Culture in the Greater Antilles. *Southwestern Journal of Anthropology,* 7 (no. 3): 248–65.

———. 1952. Porto Rican Prehistory. In *The New York Academy of Sciences, Scientific Survey of Porto Rico and the Virgin Islands,* vol. 18, pts. 3–4. New York.

———. 1953a. Guianas. In *Instituto Panamericano de Geografía e Historia, Comisión de Historia, Program of the History of America, Indigenous Period,* vol. 1, no. 7. Mexico City.

———. 1953b. The Strategy of Culture History. In *Anthropology Today: An Encyclopedic Inventory,* ed. A. L. Kroeber et al. pp. 57–76. Chicago: University of Chicago Press.

———. 1958. The Inference of Migrations from Anthropological Evidence. In *Migrations in New World Culture History,* ed. Raymond H. Thompson, pp. 63–68. University of Arizona Social Science Bulletin, no. 27. Tucson.

———. 1962. Southwestern Archaeology Today. In *An Introduction to the Study of Southwestern Archaeology* . . . by Alfred Vincent Kidder, pp. 1–53. New Haven: Yale University Press.

———. 1964. Prehistory of the West Indies. *Science*, 144 (no. 3618): 499–513.

———. 1972. *An Introduction to Prehistory: A Systematic Approach*. New York: McGraw-Hill.

———. 1976. Peopling of the Americas. *Quaternary Research*, 6 (no. 4): 597–612.

———. 1977. Pattern and Process in West Indian Archaeology. *World Archaeology*, 9 (no. 1): 1–11.

———. 1978. The La Gruta Sequence and Its Implications. In *Unidad y Variedades, Ensayos en Homenaje a José M. Cruxent*, ed. Erika Wagner and Alberta Zucchi, pp. 203–29. Caracas: Centro de Estudios Avanzados, Instituto Venezolano de Investigaciones Científicas.

———. 1979. Report to the Japan Society for the Promotion of Science. New Haven: Department of Anthropology, Yale University.

———. 1980. The Concept of Series in Bahamian Archeology. In *Proceedings of the Second Bahamas Conference on Archeology*, ed. Robert S. Carr and John Winter. *The Florida Anthropologist*, 33 (no. 3): 94–98.

———. 1982a. Ceramic and Religious Development in the Greater Antilles. *Journal of New World Archaeology*, 5 (no. 2): 45–55. Los Angeles: The Institute of Archaeology, University of California.

———. 1982b. The Olsen Collection from Ile à Vache, Haiti. *The Florida Anthropologist*, 35 (no. 4): 169–85.

———. 1983. La frontera Taína: Su prehistoria y sus precursores. In *Las culturas de América en la época del descubrimiento: Seminario sobre la investigación de la cultura taína*, pp. 25–36. Madrid: Comisión Nacional para la Celebración del V Centenario del Descubrimiento de América.

———. 1984. The Peabody Museum's Exhibits of Connecticut Archaeology and Ethnology: Past, Present, and Future. In *Connecticut Archaeology Today*, ed. Renee Kra. *Bulletin of the Archaeological Society of Connecticut*, no. 47. pp. 144–56. Washington, Conn.: American Indian Archaeological Institute.

———. 1985. Arawakan Phylogeny, Caribbean Chronology, and Their Implications for the Study of Population Movement. In *La esfera de interacción de la cuenca del Orinoco: Festschrift a Marshall Durbin*, in press. Caracas: Instituto Venezolano de Investigaciones Científicas.

———. MS. Social, Linguistic, and Stylistic Plurality in the West Indies. Paper read at the Eleventh International Congress for Caribbean Archeology, San Juan, Puerto Rico, July 28 to August 3, 1985.

Rouse, Irving, Louis Allaire, and Aad Boomert. 1985. Eastern Venezuela, the Guianas, and the West Indies. In *Chronologies in South American Archaeology*, ed. Clement W. Meighan, in press. Los Angeles: University of California.

Rouse, Irving, and José M. Cruxent. 1963. *Venezuelan Archaeology*. New Haven: Yale University Press.

Ryukyuan Archaeological Research Team. 1981. *Subsistence and Settlement in Okinawan Prehistory—Kume and Irimote*. Vancouver: Laboratory of Archaeology, University of British Columbia.

Sample, L. L. 1978. Prehistoric Cultural Relations between Western Japan and Southeastern Korea. *Asian Perspectives*, 19 (no. 1): 172–75.

Sankalia, H. D. 1962. *Indian Archaeology Today*. Bombay: Asia Publishing House.

Sanoja, Mario, and Iraida Vargas. 1983. New Light on the Prehistory of Eastern Venezuela. In *Advances in World Archaeology*, vol. 2, pp. 205–44. New York: Academic Press.

Sansom, George. 1968. *A History of Japan to 1334*. Stanford: Stanford University Press.

Sauer, Carl O. 1966. *The Early Spanish Main*. Berkeley and Los Angeles: University of California Press.

Sears, William H., and Shaun D. Sullivan. 1978. Bahamas Prehistory. *American Antiquity*, 43 (no. 1): 3–25.

Serizawa, Chosuke. 1978. The Stone Age of Japan. *Asian Perspectives*, 19 (no. 1): 1–14.

Serjeanston, S. W., D. P. Ryan, and A. R. Thompson. 1982. The Colonization of the Pacific: The Story According to Human Leukocyte Antigens. *American Journal of Human Genetics*, 34 (no. 6): 904–18.

Simpson, George Gaylord. 1949. *The Meaning of Evolution: A Study of the History of Life and of Its Significance for Man*. New Haven: Yale University Press.

Sinoto, Yosihiko H. 1983. The Huahine Excavation: Discovery of an Ancient Polynesian Canoe. *Archaeology*, 36 (no. 2): 10–15.

Smith, M. G. 1965. *The Plural Society in the British West Indies*. Berkeley and Los Angeles: University of California Press.

Sollas, W. J. 1924. *Ancient Hunters and Their Modern Representatives*, 3d rev. ed. New York: Macmillan.

Spicer, Edward M., and Raymond H. Thompson. 1972. *Plural Society in the Southwest*. Albuquerque: University of New Mexico Press.

Stark, Louisa. MS. Linguistic Evidence for Early Migrations in South America. Paper read at the annual meeting of the Society for American Archaeology in New Orleans, April 28–30, 1977.

Steward, Julian H., and Louis C. Faron. 1959. *Native Peoples of South America*. New York: McGraw-Hill.

Sturtevant, William C. 1961. Taino Agriculture. In *The Evolution of Horticultural Systems in Native America: Causes and Consequences*, ed. Johannes Wilbert, pp. 69–82. Caracas: Sociedad de Ciencias Naturales La Salle.

Suggs, Robert C. 1960. *The Island Civilizations of Polynesia*. New York: New American Library.

Sung, Wen-hsun. 1981. On Man and Culture of the Pleistocene in Taiwan [in Chinese]. In *Proceedings of the International Conference on Sinology Sponsored by the Academia Sinica*, pp. 47–62. Taipei.

Taylor, Douglas. 1951. *The Black Carib of British Honduras*. Viking Fund Publications in Anthropology, no. 17. New York: Wenner-Gren Foundation for Anthropological Research.

——. 1977a. *Languages of the West Indies*. Baltimore and London: Johns Hopkins University Press.

——. 1977b. A Note on Palikur and Northern Arawakan. *International Journal of American Linguistics*, 43 (no. 1): 58–60.

Taylor, Douglas R., and Bernard J. Hoff. 1980. The Linguistic Repertory of the Island-Carib in the Seventeenth Century: The Men's Language—a Carib Pidgin? *International Journal of American Linguistics*, 46 (no. 4): 301–12.

Taylor, Douglas, and Irving Rouse. 1955. Linguistic and Archaeological Time Depth in the West Indies. *International Journal of American Linguistics*, 21 (no. 2): 105–15.

Trigger, Bruce. 1978. *Time and Traditions: Essays in Archaeological Interpretation*. New York: Columbia University Press.

Turner, Christy G., II. 1976. Dental Evidence on the Origins of the Ainu and Japanese. *Science*, 193 (no. 4256): 911–13.

——. 1983. Dental Evidence for the Peopling of the Americas. In *Early Man in the New World*, ed. Richard Shutler, Jr., pp. 147–57. Beverly Hills: Sage Publications.

Vayda, Andrew P., and Roy A. Rappaport. 1963. Island Cultures. In *Man's Place in the Island Ecosystem: A Symposium*, ed. F. R. Forsberg, pp. 133–42. Honolulu: Bishop Museum Press.

Veloz Maggiolo, Marcio. 1980. *Las sociedades arcaicos de Santo Domingo*. Museo del Hombre Dominicano, Serie Investigaciones Antropológicas, no. 16; Fundacion García Arevalo, Serie Investigaciones, no. 12. Santo Domingo.

Veloz Maggiolo, Marcio, Elpidio Ortega, and Angel Caba Fuentes. 1981. *Los modos de vida Meillacoides y sus posibles origines (un estudio interpretivo)*. Santo Domingo: Museo del Hombre Dominicano.

Vescelius, Gary S. 1980. A Cultural Taxonomy for West Indian Archaeology. *Journal of the Virgin Islands Archaeological Society* (no. 10): 36–39. (The 1980 issue of this journal was not actually published until 1986.)

Watson, Patty Jo, Steven A. Le Blanc, and Charles L. Redman. 1984. *Archeological Explanation: The Scientific Method in Archeology*. New York: Columbia University Press.

Watson, William. 1963. Who Were the Ancient Ainu? Neolithic Japan and the White Race of Today. In *Vanished Civilizations of the Ancient World*, ed. Edward Bacon, pp. 79–104. New York: McGraw-Hill.

White, J. Peter, and J. E. Downie. 1978. Mid-Recent Human Occupation and Resource Exploitation in the Bismarck Archipelago. *Science*, 199 (no. 4331): 877–78.

Whiting, John W. M., John A. Sodergren, and Stephen M. Stigler. 1982. Winter Temperature as a Constraint to the Migration of Preindustrial Peoples. *American Anthropologist*, 84 (no. 2): 279–98.

Willey, Gordon R. 1966. *An Introduction to American Archaeology*. Vol. 1, *North America*. Englewood Cliffs, N.J.: Prentice-Hall.

Willey, Gordon R., et. al. 1956. An Archaeological Classification of Culture Contact Situations. In *Seminars in Archaeology: 1955*, ed. Robert Wauchope, pp. 1–30. Memoirs of the Society for American Archaeology, no. 11. Salt Lake City.

Willey, Gordon R., and Philip Phillips. 1958. *Method and Theory in American Archaeology*. Chicago: The University of Chicago Press.

Wilson, Samuel M. MS. Taino Elite Integration and Societal Complexity on Hispaniola. Paper read at the Eleventh International Congress for Caribbean Archeology, San Juan, Puerto Rico, July 28 to August 3, 1985.

Wright, J. V. 1972. *Ontario Prehistory: An Eleven-thousand-year Archaeological Outline*. Ottawa: National Museum of Canada, National Museum of Man, Archaeological Survey of Canada.

Yokohama, Kōichi. 1978. Early Historic Archaeology in Japan. *Asian Perspectives*, 19 (no. 1): 27–41.

Zucchi, Alberta. MS. The Meillacoid Ceramic Development and Its Relationships with the Orinoco Basin. Paper read at the Eleventh International Congress for Caribbean Archeology, San Juan, Puerto Rico, July 28 to August 3, 1985.

INDEX

Two subjects are covered here: the methods and concepts discussed in the first and last chapters and exemplified in the intervening case studies (chaps. 2–5), and the human groups that figure prominently in the case studies. In listing the former, I have lumped peoples with cultures and speech communities with languages, because each of these pairs constitutes two sides of the same coin, a people being defined by its culture and a speech community by its language. In listing the latter, I have heeded V. Gordon Childe's admonition to treat the name of each group as an adjective that needs to be accompanied by a noun indicating the kind of group to which it refers (Roger Sommers, personal communication). This has led me to omit the groups that are designated in the text solely by proper names.

200

201

DUE DATE

DEC 10 1992

DEC 18 1993

OCT 1 9 1994

OCT 19 1994

BUR   FEB 07 1997

SEP 13 2000

SEP 13 2005

201-6503

Printed
in USA